The Cause We Plead

A Story of the Restoration Movement

Beatrice Carton
Good friend
Best wishes
Jim Powell
6-18-'81

The Cause We Plead

A Story of the Restoration Movement

J. M. Powell

20TH CENTURY CHRISTIAN
2809 Granny White Pike • Nashville, TN 37204

20th Century Christian
2809 Granny White Pike
Nashville, TN 37204

Dedication

To my wife Mildred, my daughter Patsy and my son Monty, without whose encouragement and sometimes prodding this book would not have been written.

Contents

Preface

In writing this book I am deeply indebted to a host of people including encouragement from those who heard the lectures as they were given in churches and colleges across the land.

My sincere thanks go to Professor Douglas Foster, of David Lipscomb College, who has rendered invaluable assistance on an almost daily basis. He has read the manuscript and offered many useful suggestions. In addition, he has provided choice material which has made the book more useful. Too, he was kind enough to prepare the index, which was no easy task, and also to write the Foreward.

I am grateful to the late Batsell Barrett Baxter who constantly encouraged me to put my lectures in book form.

My special thanks to Mrs. Katheryn Gentry Palmer for typing the numerous revisions of the manuscript. Seemingly, her patience never ended.

Thanks also to my friend of a half century, Dan Harless, for reading the manuscript and polishing up some of my rough sentences.

Librarians at Scarritt College, Vanderbilt University, David Lipscomb College and the Disciples of Christ Historical Society, as well as Societies in New England and Great Britain were helpful in many ways to provide the materials needed. Sincere thanks to them all.

Last, but not least, I am grateful to the 20TH CENTURY CHRISTIAN for publishing and promoting the book.

J. M. Powell
Nashville, Tennessee
May 11, 1987

Foreword

J. M. Powell is known across this country and throughout the world for many good things. He has served as minister for churches in Tennesee, Georgia and Kentucky. He has been a staff writer for *Minister's Monthly, 20th Century Christian* and the *Gospel Advocate,* and continues to contribute thoughtful, scholarly material for publication. He worked for thirty-two years with the Blue Ridge Encampment, serving as its Director for a quarter century. He served as President of Ohio Valley College in Parkersburg, West Virginia for four years, and taught on the faculty of that school as well. Later he served as adjunct professor for Alabama Christian School of Religion and the Nashvile Bible School of David Lipscomb College.

In recent years, however, Brother Powell has perhaps become best known for his work on the Restoration Movement. He is eminently qualified academically for such study, having earned A.A., B.A., and M.A. degrees. In addition, he was awarded the LL.D. from Lubbock Christian College in 1984. His work is based on research at the actual sites of Restoration events in America and Great Britain, as well as intense study from hundreds of primary sources, many of which are found in his own library. When to this extensive background is added Brother Powell's great love for the principles of the leaders of the Restoration Movement, as well as his marvelous style of delivery, there is produced an unbeatable combination that has made deep impressions on countless hundreds of listeners.

Batsell Barrett Baxter wrote of Powell's work: "Brother J. M. Powell has been studying the 'Restoration Movement' through many years of his life. He has become an outstanding scholar in this important area of church history. He also has the capability of conveying this material to others in a stirring way. I have been most impressed with his messages and think they are the finest that I have heard in this important area of study."

The book you hold before you is an adaptation and expansion of J. M. Powell's Restoration lectures. He has tried to give a factual and well-documented account of the backgrounds and chief figures of the early Restoration Movement in America. After looking at a number of forerunners to the Restoration through the centuries, Powell takes a thorough look at the "big four" of the American Movement: Barton W. Stone, Thomas and Alexander Campbell and Walter Scott. A number of documents printed here have not been easily accessible to the general public before now, and endnotes have been provided for those who wish to pursue specific subjects. This book is a must for all those who have been moved by Brother Powell's presentations in the past, as well as for those who want a good solid introduction to our religious heritage or who thrill at the courage of those pioneer Restoration leaders and their message for our own times.

This book is the result of much hard work. John Waddey, Director of the East Tennessee School of Preaching in Knoxville has written concerning Powell and his efforts: "A grateful brotherhood has eagerly called upon him to share his wealth of knowledge. He is an unselfish man who gladly shares his material and his information with all who come to him. Now, the reading public is blessed that J. M. Powell has placed in writing the immense store of knowledge he has accumulated over the years. Hundreds of his hearers have urged him to do so. It would have been tragic for him to leave no permanent record of all his research. Mr. Powell has done us a great service by sharing his vast knowledge with us."

Mr. Powell has been an inspiration and a mentor to many young students of Restoration history, including this writer. He knows the facts of the Restoration Movement perhaps as well as anyone living, yet he has an exciting eagerness to learn more and understand better the essence of that great effort to please God. Through this book he will reach out with his enthusiasm for the subject to hundreds who have not had the privilege to know and hear him personally.

J. M. Powell has truly rendered a great service. At a time when churches of Christ face difficulties, it is good to look again at the story of our religious roots. Often current problems can be placed in a fuller context, and we can gain a clearer perspective of them through an understanding of our past. This book, undoubtedly, will help many to do just that.

Dr. Douglas Foster
Assistant Professor of History
David Lipscomb College

Prologue

A unique feature of the Restoration Movement is that no person is asked to give up any truth he holds. He is asked to give up those things not consistent with the Word of God.

Alexander Campbell argued that unity can be achieved if religious people will accept as matters of faith only those things that all concede to be Scriptural. In this connection he said:

> Let every sect give up its opinions as bonds of union and what will remain in common? The gospel facts alone. Every sect, Catholic and Protestants, admit all the historic facts recorded in the historical books of the New Testament. Their various interpretations, additions, and new modifications of opinions concerning these facts, and not the truth or falsehood of the narrative, create all the confusion, build the whole Babel, and set all the machinery of the contending interests in motion. Now, will not the slowest to apprehend see that, if, by any means, it could be induced to abandon their opinions, retain the plain incontrovertable facts, the strife would be over. (*Christianity Restored*, p. 121).

In a lecture at Abilene Christian College, 1920, the distinguished scholar, M. C. Kurfees said: "By a careful induction and examination of facts, it will be seen among all the things over which there is division among God's people, in no instance, when the facts are weighed with proper discrimination, are they divided over what is in the Bible or what the Bible *says*, but over what is outside of the Bible, or what the Bible does not say." (M. C. Kurfees, *Abilene Christian Lectures*, 1920-1921, pp. 35,36).

This was the thesis of Alexander Campbell when he wrote these words:

> We choose to speak of Bible things by Bible words, because we are always suspicious that if the word is not in the Bible, the idea which it represents is not there, and always confident that the things taught by God are better taught by words under the names which the Holy Spirit has chosen and appropriated than the words which man's wisdom teaches. (*Christianity Restored,* p. 125).

There is developing in our brotherhood a sectarian spirit that will eventually divide us, if indeed, it has not already done so, into various splinter parties. More and more the lines of fellowship are growing tighter in an "ever-shrinking circle." The tragedy of the situation is that many of the things that are hotly debated are matters of human opinion, and not matters of faith. (cf. Romans 10:17).

It is sometimes difficult for religious people to see the difference between faith and opinion. (cf. 2 Corinthians 4:7). Often opinions are pursued with unrelenting fervor. Unity can easily become a reality on matters of faith, but we can never agree on matters of opinion. In this connection, we think of the often quoted slogan of the pioneers: 'In faith unity, in opinion liberty, in all things charity.'

No one can truthfully say that he knows every truth that God wants him to know. No person can make that statement without violating the restoration ideal. Moreover, no one can truthfully say that he is doing everything that God requires of an individual. It is a fact that we have *access* to every truth that God wants us to know and practice. (cf. John 8:31,32).

The Restoration Movement was and is a constant search for truth. This search is a continuous thing. David Lipscomb said on one occasion that he had been reading the Bible on a daily basis for more than fifty years, but that at every reading he learned truths that he had not known before—truths that had escaped him.

A case in point: The Bible clearly teaches, and most knowledgeable Christians accept without question, that if a person believes that Jesus Christ is God's Son; genuinely repents of his sins; confesses his faith in Christ and is immersed "in the name of the Father and of the Son and of the Holy Spirit," (Matthew 28:19) he is a Christian! Please observe that all God requires of a person to believe, in order for his baptism to be valid, is that "Jesus Christ is God's Son" (Acts 8:37, KJV). This is the word of faith and whatever else a preacher might require of one is human opinion—only that and nothing more. The "opinions" of men are private property and should be regarded as such. On the one hand, they should not be made tests of fellowship nor pressed to the disruption of the church. On the other hand, "faith" is public property which should and must be shared with others. The Bible teaches us to "contend earnestly for the faith which was once for all delivered unto the saints" (Jude 3).

The Restoration ideal has been with us across the years since the First

Century. In the Eighteenth Century, there were a number of movements in Ireland, Scotland, and England, designed to reproduce the purity and simplicity of First Century Christianity. Their reach, however, was greater than their grasp, yet we must acknowledge that they paved the way for the Campbells and others in the Nineteenth Century to complete the task.

The writer has made no attempt to give an exhaustive study of the Restoration Movement. Through the years he has given lectures at home and abroad on this important phase of church history. In this book he has simply enlarged on these lectures. Too, no attempt has been made to write for the scholar but, rather, for the rank and file of church members to make them aware of their rich heritage.

This volume revolves, generally, around the "big four"—Barton W. Stone, Thomas Campbell, Alexander Campbell and Walter Scott. Even though these men, more or less, worked independently in their efforts to restore First Century Christianity, each made a special contribution to the movement.

Barton W. Stone emphasized God's love for man and His willingness to save him on the simple terms of the gospel (John 3:16).

Thomas Campbell's great passion was unity. He believed strongly that unity could be achieved among Christians on the simple basis of returning to the New Testament.

Alexander Campbell gave emphasis to the authority of the Bible in matters of faith that electrified the whole Christian world. In *The Christian Baptist* (1823-1830) his slogan was "The Restoration of the ancient order of things." This was the caption of more than thirty editorials. If a practice or teaching is not mandated by Scriptures it must be discarded.

Walter Scott provided the evangelistic zeal which assured success for the movement. When all four of the above features are combined, we have an array of material that is not found in any other single volume. This is the material that helped to mold and shape the Restoration Movement. The phrase 'The Cause We Plead' was used repeatedly in the writings of the Campbell-Stone Movement. We are appropriating it as the title of this volume.

Chapter 1

What is the Restoration Movement

That question can be answered in one sentence. It is essentially a plea for Christ. The Restoration Plea rejects all ecclesiastical trappings, human names, human creeds and human doctrines. The fundamental message of this movement is to give preeminence to Christ in all things (Colossians 1:18).

There are five words which describe and define the meaning and significance of the Restoration Movement: (1) *Search* as in "ye search the Scriptures, because ye think that in them ye have eternal life; and these are they which bear witness of me..." (John 5:39). (2) *Discovery* as in "we have found him of whom Moses in the law and the prophets wrote, Jesus of Nazareth" (John 2:43). (3) *Acceptance* "Thomas answered and said unto him, My Lord and my God" (John 20:28). (4) *Practice* as in "and whatsoever we ask we receive of him, because we keep his commandments and do those things that are pleasing in his sight" (I John 3:22). (5) *Sharing* as in "seeing that Jews ask for signs, and the Greek seek after wisdom: *but we preach Christ crucified...*" (I Corinthians 22:23).

In the past, courageous, faithful, God-fearing, Bible-believing men had a compelling desire to know the will of God. They searched the Scriptures diligently and cried out, "Eureka, I have found it!" They made the greatest discovery of their lives. They discovered the truth that makes man free. Without questions or debate, they accepted the precious truths they had discovered without delay. They put them into practice, often at the price of ridicule and scorn. But this opposition did not stop them; it spurred them on to greater zeal. This truth— this good news—was too good to keep for themselves. They began to share it with others with signal success. They felt as did the apostle Paul, "for woe is unto me, if I preach not the gospel" (I Corinthians 9:16).

1

One of the favorite scriptures of the late T. B. Larimore (1843-1929) was Romans 1:16: "For I am not ashamed of the gospel; for it is the power of God unto salvation; to every one that believeth; to the Jew first; and also to the Greek." Larimore quoted this passage many times in the course of his meetings and almost invariably he would say, "I would be afraid to be ashamed, and ashamed to be afraid to preach the gospel of Christ." Larimore summarized the Restoration principles in the following way: "Take God at his word; believe what he says; be and become what he requires; live as he directs and trust him for his promises."

Now for the answer to the question posed in the caption of this essay: What is the Restoration Movement?

I.

It is a plea for the Book of Christ: The Bible.

The Christianity of the first century cannot be reproduced without giving preeminence to the all sufficiency and the alone-sufficiency of the Holy Scriptures in matters of faith and life. Over and over again we read in the *Millennial Harbinger, Christian Messenger* and other periodicals, that congregations were established on "the Word of God alone."

Restoration involves a recognition of the *verbal, plenary inspiration* of God's Word. This is the bold affirmation of the apostle Paul: "All scripture is given by inspiration of God..." (2 Timothy 3:16, K.J.V.) By *verbal* is meant the very words of the Bible are inspired. To give one of many examples, David put it this way: "The Spirit of the Lord spake by me and His word was on my tongue" (2 Samuel 23:2). We must therefore contend for the infallible accuracy of every word of Scripture. The word "inspired" means, "God-breathed." The word *plenary* means full, complete, absolute, therefore every Scripture in all of its parts is "God-breathed" or inspired of God. Instead of saying, "The Bible contains the word of God, let us be more accurate and say, "The Bible is the word of God."

Everything must be measured and approved or disapproved by the divine standard of the New Testament. If creed and dogma do not agree with the Scriptures they must be rejected as having no light.

II.

It is a plea for the church of Christ.

By church I do not mean a denomination that might use this term. I mean what Jesus had in mind when he said, "Upon this rock I will build my church" (Matthew 16:18). I have in mind the church which was prophesied in the Old Testament (Isaiah 2:2,3); the church of which Jesus is the foundation (1 Corinthians 3:11); the church over which Christ is head (Ephesians 1:22,23);

the church of which Christ is the legislator (Ephesians 5:24); the church which was purchased with the blood of Christ (Acts 20:28); 1 Peter 1:18); and the church which Jesus will save (Ephesians 1:23); the church which will endure forever (Matthew 16:18,19).

The eloquent T. B. Larimore in carefully chosen words said: "Kingdoms may be founded, may flourish and may fall; but the church of Christ can never fall, can never fail. Atheism may assail, infidelity may sneer, skepticism may smile and anxious hearts may fear for the safety of Zion but Zion stands secure, backed by the promise of the great I Am that it shall never be destroyed, the literal, living, abiding fulfillment of the promise of the Lord Jesus Christ: 'Upon this rock I will build my church and the gates of hell shall not prevail against it.' The sun may be blotted out, the moon cease to reflect light, the stars may fall from the withering vault of night, and the heavens be rolled up like a scroll, and the wreck of matter and the crash of the worlds may come and the judgment day be set; but, when the angel of the Lord shall descend on pinions dipped in the lovelight enveloping the throne of God and, planting one foot upon the land and one upon the sea, shall declare by Him who plants his foot steps upon the sea and rides upon the storm that time was, time is, but time shall be no more—even then the church of Christ shall stand, secure as the throne of God itself: for our Savior promised long ago,'the gates of hell shall not prevail against it;' and Jehovah hath declared 'it shall never be destroyed;' and the Holy Spirit by the pen of Isaiah, the prophet, says: 'The word of our God shall stand forever': so then, whether we stand or fall, whether we do right or wrong, whether we are saved or lost, the church of Christ shall stand, having been built upon this immovable foundation." (T. B. Larimore, *Life, Letters, and Sermons*, Vol. 4, pp. 131, 132).

III.

It is a plea for the name of Christ

Three times over the name Christian is mentioned in the New Testament. (1) ". . . the disciples were called Christians first in Antioch" (Acts 11:26). Phillip Doddridge correctly renders this passage thus: "And the disciples were by *divine appointment* first named Christians at Antioch," (2) "And Agrippa said unto Paul, with but little persuasion thou wouldst fain make me a Christian" (Acts 26:28), (3) "But if a man suffer as a Christian, let him not be ashamed; but let him glorify God in name" (1 Peter 4:16).

It is evident from Scripture that the name *Christian* is in fulfillment to prophecy. Isaiah expressed it this way: "And the Nations shall see thy righteousness, and all kings thy glory, and thou shalt be called by a new name which the mouth of Jehovah shall name" (Isaiah 62:2). This prophecy declares that when the "nations" or Gentiles "shall see the righteousness," that is, accept Christ, "thou shalt be called a new name." And we are told that the Name will be given by

Jehovah himself. When the church was first established only Jews became members. After some eight or ten years, Cornelius, a Gentile, and his household accepted Christ on the terms of the gospel (Acts 10:1-48). God's people through the ages were known as *disciples, friends, brethren, saints,* etc., and this was the case until the conversion of Cornelius and his household.

J. W. McGarvey in his New Testament Commentary on Acts points out that "the new name which here and now originated proved to be the most potent name that has ever been applied to a body of men." He goes on to say, "The supposition adopted by many that this name was given by the enemies of the faith in derision is groundless." In his original commentary McGarvey remarked, "The name *Christian* embodies within itself, in a more generic form, all the obligations specifically expressed by the other names. Being derived from the name of him who is head over all things for the church, whose name is above every name, it is the title of peculiar honor and glory."

It is the one name by which all Christendom could find unity. There are solid reasons, such as the following, why the name *Christian* should be worn to the exclusion of all human designations: (1) It is the divinely appointed name (Acts 11:26); (2) It is the only name by which we can be saved (Acts 4:12); (3) It is the name into which we are baptized (Acts 19:5, 8:16); (4) It is the name in which we are authorized to glorify God (1 Peter 4:16); (5) It is the name through which we are justified (Acts 10:43); (6) It is the honorable name (James 2:7); (7) It is the name above every name (Philippians 2:9-11); (8) It is the name that fulfills prophecy (Isaiah 62:2, Acts 11:26).

Wearing the name Christian carries with it weighty responsibilities. Being a *Christian* emphasizes the purpose of one's life, namely to be faithful and dedicated to Jesus Christ and his redeeming cause. It is said that Alexander the Great had a cowardly soldier in his vast army whose name was Alexander. He called the young man into his presence and demanded that the soldier either change his conduct or his name. By the same token, the Lord expects those who wear the name Christian to live up to its ideals.

The importance and significance of the name Christian is seen in the fact that three great languages and cultures come together in this name. Our English word Christ is the translation of the Greek word "Christos." This word which means the "anointed" is the equivalent of the Hebrew word "Messiah." The "ian" ending is of Latin origin and means follower of. Hence, the word Christian means follower of Christ.

IV.

It is a plea for the authority of Christ.

Jesus said: "All authority hath been given unto me in heaven and on earth" (Matthew 28:18). The problem in the world of religion today is not one of interpretation, but one of authority. A person with average intelligence can read the Bible and understand a large measure of what he has read. But the great question is, "What is the authority behind the words read?" What question can be superior to this one of authority in religion? In Harriet Beecher Stowe's book, *Uncle Tom's Cabin,* there is the scene of the black slaves congregated in the cool of the evening trying to entertain themselves. A person who could read well opened the Bible and read these words: "Come unto me all ye that labor and are heavy laden and I will give you rest" (Matthew 11:28). An old man with furrowed cheek and bent form said: "Them is good words, but who says 'em?" All recognize that the New Testament is a good book, filled with good words. But the important matter is, "Who gives expression to these good sayings?" After Jesus had finished the sermon on the mount, "the multitudes were astonished at his teaching: for he taught as one having authority, and not as their scribes" (Matthew 7:28, 29).

The supreme task which lies ahead of us as "Christians only" is to recognize and restore the authority of Christ. "Authority" is defined as "the right to command and enforce obedience; the right to act by virtue of office, station or relation." There are two kinds of authority: *Primary* authority, the source; and *Delegated* authority, that which is transferred from the primary source to others. The source of Primary authority in Christianity is God. God has chosen to exercise his authority through certain chosen vessels.

The first delegation of authority in Christianity was from God to Jesus (Hebrews 1:1). At the transfiguration of Jesus we hear the voice of God which says, "Hear ye him" (Matthew 17:5,8). In matters of faith, we are obligated to accept the voice of Jesus above all the voices in the world (cf. 1 Corinthians 14:37).

The next delegation of authority in Christianity was from Jesus to the apostles. In transferring authority to the apostles there was no danger of errors. It was necessary to qualify them with divine power to preserve them from error. Thus, Christ promised them that the Holy Spirit would guide them in all that he had taught them (John 14:26; 16:7-15).

The apostles wrote down their revelations from God through his Spirit in the Book that we call the Bible. With the completion of the New Testament, all inspiration and revelation ceased. As John Wycliff put it in the Fourteenth Century, "The Bible is the only source of spiritual truth." The truth that makes man free is to be found in the Scriptures (John 8:31, 32). Every person has the right and duty to come to the New Testament as the only source of authority accessable to man. The Bible is the "perfect law of liberty" to which nothing can be added, and from which nothing can be rightfully taken away (cf. Matthew 18:18, 2 Timothy 2:2). No man has any right to teach or preach anything for which he has no "thus saith the Lord" (cf. Galatians 1:6-9). (Z. T. Sweeney, *New Testament Christianity,* Vol. 3, pp. 504-522).

V.

A Plea for the Creed of Christ

The word "creed" comes from the Latin verb *Credo* which means "I believe." Hence, a person's creed is what the person believes. Everyone has a creed because everyone believes something. What is the creed of the church of Christ? It might more properly be asked *who* is the creed of the church? I answer with one word—"Christ." One of the contributions that Walter Scott made to the Restoration Movement of the Nineteenth Century was his emphasis on the fact that Christ was the creed of the church of the First Century. As New Testament Christians, we can and should adopt Christ as our creed. And it becomes our duty to restore this feature of New Testament Christianity.

The New Testament gives expression to this creed in numerous places such as Matthew 16:16; John 20:30,31; 1 Corinthians 2:2, 3:11. I think it was George Combs in his book "Call of the Mountains" who said: "The living creed of the living church is the Living, ever-living son of the living God." The object of our creed is not a thing, but a person. The living, reigning, interceding Christ should be the only creed of His church. Peter gave expression to this creed when he said to Jesus: "Thou art the Christ, the Son of the living God" (Matthew 16:16). This creed has but one article of faith which can be summarized in four words: "Jesus Christ, God's Son." Walter Scott referred to this as the "Golden Oracle." It is a creed that is publically acknowledged prior to Christian baptism. This is called the "good confession" (1 Timothy 6:13). Every well-taught person, willingly and gladly, makes the good confession, "I believe that Jesus is the Christ, God's Son." That person is then baptized into the name of the Father, and of the Son and the Holy Spirit, for the remission of sins after which he receives the gift of the Holy Spirit. This matchless creed is simple, universal, comprehensive, living, heaven-born and changeless.

The apostle Paul gives expression to this creed in these deathless words: "For which cause I suffer also these things: yet I am not ashamed; for I know whom I have believed, and I am persuaded that he is able to keep that which I have committed unto him against that day" (2 Timothy 1:12). It is reported that the celebrated scholar and theologian, Johann Bengel (1687-1732) had a microscopic way of observing every word in the Greek text. He observed that Paul would not allow even a preposition to come between him and his Savior. He asserted that Paul did not say, "I know upon whom," or "in whom," but "I know whom I have believed."

In this connection we note that there are three essential requirements of a good creed and Christs meets them all. (1) *Simplicity.* The creeds of men are clothed in obscure theological terms. The creeds of men talk about Hereditary Total Depravity, Reprobation, Unconditional Election, Irresistible Grace, Final Perseverence of the Saints and a lot of other things not mentioned in the Bible. By way of contrast, Paul speaks of the "simplicity that was in Christ" (2

Corinthians 11:5). Christ and His word can be understood if there is a strong desire to do so (Matthew 5:6, Ephesians 5:17, John 17:17, Psalm 25:14). Christ our creed meets the needs of scholar and child alike. In every passage of scripture there is meat for the mature and milk for the babe in Christ. A simple minded Christian was on his way to worship. He was accosted by an infidel who sought to make sport of him. The infidel said, "Where are you going, my friend?" The Christian replied, "I'm going to worship God." "Tell me," asked the infidel, "is this God you worship a big God or a little God?" The Christian replied, "He is both a big God and a little God. He is big enough to fill the earth with his glory and little enough to abide in my heart."

(2) *Universal.* The creeds of men are not universal. They are designed for special groups. The creed of one denomination will not meet the needs of another. The religious world would never agree to unite upon any one creed of the denominational world. "Christ" is the one and only creed that can bring about the answer to our Savior's prayer for unity (John 17:21). Thomas Campbell spoke of the "horrid evils of creeds" because of their divisive nature. "Christ" the perfect creed meets the needs of all people in all ages. This creed never has to be updated or revised (Hebrews 13:8), and if adopted, will unite people on a biblical basis.

(3) *Comprehensive.* The creeds of men contain some truth but not all truth. Jesus Christ is the truth incarnate (John 14:6, 8:32). In Christ is found all truth pertaining to life and godliness (2 Peter 1:3). In Christ we are complete (Colossians 2:10, 4:12). When one accepts Christ as his creed he accepts all that the Bible says about Jesus, both in prophecy and the New Testament. He also accepts without debate the commandments of Jesus, and that means the New Testament in its entirety (1 Corinthians 14:37). He accepts the Bible from Genesis to Revelation, because of the unqualified endorsement by Christ himself. For example, he accepts the Genesis account of the creation of man, because Jesus accepted it as being literally true (Matthew19:4). One cannot be a Darwinian evolutionist or even a Theistic evolutionist and at the same time be a New Testament Christian. Acceptance of Jesus means acceptance of what Jesus endorsed.

The men of the Restoration Movement of the Nineteenth Century repeated with conviction and telling success these impressive words:

No creed but Christ.
No law but the Lord's.
No book but the Bible.
No name but the Master's.

VI.

A Plea For the Ordinances of Christ

The church has no ordinances, but Christ has three: *Baptism*, the *Lord's Supper* and the *Lord's Day* . These three ordinances have great educational value to the Christian. They are remarkable symbols which relate to Christ, the believer and the world. From the beginning the Christian religion has had its memorials and symbols.

In the gospel of Christ there are recorded three facts of the gospel. Paul tells us what these facts are in writing to the Corinthians: "Now I made known unto you, brethren, the gospel which I preached unto you, which also ye received, wherein also ye stand, by which also you are saved, if ye hold fast the word which I preached unto you, first of all that which also I received: that Christ died for our sins according to the Scriptures; and that he was buried; and that he hath been raised on the third day according to the Scripture" (1 Corinthians 15:1-4). In this passage we note that the three facts of the gospel are the *death*, *burial*, and *resurrection* of Christ. Each of the three ordinances of Christ memorializes one or more of the facts of the gospel.

Paul ranks these facts as "first of all," that is, they are the most important. Only the more important facts are memorialized. It would have been strange, indeed, if memorials had not been established to perpetuate and magnify these three gospel facts. Observe the fact: "that Christ *died* ." This is the first of the three historic facts upon which Christianity rests. Is there an institution in the Christian religion that memorializes the death of Christ? Indeed there is! It is the Lord's Supper. The Lord's Supper is a memorial to only one of the facts of the gospel—the death of Christ.

On the Lord's Day I frequently hear a brother say, "Today we observe the Lord's Supper to celebrate the death, burial and resurrection of Christ." There are a number of things wrong with that statement. For one thing, I am not sure that the word "celebrate" should be used in connection with the Lord's Supper. This is the word that is ordinarily identified with a joyous, jubilant occasion. For another thing, the chief purpose of the Lord's Supper is to emphasize only one fact of the gospel, namely, the death of Christ. "For as often as ye eat this bread, and drink of the cup, ye proclaim the Lord's death till he come" (1 Corinthians 11:26). In the same connection, we find these words: "For I received of the Lord that which also I delivered unto you, that the Lord Jesus in the night in which he was betrayed took bread; and when he had given thanks he brake it and said, this is my body which is for you: This do in remembrance of me" (1 Corinthians 11:23,24).

The Lord's Supper, then, is a *memorial* of the death of Christ. In our observance of the Supper we proclaim the Lord's death till he come again. But, the Lord's Supper is not only a memorial of the death of Christ, it is also a *proclamation* of that fact. In compliance with scripture, we participate in this sacred and impressive memorial on the first day of every week (Acts 20:7; 1 Corinthians 16:2).

The second fact of the gospel is that Christ was *buried*. After his death on the cross, he was buried in a borrowed tomb. Have we a monument that attests to this fact of history? Is there a monument in the Christian religion that memorializes the burial of our Lord? We answer in the affirmative. Baptism is the memorial. Baptism is a memorial that pictures all three facts of the gospel, as we see in Paul's letter to the Romans, "Know ye not, that so many of us as were baptized into Jesus Christ were baptized into his *death*. Therefore, we are *buried* with him by baptism into death; that like as Christ was *raised* from the dead by the glory of the Father, even so we should walk in newness of life" (Romans 6:1-4; cf Colossians 2:12). Today, when we witness a scriptural baptism, we have pictured before our very eyes the death, burial, and resurrection of Christ.

The third fact of the gospel is the *resurrection* of Christ from the dead. The first day of the week, or the Lord's Day, is the memorial of the resurrection of Christ (Mark 16:9; cf. Psalms 118:22, 23). To the Jews, the Sabbath was a memorial; to Christians, the first day of the week is a memorial. Fifty two times each year Christians celebrate the resurrection of Christ (cf Acts 20:7; 1 Corinthians 16:2; Revelation 1:10).

Concerning the ordinances of Christ, some one has suggested that (1) Baptism is a test of the loyalty of the penitent believer, (2) The Lord's Supper is the test of the loyalty of a Christian, and (3) The Lord's Day is a memorial of the resurrection of Christ. It is a time to rejoice and be glad (Psalms 118:19-24; Mark 16:9).

VII.

A Plea for Terms of Admission into Christ

Just prior to his ascension, Jesus called the eleven disciples to an appointed place in Galilee and he gave to them what is called "The Great Commission" (Matthew 28:16). Jesus said to them, "All authority hath been given unto me in heaven and earth, go ye therefore, and make disciples of all nations, baptizing them into the name of the Father and of the Son and of the Holy Spirit..." (Matthew 28:18,19). In Mark's account of this commission we find these words: "And he said unto them, go ye into all the world, preach the gospel to the whole creation. He that believeth and is baptized shall be saved; but he that disbelieveth shall be condemned" (Mark 16:15,16). Luke, in his account, adds these penetrating words: "...and that repentance and remission of sins should be preached in his name beginning from Jerusalem" (Luke 24:47).

In order to understand what is in the Lord's commission it is necessary to examine each of the three reports. We cannot take one report of it and get all that we need to know. (1) In Matthew's account we have *Teach, All Nations,*

Baptizing, into the name of the Father and of the Son and of the Holy Spirit.
(2) In Mark's account we have *Preach, Every Creature, the Gospel, Believe, Baptized and Saved.* (3) In Luke's account we have *Preach, All Nations, Repentance, Remission of sins and Beginning at Jerusalem.*

By placing together the three reports, as we would the testimony of any three witnesses testifying in court, concerning any fact to be established by testimony, we get the entire contents of this important portion of Holy writ. By way of summary, we know precisely what Jesus put into the Great Commision: (1) When the Lord parted from his apostles, after giving the commandment, (Acts 1:1-3) we have the first element, *going.* (2) On the day of Pentecost the Spirit came upon them to clothe them with authority and infallibility (Acts 1:1-8; 2:1-4), and Peter, "filled with the Holy Spirit" preached Christ to the multitude, that is, proclaimed for the first time that Jesus died, was buried, raised from the dead, and made both Lord and Christ (Acts 2:1-4, 14-36). This gives us the second element - *Preaching.* (3) When the people heard this "They were pricked in their hearts" (Acts 2:37). Why? Because they believed Peter's message. Men are not cut to the heart by a message which they do not believe. This gives us the third element - *Faith.* (4) When these believers then asked what to do the apostle told them to repent and be baptized for the remission of sins (Acts 2:38). This gives us three additional elements, namely, *repentance, baptism, and remission* (salvation). (5) We are then told that these first converts to Christianity "continued steadfastly in the apostles' teaching, and in fellowship, in the breaking of bread and the prayers" (Acts 2:41,42). Here, then, when the constitutional law of Christ's kingdom was first presented to the world, we find that the Spirit authorized the following sequence: *going, teaching (preaching, making disciples), faith, repentance, baptism, salvation (remission of sin).* (C. C. Crawford, *Sermon Outlines on First Principles,* p. 13).

The terms of salvation must be crystal clear. There are five items as suggested by Matthew, Mark, and Luke: (1) Teaching, (2) Faith, (3) Repentance, (4) Baptism, (5) Salvation. This is the scriptural order of these items. Unfortunately, this order has been tampered with by many through the centuries. Those who believe in and practice infant baptism give the order as Baptism, Teaching, Repentance, Faith, Salvation. But others who insist on believer's baptism have also rearranged the biblical order, seeing it as Teaching, Repentance, Faith, Salvation, and Baptism. As we have already seen, the arrangement of these items by the Holy Spirit Himself at Pentecost was: Teaching, Faith, Repentance, Baptism, Salvation.

This is the arrangement that is used all the way through the book of Acts in the eight conversions that are listed. While faith is not always mentioned, it is always inferred. The same is true with repentance. Without exception, however, baptism is named in each and all of the conversions listed. And something else; all of those who were converted were baptized immediately (Acts 2:41, 16:33). There are no examples in the book of Acts of deferred baptism. This tells us something about the importance that the apostles placed on baptism.

"Now if the language of Jesus can establish anything, it is certain that he has placed *faith, repentance and baptism* in the commission as conditions of *salvation* or the *remission* of sins. Can we reach the blessing promised until we comply with *all the conditions?* If we can, then this ever-present principle in God's dealings with man has been overcome, or set aside in some way." (Dr. T. W. Brents, *Gospel Sermons,* p. 59). There is perhaps more ignorance in the world today about the plan of salvation than any other subject in the Bible, hence, the importance of preaching and teaching, again and again, the conditions of pardon as established by the Holy Spirit in the New Testament.

VIII.

A Plea for the Worship Established by Christ

The true worship described in the New Testament is characterized by dignity, simplicity and beauty. This is the worship that must be engaged in if we are to have the approval of God (Matthew 4:10; John 4:24 - Note the word "must"). Before we describe this "true" worship, attention is called to other kinds of worship that must be avoided.

The Bible speaks of "will worship." To the Colossian church Paul wrote: "If ye died with Christ from the rudiments of the world, why, as though living in the world, do ye subject yourselves to ordinances, handle not, nor taste, nor touch (all which things are to perish with the using), after the precepts and doctrines of men? Which things have indeed a show of wisdom in will-worship, and humility and severity to the body: but are not of any value against the indulgence of the flesh" (Colossians 2:20-23).

The Pharisees, Essenes and Gnostics of the first century made piety hinge on outward observances and rules instead of inward conviction and principle. This sort of thing seems to have crept into the church at Colossae. "Handle not, nor taste, nor touch" is an admonition to wholly abstain from the inventions and devices of men in the worship of God. It is a fearful thing to change or modify the appointments of God. Will-worship is after man's own will. It is self-chosen, and for this single reason is a departure from allegiance to God. Monks and nuns practice asceticism for the sake of pietistic effect on themselves. Will-worship, however sincere one might be, is unacceptable to God, and must be shunned.

The Bible also speaks of "vain worship." "This people honoreth me with their lips; but their heart is far from me. But in vain do they worship me, teaching as their doctrines the precepts of men" (Matthew 15:9). In Christian worship we must have a "thus saith the Lord" for everything we do. Unless we can cite chapter and verse, our worship is vain. The word "vain" means empty. For example, in our worship on the Lord's Day we have scripture for giving of our means (1 Corinthians 16:20); prayers (Acts 2:42); and for singing Psalms, Hymns, and Spiritual Songs (Colossians 3:16, 17; Ephesians 5:19). We have authority for "singing" in Christian worship, but instrumental music in Christian worship is unauthorized in Holy Scripture. Therefore, when people attempt to worship God with instruments, we must conclude that such worship is vain. Jesus said, "But in vain do they worship me, teaching as their doctrines the precepts of men (Matthew 15:9).

Too, we note the mention of "ignorant worship" in the book of Acts. Paul, in Athens, said, "For as I passed along, and observed the objects of your worship, I found also an altar with this inscription, To an Unknown God. What therefore ye worship in ignorance, this I set forth unto you" (Acts 17:23). "Paul stood in the midst of the Areopagus" and, according to J. W. McGarvey in his commentary on Acts, addressed an audience of demon worshippers. It was said by Petronius (a Roman satirist) that it was easier to find a god in Athens than a man. These Athenians had extended their worship to include "an unknown god." This was the cue for Paul to say that he came to make known to them the very God whom they had already worshipped without knowing Him. It is important that we know God, in order for our worship to be acceptable. At the Mount of Temptation, Jesus declared, "Thou shalt worship the Lord thy God and him only shalt thou serve" (Matthew 4:10). Worship is important because we become like that which we worship (Psalm 115:8). Worship of the true and living God elevates anyone who engages in it. Heathen worship is degrading.

As a people who are part of the movement to restore First Century Christianity, we are concerned with true worship. "God is a spirit: and they that worship Him must worship in spirit and truth." This familiar passage is the Scripture that guides Bible-loving and God-fearing people who desire to worship correctly; people whose aim is to honor God. In his excellent commentary on John, the scholarly Guy N. Woods asserts: "Here, the three simple but vitally important aspects of true worship are set out: (1) We must worship God; (2) We must worship God in spirit, i.e., rationally, and sincerely; (3) We must worship God in truth, as His word directs (Colossians 3:17; John 17:17). Only those who thus do are assured of the divine approval...it is possible to worship God, and yet not worship God in harmony with his will and pleasingly in His sight."

IX.

A Plea for the Restoration of a Life That Honors Christ

"For I know," said Paul, "that this shall turn out to my salvation, through your supplication and the supply of the spirit of Jesus Christ, according to my earnest expectation and hope, that in nothing shall I be put to shame, but that with all boldness, as always, so now also Christ shall be magnified in my body, whether by life, or by death" (Philippians 1:19,20). The word "magnified" is a pivotal word in this passage. It means to "extol, laud, to cause to be held in greater esteem or respect." If ever a man lived on this earth who was completely dedicated and devoted to Christ it was T. B. Larimore (1843-1929). He magnified Christ in every sermon and every deed of his life. In a letter dated

December 31, 1895, Larimore wrote to his friend F. D. Srygley:

> Instead of writing you a New-year letter, as I have so often done, I write you as follows a few of my life rules, as they occur to me in the light of the last day of 1895 - rules which I hope to strictly observe, both to the letter and spirit, till God shall call me home: (1) Be kind; (2) Be meek; (3) Be true; (4) Be humble; (5) Be gentle; (6) Be polite; (7) Be patient; (8) Be earnest; (9) Be careful; (10) Be hopeful; (11) Be faithful; (12) Be cheerful; (13) Be grateful; (14) Be generous; (15) Be prayerful; (16) Be courteous; (17) Be unselfish; (18) Be thoughtful; (19) Be industrious; (20) Be consecrated; (21) Be conscientious; (22) Always do right; (23) Do as much good as possible; (24) Do as little evil as possible; (25) Eat to live and not live to eat; (26) If possible, be perfectly pure; (27) If not, be pure as possible; (28) Always make the best of the situation; (29) Be clean—body, soul, and spirit—clean in thought, in word, in deed— always clean; (30) Conscientiously consecrate all to Christ—head, hand, heart, body, soul, spirit—time, tongue, talent—mind, muscle, money—consecrate all to Him who gave his very life to ransom a recreant, lost and ruined race. (F. D. Srygley, *Letters and Sermons of T. B. Larimore* Vol. 1, p. 129; cf. p. 135).

As Christians, our mission on this earth is to exalt Christ in our lives; to preach Him on the widest possible scale. Someone has put it this way: "We must give Christ to the world; we cannot do more, we dare not do less." This the Restoration Movement sought and seeks to do.

Chapter 2

Early European
and American Roots

The restoration of New Testament Christianity has roots that go back through the centuries. In every century there have been God-fearing, Bible-loving men and women eager to know God's will and to make it available to others. Victor Hugo in his book, *History of Crime*, writes, "Greater than a mighty army is an idea whose time has come." Many have had the noble idea of giving the Bible to the people so that they could read their way to God. But for the most part, their reach was greater than their grasp. We must look upon them as forerunners, or harbingers, of the Restoration Movement of the nineteenth century. Preserved Smith in his book, *Age of The Reformation*, says: "In all ages Christendom has not lacked minds independent enough to cut away what they considered corrupt or rotten in ecclesiastical teaching and life."[1] Of the many, I mention a few.

I.

In the 12th century there lived in France a wealthy merchant by the name of Peter Waldo. Waldo was a man who loved God and read the Bible faithfully. He was an independent thinker whose consuming ambition was to know God and to share this knowledge with others. He sold his possessions and used the proceeds to give the Bible to the people in their vernacular. Waldo's followers were numerous and came to be known as Waldenses. A number of slogans arose among them: "Every one ought to believe, for the gospel has spoken." Sometimes they put it this way: "Scripture speaks, and we ought to believe." In their sermons they would say: "Whatever is not enjoined in Scripture must be rejected," and "The Bible is the only safe guide in religion." They rejected masses and prayers for the dead, and denied purgatory as unbiblical. They defended "lay preaching." Because of their adherence to Scripture and their determination to preach it, they were violently opposed and persecuted by the Roman Catholic Church.

The program of the Waldenses may be summarized as follows: (1) "The church must return to the pure teaching of Scripture; (2) There is no purgatory; (3) The church is not infallible; (4) Christian laymen are entitled to preach; (5) Selling one's goods and giving the proceeds to the poor is an act of Christian consecration . . ."[2]

II.

The 14th Century produced a number of truth seekers who had in mind the restoration of first century Christianity, using the Bible as a blueprint. Of these, three will be mentioned. In Italy there was Marsilius (1275-1342), an intellectual and devout man, who wanted the people, as well as himself, to know the will of God. He coined a number of slogans that are important to all of us: "The only authority in the church is Scripture, the final seat of authority being the New Testament." Concerning the mission of the church he said: "The church should concern itself with the spiritual welfare of mankind." The late, distinguished G. C. Brewer used to put it this way, "The whole duty of the whole church is to preach the whole gospel to the whole world." Marsilius was bold in his opposition to the many false claims of the Roman Catholic Church. He believed in the right of private judgment. He stoutly maintained that priests had no power of physical force to compel men to obey Scripture. "No bishop or Pope has authority to define Christian truth as contained in the New Testament or to make binding laws." He was bold to say that "Peter had no higher rank than any other Apostle and that there was no Bible evidence that he was ever in Rome."[3] We owe this man a debt of gratitude for his brave and heroic efforts to put the Bible into the hands of the common people. In a remarkable way, he helped to pave the way for the Restoration Movement.

Also in this century lived William of Occam, (c. 1300-1349) a distinguished scholar and professor at Oxford University in England. He was the most powerful critic in his day of the Catholic Church. As a theologian, he was widely known and highly respected. He was a man willing to speak his mind when it was not popular to do so. As pointed out by Williston Walker in *A History of the Christian Church* Occam said, "Scripture, and not the decisions of councils and popes, is alone binding on the Christian."[4] No wonder that Luther, in this respect, could call him "dear master."[5] We are indebted to Occam for his insistence that "Scripture is the final seat of authority for the church." A bold statement for the age in which it was made!

Another harbinger of the Restoration Movement was John Wycliff (1324-1384). In Oxford, Wycliff rose to great scholarly distinction, lecturing to large classes, and was looked upon as the ablest theologian in the University. Even though he was a priest in the Catholic Church, he did not withhold his criticism of the church when he felt that it was teaching and practicing things contrary to the New Testament. "The Scriptures," he taught, "are the only law of the church."[6] He boldly taught that a papal decree had no validity except as it was consistent with the Scriptures. He attacked the Romish doctrine of transubstantiation, suggesting that the bread and wine remained unchanged. He also asserted that in the primitive church there were only two classes of officers - elders and deacons. He referred to the Bible as the only source of spiritual truth. By this he meant that God, Christ, and the Holy Spirit speak to people only through the book that man calls the Bible. He said, "Scripture is the property of the people." Convinced that the Bible is God's law, he determined to give it to the people in the English language. Between 1382 and 1384, the Bible was translated from Jerome's Old Latin Vulgate into the language of the people[7] Thus, for the first time in history, English speaking people were able to read the Bible in their native tongue. Wycliff boldly denounced various doctrines of the Catholic Church that he considered out of harmony with Bible teaching. He attacked the Pope — his avarice, his tyranny, and his usurpation. He referred to him as antichrist. "He lashed his bishops, contrasting their pomp and luxury with the simplicity of the New Testament bishops." Because of this the Pope ordered his imprisonment. Wycliff was literally hounded to death by the Catholic Church of which he was a member. He died in 1834, and forty years later his bones were dug up and burned, and the ashes thrown into the River Swift.

> The Avon to the Severn runs,
> The Severn to the sea;
> And Wycliff's ashes spread abroad,
> Far as the waters be.

Wycliff was not only "The morning star of the Reformation," he was in deed and truth one of the brightest harbingers of the Restoration Movement. The words of the great scholar and translator of the Scriptures could hardly be improved upon when we are thinking of how to study the Bible.

> It shall greatly help ye to
> understand Scripture,
> If thou mark
> Not only what is spoken or wrytten,
> But of whom,
> And to whom,
> With what words,
> At what time,
> Where,

To what intent,
With what circumstances,
Considering what goeth before
And what followeth.[8]

III.

The 15th Century produced three notable men that helped to bring on the Restoration Movement of which we are a part. First of all, I mention John Huss of Bohemia (1373-1415), a professor in the University of Prague, and a disciple of John Wycliff. He was born in 1373 and ordained to the priesthood in 1401; he believed that the true head of the church was not the Pope, but Christ. As a preacher, he gained immense popularity through his fiery sermons. With Wycliff, he believed Scripture to be the only source of authority in the church.

Huss was a devoted disciple of Wycliff. Preserved Smith points out that "almost the whole content of his lectures," at the University of Prague, "as of his writings, was borrowed from Wycliff, from whom he copied not only his main ideas but long passages verbatim and without specific acknowledgement."[9]

Starting a campaign against indulgences, Huss fell under the ban of his church superiors. He was excommunicated by the Pope and was summoned before the Council of Constance. In spite of the fact he had been promised safe conduct to and from the Council he was tried, condemned and burned at the stake July 6, 1415. The charge against him was that of heresy. His heresy was simply saying that only Christ is the head of the church, and not the Pope.[10] Let it be said to the everlasting credit of Huss that he died with steadfast courage, love to his friends and forgiveness to his enemies. We are enjoying freedoms today because of the courage and faithfulness of this remarkable man.

Wycliff in England and Huss in Bohemia were paralleled in Italy by Jerome Savonarola (1452-1498) whom "Luther proclaimed as a proto-martyr of the Reformation." At the age of thirty, Savonarola came to Florence where he spent the rest of his life. He was "a second John the Baptist pleading for a return to the purer life of early Christianity." He castigated the sins and wrongs of the church and world, drawing from the Bible lurid prophecies of danger and woe that would come to pass unless the people repented. For twenty years in the Cathedral of Florence this man preached the Bible as he understood it, and he did so with telling effect. His preaching produced a religious and moral revival.

Roman scandals were notorious throughout Italy. Papal corruption and immorality reached their height during the Pontificate of Alexander VI, "a monster of all the vices." It was not without reason that Savonarola denounced Rome and its clergy, quoting a common saying of the time, "If you want to ruin your son, make him a priest."[11] His preaching made him a bitter enemy of Pope Alexander.

When the Pope found that he could not bribe the powerful preacher with the offer of a cardinal's hat, nor reduce him to silence by repeated admonitions, he excommunicated him. At length, Savonarola was tried for heresy. On May 23, 1498, with two of his followers, he was hanged, then burned, and his ashes thrown into the Arno River. What was his crime? Pleading for the primitive faith of the Bible against the traditions of the Catholic Church.

There were other men, less renowned, however, than Wycliff, Huss and Savonarola, who helped to snatch the Bible from the clutches of Rome and put it into the hands of the people. Among them was John Wessel (d. 1482) in Germany, a teacher of theology at several leading universities. He regarded the Bible as the only rule of faith. He rejected the alleged infallibility of the Pope, along with many other tenets of the Roman Church. He repudiated the authority of the church to interpret the Scriptures for believers. Because of his stand for the Bible and the right of the people to read it, he was looked upon as a heretic. He died in prison in 1482. Yet, he must be regarded with those other men as a harbinger of the Restoration Movement.

Martin Luther declared that if he had "read sooner the works of Wessel it might have been plausibly said by his enemies that he borrowed everything from them."[12]

IV.

The 16th Century is also important in the search for religious truth. In this century, many contributed to the wide distribution of the Word of God. Among that number I mention the following: Martin Luther, Philip Melancthon, Erasmus, Ulrich Zwingli, Oecolampadius, John Calvin, John Knox and others. It is true that these men accomplished much in the way of clearing the atmosphere. Luther translated the New Testament into German in 1522, and ten years later he completed the translation of the entire Bible into his native tongue. He often said to his followers, "Call not yourselves Lutherans, but call yourselves Christians." All of these reformers maintained that authority resided not in the church but in the Bible, exercising the right of private judgment. "The Pope," said Luther, "is no judge of matters pertaining to God's Word and faith. But the Christian man must examine and judge for himself."[13] A grave mistake made by the reformers is that they made no distinction between the Old and New Testaments. This distinction came later.

In spite of the valuable contributions the Reformers made, the end results were disastrous. Their efforts crystalized into warring denominations— denominations entrenched behind elaborate credal formulas. But out of the morass of the German Reformation, there emerged several Biblical principles that we hold dear:

1. Plenary verbal inspiration of the Scriptures (2 Timothy 3:16).
2. Authority of the Scriptures (Matthew 28:18).

3. All sufficiency and alone sufficiency of Scripture in matters of faith (2 Timothy 3:17).
4. Luther's definition of the church: "the church is a priesthood of believers (this based on 1 Peter 2:5).
5. The right of private judgment (cf. Acts 17:11).
6. *Sola Scriptura*, only the Scripture.

Close on the heels of the Reformation of the 16th Century there arose in Switzerland a group of people who were called by their enemies Anabaptists, a word that means "rebaptizers." In searching the Scripture, they reached the conclusion that the primitive church had been composed only of penitent believers. Hence, they rejected infant baptism as being no baptism at all. They insisted that adults who had been "baptized" as infants had to be rebaptized, or rather "baptized."

Perhaps more thoroughly than any of their contemporaries they read the Bible in order to recover the pattern of the early church. The great word with them was "restitution," a word later to be used by the Glasites in Scotland. The Campbells, and others, used the words "restoration" and "reformation." In New England, Elias Smith used the word "freedom." Others have used the word "reproduction." All had in mind reproducing the church of the first century, using the New Testament as a blueprint.

It is needless to say that the Anabaptists were bitterly opposed by both Protestants and Catholics. "The Zurich government, in March, 1526, ordered Anabaptists drowned in hideous parody of their belief in "immersion."[14]

The Anabaptists divided church history from the time of Christ to the 16th Century into three periods: "The 'Golden Age,' the 'Fall,' and the 'Restoration.' The Golden Age lasted from the Apostles until the reign of Constantine, who was responsible for the onset of the Fall. "New Testament Christianity was believed to have flourished in the Golden Age. The second part of Christian history, called the Fall, corresponded to the Middle Ages. It began in A. D. 407 with the edict of Innocent I making infant baptism compulsory. The third period, the Restoration, began with the 16th Century Anabaptists, and their efforts to restore New Testament Christianity."[15]

The following tenets show how close the Anabaptists were to New Testament teaching:

1. They were strong in their opposition to a state church.
2. They chose to set themselves apart as independents.
3. They viewed the Bible as the sole law of the church.
4. "The proper order of Christian development is preaching the word, hearing, belief, baptism, works."[16]
5. They believed that the Church of the New Testament included more than clergy.
6. They made no distinction between clergy and laity.

7. They believed that the church must follow the teaching of the New Testament in matters of faith. They thus made a distinction between the Old and the New Testaments.
8. They believed that the church was made up only of immersed believers.
9. They taught "the priesthood of believers."
10. They observed the Lord's Supper each Lord's Day. They looked upon it as being a Memorial rather than a sacrifice.
11. They maintained that Christians should not bear arms or hold public office.
12. They did not use instrumental music in worship.

V.

Following on the heels of the Reformation of sixteenth century, there arose in England religious leaders who believed the English Reformation, under Henry VIII, had not gone far enough in its reform. They had a consuming desire to purify the church, as it then existed, and restore it to its primitive apostolic state. Those Puritans insisted on a return to the Scriptures for everything done in religion. For this, many suffered persecution and even death.

Among those who led in the attempt to purify the church were: Lawrence Humphrey (1527-1590), Thomas Sampson (1517-1589), John Gough (c. 1540-1571), and William Fulke (1538-1589).

The Puritans insisted on simpler practices in worship. For them, the Bible was supreme in matters of faith and life. They insisted that the Bible superseded any claim of the church to define and interpret what one must believe. They believed this was an individual responsibility and duty. They insisted that every one has the right to read the Bible for himself and thereby know God's will.

They sought to purge from worship everything that smacked of Romanism. They objected to showy clerical dress as being inconsistent with the Biblical teaching of the priesthood of believers. They looked upon the sign of the cross as superstitious. John Gough, a noted Puritan of the day, wrote:

> It is evident that the right life of a Christian consisteth not either in multitude of people, prescription of time, forefathers, nor outward ceremonies, but only in virtuousness of life, leaving our own dreams and inventions, and in following the sacred and holy Scriptures, setting the same always before our eyes as our only lodestar to follow, and touchstone to try all doctrine by. For whatsoever is not contained in God's book (I mean the Holy Bible) no Christian is bound of necessity to do. Neither (as I said before) need we to run into any cloister to seek a perfect life, seeing it is the duty of all Christians (of what estate or degree soever he be) to

live in the fear of God, and in such sort as in this godly work following is most lively and Christianity set forth. So that in that matter I shall not need anything to entreat of.[17]

To show further the reverence the Puritans had for the word of God the following is noted from William Fulke: "The church of God is the house of God, and therefore ought to be directed in all things according to the order prescribed by the Householder himself, which order is not to be learned elsewhere, but in the holy word."[18]

There is no question but that the men and movements mentioned above helped lay a foundation for the Restoration Movement of the 19th Century. Alexander Campbell said, "I am greatly indebted to all Reformers from Martin Luther down to John Wesley. I could not enumerate or particularize the individuals, living or dead, who have assisted in forming my mind. I am in some way indebted to some person or other for every idea I have on the subject. When I begin to think of my debt of thought, I see an immense crowd of claimants."[19]

VI.

In the 17th Century, there was widespread interest in the Bible. Many notable persons contributed to the acceleration of the search for the truth. In England, there was William Chillingworth (1602-1644). He grew up as a Catholic, but later embraced Protestantism. He had a healthy respect for the Word of God, insisting that "The Bible, and the Bible alone, is the book of Protestantism." "I am fully assured," he said, "that God does not and, therefore, that men ought not, to require any more of any man than this—to believe the Scripture to be God's word, to endeavor to find the true sense of it, and live according to it."[20] In Germany, Rupertus Meldenius was shouting from the house top, "In essentials unity; in non-essentials liberty; in all things charity." This slogan was heard in Germany and all of western Europe. It crossed the Atlantic and was heard in the New World. In the 19th Century, it was used effectively by the Campbells and other personalities of the Restoration. Thomas Campbell put it this way: "In faith unity; in opinion liberty; in all things charity."

John Locke, the intellectual to whom Alexander Campbell referred as the "Christian Philosopher," was sending out Bible tracts on a wide scale in his native England. He wrote four pamphlets on the subject of Toleration. In the first Essay *Concerning Toleration* Locke suggests the possibility of one becoming a Christian, worshipping and living as a Christian without ever becoming a member of any denomination. When Thomas Campbell was twenty years of age in 1783, he enrolled as a student at Glascow University. There he came under the influence of the Lockean philosophy which, no doubt, changed his religious views. Campbell was so engrossed with this particular essay that in 1844, in America, he ran it serially in *The Millenial Harbinger* for the whole country to read and absorb. Lester McAllister points out that "it was from Locke's *Essay Concerning Human Understanding* that the basic ideas concerning reason and faith were derived by Thomas Campbell." The thesis was that faith is the assent to any proposition not made by the deduction of reason, and that it comes to people through revelation (cf. Romans 10:17). Locke wrote an essay entitled *Reasonableness of Christianity* which also made a great impact on the Campbells. It is beyond question that Thomas Campbell guided his son, Alexander, in the study of these writings.[21]

Alexander Campbell had this to say about John Locke: "That far-famed and greatly renowned Christian philosopher, John Locke, the author of Religious Toleration in 1689, the ornament of his country and humanity itself, spent the last fourteen or fifteen years of his great and useful life in reading scarcely any other book except the Scriptures. The day before he died, (so earnest was he for the comfort of his friends and the diffusion of Christian knowledge among them) he exhorted all about him to read the Holy Scriptures, exalting the love which God showed to man in justifying him by faith in Jesus Christ and returning him thanks for having called him to the knowledge of that divine Savior. To a person who asked him which was the shortest and surest way for a young gentleman to attain the true knowledge of the Christian religion, in the full and just extent of it, he replied, 'Let him study the Holy Scriptures, especially the New Testament. Therein are the words of eternal life. It hath God for its author - salvation for its end - and truth, without any mixture of error, for its matter.' Locke was a friend to God and man. Though dead, he still recommends to us, and to all future generations, to read the Scriptures. He walked with God."[22]

Something else happened in the 17th Century that helped to bring on the Restoration Movement. In 1680 the Independent Movement sprang up in Scotland. People began to think for themselves and read the Bible in an effort to know the will of God. Independent churches were established. Human names, human creeds and human doctrines were discarded. They purported to take the Bible as their only guide in matters of faith and life. The road was rapidly being paved for the Campbells, and others, to bring to America and the world the pure religion of Christ.

VII.

We come now to the 18th Century—a century of numerous independent movements which desired to reproduce the Christianity of the first century. In 1728, there began a movement in Tealing, Scotland, under the leadership of John Glas (1695-1773). Glas was educated at St. Andrews and the University of Edinburgh, and was ordained as a minister in the Church of Scotland in 1719. Under pressure, Glas left the Church of Scotland in 1728. He was opposed to the State Church, believing strongly that there should be a separation between church and state. He espoused independent views and a return to

New Testament teaching. He began to establish independent churches, repudiating human creeds, human names and human doctrines.

On one occasion Glas visited Edinburgh and, while there, he met Robert Sandeman (1718-1771), a student at the University. In time, Robert married the daughter of Glas. Robert Sandeman not only had a brilliant mind but an outgoing personality. About 1755 he joined his father-in-law and together they set out to "restore primitive New Testament practices."[23]

It was Sandeman who took the lead in this movement and gave it "theological content." Among the beliefs Glas and Sandeman came to hold are the following:

1. They emphasized the difference between the Old and New Testament.
2. They believed in church autonomy.
3. They observed the Lord's Supper on the first day of each week.
4. They refused to refer to the Lord's Day as the "Christian's Sabbath."
5. They believed that faith comes as a result of evidence or testimony.
6. They believed in the possibility of restoring the New Testament church.
7. They advocated the "holy kiss," the love feast and foot washing.

Glas and Sandeman saw nothing wrong with the Presbyterian practice of infant baptism. Robert Carmichal and Archibald McLean, two astute Bible students identified with this movement, discovered that baptism was for the penitent believer. Carmichal went to London and was immersed by a Dr. McGill. On returning to Edinburgh, he immersed McLean and six other believers. They separated from the "Glasites" or "Sandemanians," as the movement was variously called. The followers of Carmichal and McLean became known as "Old Scotch Baptists." Churches were established in Glascow, Dundee, Montrose, and various other places. In time, "Old Scotch Baptist" churches were established in the United States. Henry Errett, father of Isaac Errett, served such a church in New York City.

In 1763, Sandeman came to America where he established congregations in Boston, Massachusetts, Portsmouth, New Hampshire, and Danbury, Connecticut. He settled in Danbury and remained there until he died. The following is the inscription upon the stone which marks the place in the old Wooster Street burial ground, where Robert Sandeman was laid to rest:

Here lies
until the resurrection
the body of
ROBERT SANDEMAN,
a native of Perth, North Britain,
who in the face of continual opposition
from all sorts of men,

long and boldly contended for the ancient Faith
that the bare work of Jesus Christ,
without a deed or thought on the part of man,
is sufficient to present the chief of sinners
spotless before God.
To declare this blessed truth
as testified in the Holy Scriptures,
he left his country, he left his friends,
and after much patient suffering finished his labors at Danbury
April 2, 1771.
Age 53 years."

Archibald McLean became the dominant leader in this "Scotch Baptist" movement. It was the works of McLean that had revolutionized the views of William Jones, the author of the *History of the Waldensess*. Jones was baptized in Chester in 1786, and was, in 1809, presiding over the Scotch Baptist church in London. Years later, William Jones came under the influence of Alexander Campbell. It came about this way: P. C. Wyeth from Bethany, Virginia, was on a journey to Europe. In London, he attended the Scotch Baptist church where Jones was the preacher. Jones was surprised to hear from Wyeth the particulars of so extended a reformatory movement in America and, conceiving that in its general features it agreed with that attempted by Archibald McLean and the Scotch Baptist churches, at once opened a communication with Mr. Campbell. He obtained some of Campbell's works, with which he was so much pleased that he determined to reproduce them in England in a periodical which he entitled *The British Millennial Harbinger*.[24] The British Harbinger continued for many years under the editorship of Jones, then James Wallis, and finally, David King.

John Glas died at Dundee, Scotland in 1773. His tombstone in that city bears the following inscription:

John Glas, minister of the Congregational church in this place, died 2nd November, 1778. Aged 78 years. He long survived Katherine Black, his beloved wife, (enterred also in the same grave) and all his children, Fifteen in number, many of whom arrived at mature age: and nine lie here beside their parents. His character in the churches of Christ is well known and will outlive all monumental inscriptions."

Robert Haldane (1764-1842) and his brother James (1768-1851) were two Scotchmen who had a tremendous influence on Thomas and Alexander Campbell. These men were wealthy members of the Church of Scotland. They became interested in the study of the Bible and, in time, used their talents and money to establish independent churches patterned after the New Testament. Greville Ewing (1767-1841) came under the influence of the Haldanes and joined forces with them to give the Bible to the people on the widest possible scale.

The year of 1799 is the year that is important in the lives of the Haldane brothers. This is the year that they, along with Greville Ewing, left the Church of Scotland and became independents. They went out with an open mind and an open Bible. They went out willing to follow the truth wherever it led them. This is true discipleship. The Tabernacle, or Circus Church, was constituted in Edinburgh, January, 1799, with some 310 members. James Haldane was selected as the preacher and served well for the next half century. According to the customs of the day he was ordained on Sunday February 3, 1799, in a five hour ceremony.[25]

Greville Ewing had preached for a number of years at Lady Glenorchy's Chapel. In May, 1799, he removed to Glasgow. Robert Haldane had purchased "the Circus in Jamaica Street," Glasgow, at the cost of 2000£, and converted it into a Tabernacle for a congregation, of which Mr. Ewing was to be the pastor."[26] Ewing preached for the independent congregation and presided over a training school for preachers.

Congregations and schools sprang up in various parts of Scotland with the Haldanes underwriting, for the most part, the expenses.

The Haldanes were deeply concerned over the formalism and sterility of the established church. Too, they were alarmed by the rationalistic theology of the day. It was not until 1808 that the Haldanes discovered that the immersion of penitent believers was the teaching of the New Testament. They attended to this matter with great haste to the effect that hundreds of people were scripturally baptized. Greville Ewing did not follow them in this change and, for this and other reasons, relations became strained.

Garrison and DeGroot bring out the fact that "the feature of the Haldane impulse which they embodied was the determination to restore the exact pattern of the primitive church in structure, ministry, ordinance and worship. The evangelistic zeal was lost. A few years later, two of the churches—one in Edinburgh, the other in New York—exchanged letters arguing earnestly, but very courteously, as to whether the New Testament commanded the service of public worship be opened with a hymn or a prayer. Each quoted appropriate texts of Scripture: "First of all supplications, prayers, intercessions and giving of thanks" (1 Timothy 2:1) meant prayer first; "Enter into the courts with praise" (Psalm 100:4) meant hymns first.[27]

Another reformer in the eighteenth century to help pave the way for the restoration movement was John Wesley (1703-1791).

In the 1760's, two or three disciples of Wesley came to America as missionaries. In 1769, Wesley sent two more men. In 1771, Francis Asbury arrived. The zeal of the Methodist missionaries produced signal success. The so-called Christmas letter of John Wesley is one of the notable documents of church history. It is so important that it is quoted in full.

TO DR. COKE, MR. ASBURY,
And Our Brethren in North America
Bristol, September 10, 1784

By a very uncommon train of providences many of the provinces of North America are totally disjoined from their mother country, and erected into independent states. The English government has no authority over them either civil or ecclesiastical, any more than over the states of Holland. A civil authority is exercised over them, partly by the congress, partly by the provincial assemblies. But no one either exercises or claims any ecclesiastical authority at all. In this peculiar situation some thousands of the inhabitants of these states desire my advice; and in compliance with their desire, I have drawn up a little sketch.

Lord King's "Account of the Primitive Church" convinced me many years ago that bishops and presbyters are the same order, and consequently, have the same right to ordain. For many years I have been importuned, from time to time, to exercise this right, by ordaining part of our travelling preachers. But I have still refused, not only for peace' sake, but because I was determined as little as possible to violate the established order of the National Church to which I belonged.

But the case is widely different between England and North America. Here there are bishops who have a legal jurisdiction: in America there are none, neither any parish ministers. So that for some hundred miles together, there is none either to baptize, or to administer the Lord's Supper. Here, therefore, my scruples are at an end; and I conceive myself at full liberty, as I violate no order, and invade no man's right, by appointing and sending labourers into the harvest.

I have accordingly appointed Dr. Coke and Mr. Francis Asbury to be joint superintendents over brethren in North America; as also Richard Whatcoat and Thomas Vasey to act as elders among them, by baptizing and administering the Lord's Supper. And I have prepared a liturgy little differing from that of the Church of England (I think, the best constituted national church in the world) which I advise all the travelling preachers to use on the Lord's Day, in all the congregations, reading the Litany only on Wednesdays and Fridays, and praying extempore on all other days. I also advise the elders to administer the Supper of the Lord on every Lord's Day.

If any one will point out a more rational and Scriptural way of feeding and guiding those poor sheep in the wilderness, I will gladly embrace it. At present, I cannot see any better method than that I have taken.

It has, indeed, been proposed to desire the English bishops, to ordain part of our preachers for America. But to this I object. (1) I desired the bishop of London to ordain only one; but could not prevail. (2) If they consented, we know the slowness of their proceedings; but the matter admits of no delay. (3) If they would ordain them now, they would likewise expect to govern them. And how grievously would that entangle us! (4) As our American brethren are now totally disentangled both from the state, and from the English hierarchy, we dare not entangle them again, either with the one or the other. They are now at full liberty, simply to follow the Scriptures and the primitive church. And we judge it best that they should stand fast in that liberty, wherewith God has so strangely made them free.

John Wesley

The letter points out a number of things important to students of the restoration movement. For example:

1. Bishops and presbyters are of the same order.
2. The Lord's Supper to be administered on every Lord's Day. In this connection Wesley said, "If any one will point out to me a more rational and Scriptural way of feeding and guiding those poor sheep in the wilderness I will gladly embrace it'.
3. You are now at liberty, simply to follow the Scriptures and the primitive church.

This letter was written by John Wesley from Bristol England, September 10, 1784. It was delivered to America by Dr. John Coke and read to a group of Methodist ministers in Baltimore, Maryland, December 24, 1784.

John Wesley, in his understanding of things, was seeking to restore New Testament teaching. This is evidenced by some of the things said in his Christmas letter, and by the following:

1. "We are buried with him"—alluding to the ancient manner of baptizing by immersion. Notes on New Testament, Romans 6:4'.[28]
2. John Wesley said: "Would to God that all party names and unscriptural phrases and forms which have divided the Christian world were forgotten. . . .with regard to the name Christian, I say, there is none like it; give it to me and in his life and death I would glorify God in this name."[29]
3. "The late, venerable and most eminent divine, the Rev. John Wesley, who was a lover of music and an elegant poet, when asked his opinion of instruments of music being introduced into the chapels of the Methodists said, in his terse and powerful manner, 'I have no objection to instruments of music in our

chapels, provided they are neither heard nor seen."[30]
4. He is frequently quoted as saying: "We ought to be downright Christians." This is one of the sayings of Wesley that arrested the attention of James O'Kelley.

During the famous Christmas conference mentioned above the name "Methodist Episcopal Church" was adopted. Coke and Asbury were appointed as "superintendents." Dr. Coke returned to England and Francis Asbury conferred upon himself the title of "bishop." As bishop, Asbury had three rules: "Pay, pray, obey."

The Methodist Episcopal Church immediately began to have internal strife. There was considerable opposition to the "Episcopal" type of government that had been adopted. It was believed that this was contrary to New Testament teaching. The leader in this opposition was James O'Kelley (1735?-1826). It is not known when or where O'Kelley was born. Some think he was born in Ireland, others think he was born in Virginia. It is generally believed that he died in 1826. He was buried in Chatham County, North Carolina. Friends erected a monument over his grave. The shaft bears this inscription:

Erected by his Christian friends
to the memory of Rev. James O'Kelley
of North Carolina. The Southern Champion of Christian Freedom.

It seems that no date of his birth and death are given on the tombstone.

James O'Kelley was a man of commanding personality, and keen intellectual acumen. He was a man who stressed the importance of Christian freedom and wanted this idea to be the ruling principle of church government. At the general Methodist Conference in 1792, O'Kelley introduced a resolution that would permit a preacher the right to appeal an appointment received from the bishop. The resolution was voted down. O'Kelley served notice that he was through with the conference. He, of course, had many sympathizers. This break with the Conference is generally known in church history as the "O'Kelley secession." There were more than 6000 people involved in this secession. Rice Haggard comes into prominence at this time.

In 1794, at Old Lebanon Meeting House in Surry County Virginia, some six thousand people met to decide their future course. Rice Haggard stood up with a copy of the New Testament is his hand and said" "Brethren, this is a sufficient rule of faith and practice, and by it we are told that the disciples were called Christians, and I move that henceforth and forever the followers of Christ be known as Christians simply." Then a preacher from North Carolina moved that the Bible should be their creed. Both motions were carried unanimously.[31] Thus began in America the first well-defined movement to restore New Testament Christianity. They left that place with hearts aflame. They carried with them what became known as the "Five Cardinal Principles of the Christian Church':

1. The Lord Jesus Christ is the only Head of the Church.
2. The name Christian to be worn to the exclusion of all party and sectarian names.
3. The Holy Bible, or the Scriptures of the Old and New Testament our only creed, and a sufficient rule of faith and practice.
4. Christian character, or vital piety, the only test of church fellowship.
5. The right of private judgment, and the liberty of conscience, the privilege and duty of all.[32]

This brings us to the nineteenth century when the Restoration Movement reached full flower under the teaching of the Campbells, B. W. Stone, Walter Scott and scores of others.

3. The Holy Bible, or the Scriptures of the Old and New Testament our only creed, and a sufficient rule of faith and practice.
4. Christian character, or vital piety, the only test of church fellowship.
5. The right of private judgment, and the liberty of conscience, the privilege and duty of all.[32]

This brings us to the nineteenth century when the Restoration Movement reached full flower under the teaching of the Campbells, B. W. Stone, Walter Scott and scores of others.

Endnotes

1. Preserved Smith, *The Age of the Reformation*, pp. 34-35.
2. Lars P. Qualbin, *A History of the Christian Church*, p. 182.
3. Williston Walker, *A History of the Christian Church*, pp. 264-65.
4. Ibid., p. 252.
5. Ibid.
6. Ibid., p. 269.
7. Ibid.
8. Wilbur M. Smith, *Profitable Bible Study*, p. 38.
9. Smith, *Age of the Reformation*, p. 273.
10. Walker, *Christian Church*, p. 273.
11. Stevenson, *Story of the Reformation*, p. 17f.
12. George Fisher, *History of the Christian Church*, p. 276f.
13. Roland H. Bainton, *The Reformation of the Sixteenth Century*, p. 61.
14. Walker, *Christian Church*, p. 327.
15. Lynn A. McMillan, *Restoration Roots*, p. 11.
16. Walker, *Christian Church*, p. 326f.

17. John Gough, *Prologue to Erasmus' Enchiridian*, in Leonard J. Trinterud, *Elizabethan Puritanism*, p. 38.
18. William Fulke, *A Brief and Plain Declaration*, in Trinterud, *Elizabethan Puritanism*, p. 243.
19. B. B. Tyler, *History of the Disciples of Christ*, p. 43.
20. Fisher, *History*, p. 600.
21. Lester McAllister, Thomas Campbell, Man of the Book, p. 126.
22. *Millennial Harbinger*, 1845, p. 143.
23. McAllister and Tucker, *Journey in Faith*, p. 94.
24. Richardson, *Memoirs*, (vol. 2), p. 396.
25. Alexander Haldane, *Memoirs of Robert and James Haldane*, p. 217f.

Chapter 3

The New England Movement

The idea of restoration was held by many men through the centuries. At the dawn of the nineteenth century it was an "idea whose time had come." The time was right - the world ready and waiting - for another great religious awakening....It came with force and vigor which shook the foundation of the Christian world.[1]

People in all religious groups were growing tired of the status quo. There was widespread hunger for something better. There was dissatisfaction everywhere. C. C. Crawford mentions a number of conditions which made this movement possible:

1. "Dissatisfaction with human creeds."
    At best, these documents were but expressions of human opinion. They completely set aside the authority of Christ.
2. "The dogma of total depravity."
    It was taught everywhere that man was conceived and born in sin, totally dead and totally depraved. Men were taught that they could do nothing to obtain salvation. They had to wait and agonize in the hope that God would perform a miracle to bring deliverance from their sins. It was believed that man could do nothing. The whole responsibility, with reference to salvation, lay in God's hands. This was Calvinism. The following doggerel denotes the feeling of the time about salvation:

    If you seek it, you can't find it,
    If you find it, you can't lose it,
    If you lose it, you never had it.

3. "The mystical conception of conversion."
Calvinism was the prevailing theology of the day, which meant that man was uncertain as to whether he was among the "elect" or not. Too, religion was something better felt than told. A person had to have an experience of some kind, such as a dream or vision, hearing a voice, or seeing a strange light. These would determine one's spiritual status.

> Tis a point I long to know;
> Oft it causes me anxious thought;
> Do I love the Lord or no?
> Am I his, or am I not?

4. "General neglect of the Bible."
The Bible had been buried under the rubbish of Catholicism and denominationalism. The Bible was looked upon as a "dead letter." Preachers believed that the Holy Spirit told them what to say. The people, as well as preachers, knew little or nothing about the Bible. Nothing was known about the proper division of this book. The apostolic terms of salvation were unknown or, at least, disregarded.
5. "Rampant sectarianism."
Creedal formulas divided the people. Each group thought its creed was better than the others. There was much strife between the various churches. This was especially true of Methodists and Baptists.
6. "General religious stagnation and a widespread decadence of morals."
A wave of infidelity was sweeping across the land (*The Restoration Plea*, pp. 23-26).
These were the conditions in America that provided a fertile field for the restoration movement of the nineteenth century.[2]

When Abner Jones (1772-1841) was eight years old, his father, Asa, moved the family from Massachusetts to the "frontier in Central Vermont."[3]

The brooding presence of the primeval forest, the harshness of the new home's climate and terrain, the constant labor necessary to preserve life, their almost complete isolation from other human companionship, all made deep and lasting impressions on young Abner's mind, helping to give it an unusual depth of thoughtfulness and intensity of feeling, hardening it with strength of will and self-reliance.[4]

The Jones family began attending a Baptist church. The only view of

Christianity they heard was the "fearful doctrine of Calvinism."[5] In 1786, Asa Jones died, leaving his family to fend for themselves in the harsh wilderness of Central Vermont.

Abner's life was nurtured in all the hardships of life on the frontier. He attended school only for a few weeks in his life yet, in time, he gained the reputation of a polished scholar. "He drove himself to master Latin, Greek, Hebrew." "His son authored a Hebrew grammar, Jones might have been the most thoroughly and impressively self-educated man in America. With his meager public schooling, he yet attained a level of scholarship that few graduates (or even professors) could approach."[6]

In 1793, he accepted a teaching position in Woodstock, Vermont. In that same year, Abner was baptized by a Baptist preacher. After his baptism, Abner made an extended trip to visit churches in New Hampshire. In New Saulsburg, he met (for the first time) a young preacher by the name of Elias Smith.[7]

As a young man of twenty-one with a keen intellect, "he discovered that the Bible did not teach the terrible Calvinist doctrines that had made his childhood so miserable and wrapped in cloud the character of God."[8]

Later, Jones wrote:

> I felt my mind much tried about what my brethren called the great mysterious doctrines of the gospel, viz, election, reprobation, decrees, for I plainly discovered that they preached complete contradictions on the subject, and I read that no lie is of the truth and contradictions must be lies. Thus, my mind was in great perplexity concerning these things, which caused me to review them, and compare them by the scriptures of truth, yea, in short, I took a review of all that I had professed to believe before, and I found I had embraced many things without proper examination. I then drew up a determination to believe, and practice, what I found required in the Bible, and no more. There was a Baptist minister that occasionally preached with us in Hartland who often made use of the following expression: I will have nothing but what I can bring thus saith the Lord, and thus it is written. This put me on search to compare what he preached and practiced with the Scripture.[9]

After teaching for some time, Jones studied medicine for two years at Grafton, New Hampshire, and began to practice in Lyndon, Vermont, in 1798. But Jones was more interested in preaching the wonderful truths of the New Testament than in the practice of medicine and began to preach. However, he returned to medicine from time to time. As a preacher, he now aligns himself with the Freewill Baptists, but with the stipulation that he would be only a "Christian." He was greatly disturbed "in regard to sectarian names and human creeds."[10]

Jones was also disturbed about the Baptist name. "The first thing I thought of was the name of our denomination, viz, Baptist. When I searched the New Testament through, to my great astonishment, I could not find the denomination of Baptist mentioned in the whole of it. I only found John the baptist in all the New Testament. Christ did not call his disciples baptists; the Christian churches in the apostolic time were not called baptists. . . .the disciples were called Christians at Antioch. After this search, I denied the name 'baptist,' and so I have continued to do so unto this day."[11]

In 1801, in Lyndon, Vermont, where Jones made his home at the time, "there were about a dozen of us who covenated together in church by the name Christians only."[12] This was, perhaps, the first Christian church to be established in New England. In the months that followed, Christian churches were established in many places in Vermont and New Hampshire.

Abner Jones spent his days preaching the Word of the Lord. Some months he would preach more than once per day and travel on horseback over two hundred miles. Jones died in 1841 and was buried in Exeter, New Hampshire.

Elias Smith (1719-1846) "moved with his family to Woodstock, Vermont, in 1782, or just two years after the Jones family moved there."[13] Smith and Jones worked together for approximately forty years in an effort to bring New Testament Christianity to New England.

The father of Elias was a member of the Baptist church and his mother was a Congregationalist. As a child, Elias was sprinkled according to the practice of his mother's church. In 1789, Elias was immersed and received as a member of the Baptist church in Woodstock, Vermont. Because of his convictions, Elias began preaching in 1790. His first sermon was titled. "Search the Scriptures." "This title well described the mental activity at this time as he had (in eighteen months) committed most of Romans through Revelation to memory."[14]

In August, 1792, Smith was ordained a Baptist minister in Lee, New Hampshire, in the presence of an estimated three thousand people.[15]

In 1792, Smith began the study of the Freewill/Calvinism controversy. . . . Previous to this, he had settled the question of baptism: "I searched the New Testament carefully and found infant baptism not there," he wrote.[16]

In time, there was an open break with the Baptists. He left the Baptist church suggesting the following reasons:

1. Their name Baptist, which is unscriptural. One man was called a baptist, but no churches.
2. Articles, which are an addition to the perfect law of liberty; these they held and I disowned them.
3. Association of churches, which is contrary to the New Testament, and anti-christian.
4. Holding to the necessity of a college education to be ministers of the gospel. This is contrary to the New Testament.
5. The Baptists held to missionary societies, which is nothing more or less than the old Jesuits plan invoked first by a monk.

6. The Baptists hold to councils to ordain ministers and settle disputes. These are unscriptural.
7. They hold to installing, or re-installing ministers, a practice not intimated in any part of the Bible.[17]

In his preaching and writing, Smith made a strong appeal for the non-sectarian name "Christian." "He was the first to advance the all sufficiency of the name 'Christian' in 1802 in Epping, New Hampshire. There was no need to add the word Baptist, Methodist, etc., to the name Christian." Elias Smith, writing in The Morning Star and City Watchman, July 2, 1827, said that he "was the first in New England, who made a public declaration of being a Christian only, without knowing there was another person on earth of his mind."[18]

In order to augment his income, Elias Smith became a "Botanic physician." He studied a few weeks with one Dr. Samuel Thomson of Boston.

> In November of this year, 1816, having paid attention to disease and medicine, I began to minister to the sick occasionally as Dr. Thomson taught me, knowing but little as to theory or practice. Though a new beginner, I had considerable practice, as those attended found great relief as my medicine made no mistake.[19]

Smith continued to preach and establish Christian churches. The most significant contribution that Smith made was the founding of the paper, *Herald of Gospel Liberty*.

The first issue of this paper came from the press September 1, 1808, at Portsmouth, New Hampshire. On the front page were these words: "A religious newspaper is almost a new thing under the sun; I know not but this is first ever published in the world." Smith was probably right in this claim. The name "Herald of Gospel Liberty" throws abundant light on the movement it represents. "Liberty was the keynote liberty of the Christian man from the trammels of traditional creeds, and liberty of the Christian congregation from the bonds of ecclesiastical organization."[20]

Smith had a brilliant mind, but an unstable one. He was embroiled in various "conflicts from childhood to old age."[21] Elias Smith lapsed into Universalism more than once, but always returned to the Christian fold.

In 1817, Smith had more misgiving about his personal beliefs. His problem of Calvinism still bothered him. In running from it once, he had gone into Universalism. Smith said, "In the days of my ignorance, I embraced Calvinism, and when I understood the extent of it, Universalism was at the end."[22]

There seemed to Smith for a time to be no alternative - it was either Calvinism or Universalism. This problem continued to plague him. On October 1, 1817, Smith published in his paper that he had gone into Universalism. This was the last number that he ever published.[23] He sold his paper the following year. It not only changed name, editors, owners, and locations, it also changed its original objectives. The paper exists today as the chief organ of the United Church of Christ, with the name *Christian*.

Even though Smith returned to the fold in 1823, he found that his brethren were slow to receive him. After all, this was the third time that he had gone into Universalism and returned. But he continued to serve in a limited way until his death in 1846. His mortal remains lie buried in a cemetery in Lynn, Massachusetts.

His straying into Universalism is strange, indeed, when we realize that his preaching had been so strong against it. In 1805, he published a book called *Smith's Eight Sermons*, sub-titled *The Doctrines of Universalism Overthrown By The Word of God*. In the first of the five sermons, he says:

> Universalism is founded on Calvinism and Arminianism. It is a three-headed monster, the bastard child of its mother, Calvinism, and father, Arminianism. These two systems are as opposite to each other as a father and mother are and on this account they have produced this child, which is as different from the scriptures as they are. They are as different from the Scriptures as light is from darkness. When Calvinism and Arminianism are dead, Universalism will be left to the world, a poor orphan monster, and will die for want of friends.[24]

In this series of sermons, Smith refers to Universalism as "an invention of the devil." Yet, three times over, he embraced it, but let it be said to the everlasting credit of Smith that he finally renounced it.

On March 7, 1826, a letter written by Smith appeared in the *New England Galaxie*. On December 25, 1826, the letter appeared in Barton W. Stone's *The Christian Messenger*, which reads:

> Dear Brother H. - By a letter of yours to Brother W., I find some questions which you wish to be answered, and think it best for me to answer them as there will (in that case) be no mistake or misunderstanding. I am ready to answer them in such a manner as to leave no doubt in your mind as to my understanding of your questions.
>
> As to the final and eternal salvation of all men: After great study and prayerful search of the Scriptures, particularly the New Testament, I am satisfied that the New Testament does not teach that doctrine. It is not true, as it does not produce that effect on those who receive it, which the Apostle's doctrine produced. Their doctrine, when received, produced a change in all who loved it. Universalism produces no change for the better in such as receive and loved it. Experience of the apostles doctrine will do without anything else — Universalism will not satisfy — 'Christ in you the

hope of glory.' I do not know that there is any Universalism in me;. . . almost three years ago I renounced Universalism, publicly, in your hearing. . . but the opposition I met discouraged me, and I partially receded, but have never been satisfied as before.

Whether I may live to redeem the time, seemingly lost, is to me unknown. . . whether I shall ever find an open door among the Christian brethren, therefore, is unknown to me; though nothing would be more grateful to me, than for once, at least, to stand in that assembly and, once more, preach Christ. . . all that I have written is but a sketch of an abundance which I must keep back for want of time and room. You are at liberty to make use of this as you think is wisdom. I hope to see you soon. Elias Smith"[25]

In the *Christian Messenger* of July 25, 1827, Barton W. Stone writes:

"We have lately had the pleasure of perusing a letter from Elder Elias Smith, to Elder T.M. Allen, dated Boston, April 30, 1827, from which we make the following extracts which we are sure will be read with pleasure.

I will give you a short account of my progress since leaving Universalism, which was 16 months ago. I began first to preach or 'do my first works' and preached to a few only; sometimes in Boston, and in Roxbury (near Boston). A few brethren knew the voice and attended with me. The leading members were, in general, against me, though they had prayed for my return. Some influential brethren who heard me labored for a union between them and me, but to no purpose. . . . .since last August I have baptized 20; these, with others, amounts to 40. . . The first of the month we moved our meeting to a very large hall — three times as large as the other, yet, as many meet as can be seated with comfort. . . [26]

In the same issue of the Messenger there is a notice of *The Morning Star*, a periodical, edited monthly by Elder Elias Smith. Stone recommends it "to the patronage of the friends of truth."[27]

Alexander Campbell issued an Extra in December, 1837, against Dr. John Thomas' teaching as follows: "Like Elias Smith, from whom he has quoted, but not borrowed anything, he has run into the grossest materialism and become a factionist of the most indomitable spirit. I pray he may not run with Elias into universal skepticism, from which the unfortunate old gentleman has not yet fully recovered when I saw him last year in Boston."[28]

"Smith had a brilliant mind, but an unsteady one. Where Jones sometimes let timidity prevent him from forming a decisive opinion on a subject, Smith rashly adopted opinions without sufficient knowledge or thoughtfulness."[29]

"Of the two, Smith seems to have been the bolder in thought, Jones the bolder in action."[30] These worked together for nearly forty years. "Smith and Jones enriched and balanced each other's personalities. Smith's boldness encouraged his hesitant companion, and Jones' gentleness soothed the passions of his friend."[31]

The doctrinal position of Elias Smith and the New England Restoration Movement is stated as follows:

> That my friends and enemies may know how my mind stands, as it respects the commands and doctrines of men and the scriptures of truth, I here present them with my solemn protest, against all man-made systems of doctrine, and invented power, contrary to Christ and the scriptures of truth, that they may have my mind, when my race on earth is run and my course is finished.
>
> I do, in the first place, publicly declare that the Holy Scriptures which contain a revelation of the will of God are the only sure authentic and infallible rule of the faith and practice of every Christian, by which all opinions are to be fairly and impartially examined and, in consequence of this, I do protest against setting up and allowing decrees of any man, or body of men, as of equal authority and obligation with the Word of God.
>
> I do further assert and maintain, according to the doctrines of Christ and the Apostles, and the practice of Christians in the first century, that in all things essential to the faith and practice of a Christian, the Scriptures are plain and easy to be understood by all who diligently and impartially read and study them, and that charging the Scriptures with obscurity and uncertainty is contrary to the plain declaration of the Scriptures and is an abuse of the rule given by Christians to walk by, and an insult upon that Holy Spirit by which the authors of them were guided, and a wicked reproach thrown upon them ignorant, corrupt and wicked hirelings to draw men into a slavish dependence on them; that by thus representing the Scriptures as a dark book...
>
> I do further assert that every Christian is under an indispensable obligation to search the Scriptures for himself....that he hath an inalienable right impartially to judge of the sense and meaning of it, and to follow the Scripture wherever it leads him...
>
> I do further assert and maintain that every Christian hath an equal right to the peaceable and constant possession of what he believes to be truth contained in the Scriptures...[32]

Smith's beliefs are further set forth in his dictionary of the Bible published in Philadelphia, 1812. He tells how he came to write this book:

In February, 1812, I began to write my New Testament Dictionary, having obtained a considerable number of subscribers for the same. In March, I had only fifty pages written. About this time, my printers began upon it and I wrote for them constantly for about five months. In August it was all printed. This was the most difficult piece I ever undertook to write. Eleven hundred and eight words were written upon . . . [33]

His comments on the word "Fables" are as follows:

Fables, 1. idle groundless stories or things mentioned which never existed; being invented by cunning men, to deceive and take advantage of the ignorant, 2 Peter 1:16.[34]

In giving examples of fables he says, "These fables are such doctrines and laws as are not mentioned in Scripture. I will name a few of the many: Original sin, Purgatory, Total Depravity, Transubstantiation, Consubstantiation, Creeds, Disciplines, Prayer Book, Infant Baptism. All these things are fables as they are not mentioned in Scripture; and all these things men love who cannot endure sound doctrine."

In a sermon on Baptism preached at Norwood, (N.H.), July 12, 1802, Elias Smith said, "How can any person have the boldness to stand before an assembly of people and tell them that infants are subjects of baptism, when every place in the New Testament where the subject of baptism is mentioned is always said to be a believer? If any person will deny these it is evident that he must be a friend to anti-Christ's baptism, and not to Christ's! If one proof could be produced in favor of infant baptism from the Scriptures, I would gladly allow the practice. But there is not a man on earth who can produce one positive declaration in all the Scriptures in favor of it. Infant baptism is a part and pillar of popery, and when Mystery Babylon falls, infant baptism will be found in its ruins."[35]

Before closing this section allow me to inject a personal note. It was my privilege to spend most of the summer of 1977 in New England. In connection with my lectures on the restoration movement in Vermont, Massachusetts, New Hampshire and Connecticut, I had time to do considerable research in preparation for this book.

In Vermont, I visited Woodstock, where both Abner Jones and Elias Smith lived as young men and later preached. Smith established a Christian Church there in 1810. Some four years later, there was a congregation that numbered about 100.

Within the next few years, "the Christians baptized 367 people in Woodstock and surrounding towns." Many years ago a congregation met in the court house until 1825. "The Christians purchased a lot on Pleasant Street, the main road through town, for the considerable sum of $200.00 on August 1, 1826. Within two weeks they laid the cornerstone, and they completed the entire building by the end of the year. Abner Jones preached the dedicatory sermon on January 18, 1827." The building still stands, but owned and used by Masons.

It was at Woodstock that I visited the Historical Society and secured a copy of *Memoirs of Abner Jones*. In every Historical Society in New England, there were numerous books, papers by and about both Jones and Smith. At Worcester, Massachusetts, I visited the American Antiquarian Society, where is housed more books and publications written prior to 1820 than any other library in America. I was amazed to find such a vast amount of Jones-Smith material, which was made available to me for examination. Through the good graces of the society, I was able to secure a copy of the first issue of *Herald of Gospel Liberty*. There were scores of sermons by both Jones and Smith. I had a number of copies made. One was "A Sermon on Baptism, preached at Norwood, July 12, 1802; delivered at the baptizing of Mrs. Stokes, by Elias Smith, preacher of the Gospel, in Portsmouth, New Hampshire."

In the introduction of the sermon, Smith says, "In attending to this text, I shall endeavor to explain seven particulars:

I.   I shall prove from the Scriptures that there is but one baptism, which is water baptism.
II.   I shall shew who is the author of it.
III. Who is the scriptural subject.
IV.   What is the scriptural mode.
V.   Who is the administrator.
VI.   The name in which it is done.
VII. The design of the ordinance.

Smith discussed each of the seven points with unusual skill and understanding. It is well to remember that this sermon was preached in 1802, long before the Campbells came to America. As a matter of fact, Alexander Campbell was only a youth of twelve at his home in North Ireland. With reference to the first point, Smith says that there were only two examples of "baptism of the Holy Ghost" mentioned in Scripture: The day of Pentecost in Acts 2 and "Cornelius and his friends" in Acts 11. He points out that the Baptism of the Holy Ghost was a promise to a select few in the apostolic age and not a command to all. Said he, "There is no such baptism in the present day." The baptism of the New Testament "must be a baptism of water."

With reference to the subject of baptism: "According to the New Testament the subject of baptism is a believer in Christ; for the subject is one who submits to the law of the King. An infant cannot submit to him."

Smith was very articulate when he spoke about "the mode of baptism." He said, "To many this is wholly a matter of indifference." But he goes on to say that "the person who asserts this must be either ignorant of the nature of mode, or mean to deceive others in saying so; for baptism depends wholly on the mode; take that away, and there is nothing left of baptism, but the name." Smith was bold to say that "baptism is by burying the believer under water, and raising him out of it again." "This," said he, "is the only scriptural mode of baptism." He proves his contention first from Scripture, by citing such passages as Romans 4:4 and Colossians 2:12.

The "places" where people were baptized prove that they were immersed. He quotes Matthew 3:6; Mark 1:5, 9, 10. He pointed out that some who opposed immersion said that the River Jordan was not more than ankle deep. This kind of reasoning was engaged in simply "to evade the force of truth." "Any person of common sense must know that the people did not go into a meeting-house and have their children sprinkled; but that the people themselves were baptized in rivers, where there was "much water." Another argument used to prove the "mode of baptism" was immersion he cited Acts 8:36-39, and elaborated on this passage at length. In concluding, in this connection, Smith shows his familiarity with the writings of scholars by quoting from Calvin, Mosheim, Leighton, Watts, Burkett and others to strengthen his contention.

Concerning the design of baptism, Smith suggests that "one reason, among many, why there is such contention about baptism is that the design of the ordinance is not understood. . ." Smith said, "The design of this one baptism is to represent a burial and resurrection, and to make a distinction between those who believe in Christ, and those who do not." He went on to say that a "burial supports a death." "This one baptism is meant to point out three deaths and resurrections:

1. The death and resurrection of Christ.
2. Our death to sin and resurrection to newness of life (Romans 6:3,4).
3. The death of our bodies, and their resurrection to immortality at the last day.

Smith concludes by saying, "When a believer is baptized according to the Scripture rule, he tells the beholders by his conduct, first, that he is dead to his old conduct, sentiments, conversation, and company. . ." "When the person is raised out of the water, this is to show that he has a new principle in his heart—new sentiments—new conversation—and new company. How different is this baptism, from that which men have invented." For a clincher, Elias Smith quotes Galatians 3:27, "For as many of you as have been baptized into Christ, have put on Christ."

In Portsmouth, New Hampshire, there is still standing a church building built by Elias Smith. It is a typical New England wood structure; used now by a group of Baptists. Also, on Jeffrey Street, there is a marker on the spot where Elias Smith lived and where the Herald of Gospel Liberty was first printed.

This New England movement owes its primary significance to the fact that men and women were looking in the direction of the New Testament order of things and away from sectarianism. The chief contribution of this movement was the direction in which it went. Others who followed them picked up where they left off and went forward to greater accomplishments.

Endnotes

1   C. C. Crawford, *The Restoration Movement*, p. 22.
2   Ibid, pp. 23, 24.
3   James Gardner, Unpublished Manuscript, 'The Christians of New England,' p. 7.
4   Ibid, p. 8.
5   Ibid, p. 9.
6   Ibid, p. 23.
7   Ibid, p. 10.
8   Ibid, p. 11.
9   Abner Jones, *Life, Experiences, Travels and Preaching* p. 59.
10. A. H. Newman, *A History of The Baptist Churches in the United States*, p. 501.
11. Abner Jones, *Memoirs*, pp. 59, 60.
12. Ibid, p. 102.
13. James Gardner, *The Christians of New England*, p. 16.
14. Robert W. Lawrence, *Elias Smith - Pioneer in Religious Journalism*, North Atlantic Christian, April/May 1962.
15. Ibid.
16. Ibid.
17. Elias Smith, *Life, Conversion, Preaching, Travel, Suffering*, p. 343.
18. Garrison-DeGroot, *The Disciples of Christ—A History*, p. 82.
19. John W. Neth Jr., *Elias Smith, Medicine Man*, The Harbinger and Discipliana, October, 1957, p. 55. At Dartmouth College library the author saw a volume titled, 'The American Physician' written by 'Dr. Elias Smith.'
20. Garrison-DeGroot, p. 90.
21. James Gardner, p. 27.
22. Elias Smith, *Life, etc.* p. 400.
23. Earl West, *Search For The Ancient Order*, Vol. 1, p. 15.
24. Elias Smith, *Smith's Eight Sermons*, p. 4 of Sermon 1.
25. Barton W. Stone, *The Christian Messenger*, Vol. 1, p. 46.
26. Ibid, p. 215.
27. Ibid, p. 216.
28. Alexander Campbell, *Millenial Harbinger, 1837*, p. 578.
29. James Gardner, p. 27.

30. Garrison-DeGroot, *History*, p. 89.
31. James Gardner, p. 28.
32. Elias Smith, *Life, etc.*, pp. 402, 403.
33. Elias Smith, *Life, etc.*, pp. 394. 396.
34. Smith's Dictionary, *Fable*, pp. 167, 168.
35. Elias Smith, *Sermon on Baptism*, p. 10.

Chapter 4

Barton W. Stone, Apostle of Love

Years ago I heard Carl Sandburg make a speech using as his subject Abraham Lincoln. In the course of the lecture he referred to Lincoln as a man of "Velvet and Steel." Barton Warren Stone (1772-1884) was such a man. He was by nature gentle, refined, and kind. But he was also a man of mighty convictions, with the boldness and courage of a lion. He is the first of the so called "big four" in the movement who attempted to restore first century Christianity in America.

Barton W. Stone was born on a large farm near Port Tobacco, Maryland, December 24, 1772. His father was John Stone, a man of considerable wealth and influence. Barton was the direct descendent of William Stone, the first Protestant Governor of Maryland. A close relative, Thomas Stone, was a member of the Second Continental Congress and one of four men from Maryland to sign the Declaration of Independence.[1] John Stone died at the outbreak of the Revolutionary War. Mrs. Stone disposed of the property and, with her seven children, moved to Pittsylvania County, Virginia, just across the line from North Carolina. Barton was seven years old at the time.[2]

John Stone had provided that his estate be divided equally among the widow and children. At the age of fifteen, Bart (as he was called at the time) received his portion. He quickly decided to use it to secure the best education possible. He had a strong desire to study law and perhaps get involved in politics.

In 1790, at the age of eighteen, Bart enrolled at the noted Guilford Academy, near Greensboro, North Carolina. The school was under the direction of Doctor David Caldwell (1725-1824), a Presbyterian preacher and educator of considerable note. Dr. Caldwell had graduated with honors from what is now Princeton University. At the school were some fifty students, many of whom were studying for the Presbyterian ministry.

Bart applied himself diligently in his studies of English, Latin, Greek, and other subjects. He practiced self-discipline, giving himself wholly to academic matters. He had no particular interest in religion at this time.

In the Spring, James McGready (1760-1817), a noted Presbyterian preacher, came to the area and conducted a revival. Thirty of the Guilford students "embraced religion." Ben Reynolds, Bart's roommate, prevailed upon him to attend the revival. Bart later related what happened, "I consented and walked with him. A crowd of people had assembled, the preacher came - it was James McGready, whom I had never seen before. He arose and looked around the assembly. His person was not prepossessing, nor his appearance interesting, except his remarkable gravity, and small piercing eyes. His coarse, tremulous voice excited in me the idea of something unearthly. His gestures were the perfect reverse of elegance. Everything appeared by him forgotten but the salvation of souls. Such earnestness, such zeal, such powerful persuasion, enforced by the joys of Heaven and miseries of hell, I had never witnessed before. My mind was chained to him. . . . His concluding remarks were addressed to the sinner to flee the wrath to come without delay. Never before had I comparatively felt the force of truth."[3]

From this time on, Bart thought less and less of law and more and more about religion. About a year after the McGready meeting, another Presbyterian preacher by the name of William Hodge came to the community. "Great excitement was among the people." Bart heard Hodge preach on the "Love of God." His text was John 3:16. This sermon proved to be a turning point in his life. It was at this time that Stone joined the Presbyterian church and decided to give up law and become a preacher. Encouraged by David Caldwell, Stone applied for a license to preach. To secure the license, he was to appear before the Orange Presbytery and present a sermon on the "Trinity." Stone had problems with this subject. The theological treatises that he read on the subject were more confusing than enlightening, but when he was examined by "Old father Patello" on the subject, his answers were satisfactory.

Stone finished his courses at Guilford Academy and, having to wait until his license could be confirmed by the Presbytery, he made a visit to his brother in Georgia. While there, he was invited to teach in Succoth Academy at Washington, where he remained for one year as "Professor of Languages." Hope Hull (1763-1818), a Methodist preacher, was principal of the Academy. In 1792, Hull had supported James O'Kelley in his opposition to Frances Asbury's autocratic rule.

Stone returned to North Carolina and received his license from Henry Patillo (1726-1801), and immediately began to preach throughout the area. He continued to apply himself to mental and spiritual improvement. His mind was confused by many of the abstruse doctrines of Presbyterianism. Though he admitted them to be true, he could not satisfactorily reconcile many of them with many other things plainly taught in the Bible.

In the first part of May, 1796, Stone and a companion, Robert Foster, started out toward the west on their horses. On May 23, Robert Foster left Stone, who then traveled alone to Knoxville. Traveling in those days through the wilderness was considered dangerous because of the hostile Indians. Stone left Knoxville headed for the Cumberland River; eventually reaching Bledso's Lick near Gallatin, in Sumner County. He was but a few miles from Nashville, "which, at that time, was a poor little village, hardly worth notice."[4] He stopped at Mansker's Creek where he preached a strong sermon against dancing, which created much opposition among some of the listeners.[5]

In company with another young Presbyterian preacher by the name of John Anderson, Stone travelled to Bourbon County, Kentucky. Anderson returned to North Carolina and Stone remained at Cane Ridge and Concord where there were two Presbyterian churches seeking a minister. The year was 1796 and Stone was 24 years old. For the next two years, he preached at these churches on alternate Sundays. In 1798 he was duly ordained by the Transylvania Presbytery.

At this time Stone was still having serious doubts about The Trinity, Reprobation, Predestination, and other matters in the Westminster Confession of Faith. Prior to going before the Presbytery, he took aside Dr. James Blythe and Robert Marshall and told them of his difficulties. They asked him how far was he willing to receive The Confession. Stone told them, "As far as I see it consistent with the Word of God." The answer was satisfactory. He then went before the whole body and was asked, "Do you receive and adopt the Confession of Faith as containing the system of doctrine taught in the Bible?" Stone answered, "I do, as far as I see it consistent with the Word of God." Again, his answer was satisfactory and he was ordained.[6]

Stone was out of sympathy with all five points of Calvinism: Inherited Sin, Total Depravity, Irresistible Grace, Predestination, Unconditional Election and the final Perseverance of the Saints. He believed that God did love the whole world, and that the reason he did not save all was due to unbelief. Saving faith is produced by testimony revealed on the pages of Holy Writ. When we read the Bible, believe and obey it, we become children of God. This was his firm belief and conviction.

Stone delivered his soul with reference to Calvinism in these words: "Let me here speak when I shall be lying under the clods of the grave. Calvinism is among the heaviest clogs on Christianity in the world. It is a dark mountain between Heaven and earth, and is amongst the most discouraging hindrances to sinners in seeking the Kingdom of God and engenders bondage to gloominess to the Saints. Its influence is felt throughout the Christian world, even where it is least suspected. Its first link is total depravity. . . ."[7]

Religious excitement was evidenced everywhere among the various denominations around the turn of the century, particularly in Kentucky and Tennessee. In the spring of 1801 Stone heard that his friend, James McGready, was in a great revival in Logan County, Kentucky. McGready was the pastor of three churches in the county: Red River, Gasper River, and Muddy River. Stone went down to attend the Camp Meeting that was in progress. Multitudes came together and continued a number of days. The things that Stone saw "baffled description." Though "Stone saw much in Logan county that he regarded as fanaticism, he became convinced that, on balance, the good far outweighed the bad."[8]

With his heart fired with the love of God, Stone returned to Bourbon County determined to create a revival among his own people. He preached Sunday morning at Cane Ridge on the Great Commission, "Go ye into all the world and preach the gospel to every creature. He that believeth and is baptized shall be saved; but he that believeth not shall be damned" (Mark 16:15,16). Sunday night he preached at Concord. Even though excitement was in the air and an "awakening" was about to take place, Stone went hurriedly to Muhlenburg County, Kentucky, and on July 2, 1801, he married Elizabeth Campbell. Immediately after the wedding, the bride and groom returned to Cane Ridge for the great revival that would shortly come.

This revival began on the third Lord's Day in August, 1801. The roads around Cane Ridge were literally crowded with wagons, carriages, horsemen and footmen moving to the camp ground. Estimates as to the number in attendance go as high as twenty to thirty thousand. Four or five preachers would be speaking at the same time in different parts of the encampment. Methodists, Baptists and Presbyterians cooperated in the preaching. During the meeting emotions ran high, resulting in "a display of acrobatic conversions." There were five general types of "bodily agitations" that were prevalent: (1) The falling exercise. This was the most common. The subject would cry out in a piercing scream, then fall flat on the ground and lying for several minutes, as though dead; (2) The jerks. In this exercise, various parts of the body would jerk violently to one side and then to the other; (3) The dancing exercise. This would begin with the jerks and then pass on to dancing. Usually, they would dance until they fell exhausted to the ground; (4) The barking exercise. This was really the jerks, but when a person's body jerked suddenly and violently, it caused a big grunt which appeared to be barking to the observer; (5) The laughter and singing exercises were just what the terms signify.[9] This emotional upsurge continued for a week. It would have continued longer but the food gave out and the meeting was forced to close in spite of the fact that there had been "three thousand conversions."

Stone was a firm believer in the universality of salvation. He believed that God loved all and wanted all to be saved on the simple terms of the gospel. He was not alone in his belief. He was surrounded by men that he considered strong, such as Richard McNemar, John Thompson, John Dunlavy, David Purviance, and Robert Marshall, all ministers in the Presbyterian church. A.W. Fortune observes that "the most important result of the Cane Ridge Revival was not the spiritual awakening which it produced . . . It led to an ecclesiastical revolt which spread through the churches of Kentucky."[10] Stone and the men around him preached a doctrine of salvation that was contrary to every point in Calvinism. This, of course, brought resistance from the Presbyterian church as a whole.

The revival preachers were tried for heresy in the synods and presbyteries for teaching things contrary to the Westminster Confession of Faith. Richard McNemar was singled out and tried first. He was summoned before his Presbytery to answer the following charges:

1. He reprobated the idea of sinners attempting to pray, or being exhorted thereto, before they were believers in Christ.
2. He condemned those who urged that convictions are necessary or that prayer is proper in the sinner.
3. He expressly declared at several times that Christ has purchased salvation for all the human race, without distinction.
4. He expressly declared that the sinner has power to believe in Christ at any time.
5. That the sinner has as much power to act faith as to act unbelief, and reprobated every idea in contradiction thereto, held by persons of a contrary opinion.
6. He has expressly said that faith consisted in the creature's persuading himself assuredly that Christ died for him in particular; that doubting and examining into evidences of faith were inconsistent with, and contrary to, the nature of faith.[11]

For preaching anti-Calvinistic doctrine, McNemar was put through a fiery ordeal. Based on the hostility of the Synod of Kentucky against him, the other four - Marshall, Dunlavy, Thompson and Stone - "withdrew from their jurisdiction, but not from their communion." These five men immediately wrote a letter of protest, which is given in full in A.W. Fortune's *The Disciples in Kentucky,* pp. 40,41.

Stone and the others withdrew from the Synod of Kentucky, but they wanted it understood that they had not renounced the Presbyterian church. This is indicated by the fact that they created their own Presbytery called The Springfield Presbytery.

The group published a pamphlet titled *An Abstract of an Apology for Renouncing the Jurisdiction of the Synod of Kentucky, Being a Compendious View of the Gospel and a Few Remarks on The Confession of Faith.*[12] "In this were set forth the causes which led to the separation; their objection to The Confession of Faith of human origin, and particularly that of the Presbyterians; and a declaration of their entire abandonment of all authoritative human creeds, and their adhesion to the Bible alone as the only rule of faith and practice in religion. This was the first public declaration of religious freedom in the Western Hemisphere; the first in the world since that of the intrepid Luther was nullified by the Yoke of Bondage framed at Augsburg. This was the beginning of that vast and mighty moral revolution connected with the present age and which has since been turning and overturning in its onward progress and promises such glorious results under the guidance of him who overrules all the grand events of the time."[13]

In this *Apology*, the ministers set forth with clarity their objections to *The Confession of Faith* and their abandonment of everything but the Bible as their rule of faith and practice. David Purviance, a candidate for the Presbyterian ministry, joined Stone and the others, thereby expressing his devotion to the things for which they stood.

Not long after his separation, Stone went before his congregation and informed them he could no longer preach to support Presbyterianism. Stone cooperated with his associates in the *Springfield Presbytery* in preaching and establishing churches with the Bible as their only guide. However, within a year's time, it was decided that such an organization was unscriptural and should be abandoned. The group divested itself of all party names and adopted the name "Christians," trusting alone in God and the word of his grace. At this time, they published a pamphlet on the name "Christian" written by Rice Haggard (1769-1819).[14] The Christians were maligned and their swift annihilation was prophesied. In spite of much opposition, however, they advanced, and churches and preachers multiplied.

In their next annual meeting at Cane Ridge, on June 28, 1804, an important document was read and adopted. The document was titled "The Last Will and Testament of the Springfield Presbytery," and is here given in full:

THE LAST WILL AND TESTAMENT
OF THE SPRINGFIELD PRESBYTERY

The Presbytery of Springfield, sitting at Cane Ridge, in the county of Bourbon, being through a gracious Providence in more than ordinary bodily health, growing in strength and size daily; and in perfect soundness and composure of mind; and knowing that it is appointed for all delegated bodies once to die; and considering that the life of every such body is very uncertain, do make and ordain this our last Will and Testament, in a manner and form following, viz:

Imprimis. We will, that this body die, be dissolved, and sink into union with the Body of Christ at large; for there is but one Body, and one Spirit, even as we are called in one hope of our calling.

Item. We will, that our name of distinction, with its Reverend title be forgotten, that there be but one Lord over God's heritage, and his name one.

Item. We will that our power of making laws for the government of the church, and executing them by delegated authority, forever cease; that the people may have free course to the Bible, and adopt the law of the Spirit of life in Christ Jesus.

Item. We will, that candidates for the Gospel ministry henceforth study the Holy Scripture with fervent prayer, and obtain license from God to preach the simple Gospel, with the Holy Ghost sent down from heaven without mixture of philosophy, remorse, deceit, traditions of men, or the rudiments of the world. And let none henceforth take this honor to himself, but he that is called of God, as was Aaron.

Item. We will, that the church of Christ resume her native right of internal government—try her candidates for the ministry, as to their soundness in the faith, acquaintance with experimental religion, gravity and aptness to teach; and admit no other proof of their authority but Christ speaking in them. We will, that the church of Christ look to the Lord of the harvest to send forth laborers into his harvest; and that she resume her primitive right of trying those who say they are apostles and are not.

Item. We will, that each particular church, as a body, actuated by the same spirit, choose her own preacher, and support him by a free will offering, without a written call or subscription—admit members—remove offenses; and never henceforth delegate her right of government to any man or set of men whatever.

Item. We will, that the people henceforth take the Bible as the only sure guide to heaven; and as many as are offended with other books, which stand in competition with it, may cast them into the fire if they choose; for it is better to enter into life having one book, than having many to be cast into hell.

Item. We will, that preachers and people, cultivate a spirit of mutual forbearance; pray more and dispute less; and while they behold the signs of the times, look up, and confidently expect that redemption draweth nigh.

Item. We will, that our weak brethren, who may have been wishing to make the Presbytery of Springfield their king, and wot not what is now become of it, betake themselves to the Rock of Ages, and follow Jesus for the future.

Item. We will, that the Synod of Kentucky examine every member, who may be suspected of having departed from the Confession of Faith, and suspend every such suspected heretic immediately; in order that the oppressed may go free, and taste the sweets of gospel liberty.

Item. We will, that Ja——- ————, the author of two letters lately published in Lexington, be encouraged in his zeal to destroy partyism. We will, moreover, that our past conduct be examined into by all who may have correct information; but let foreigners beware of speaking evil things which they know not.

Item. Finally we will, that all our sister bodies read their Bibles carefully, that they may see their fate there determined, and prepare for death before it is too late.
Springfield Presbytery

June 28, 1804 L.S.

Robert Marshall B.W. Stone
John Dunlavy John Thompson
Richard M'Nemar David Purviance Witnesses[15]

The importance of this "Will" lies in the fact that it appeals directly to the Bible and the right and duty of every individual to read and follow it for himself or herself. Complete independence of each local congregation is asserted. The desire for the unity of God's people is expressed. There is also a repudiation of "church sessions, presbyteries, synods, general assemblies, etc." as without precept or example in the New Testament. "This document ranks in importance next to Thomas Campbell's *Declaration and Address.*"[16]

The "witnesses" for a time "boldly preached the sufficiency of the gospel to save men, and that the testimony of God was designed and able to produce faith, and that sinners were capable of understanding and believing this testimony and acting upon it by coming to the Savior and from him obtaining salvation and the Holy Spirit."[17] This departure from the doctrine of the Westminster Confession of Faith brought forth strong opposition from the Confession's supporters.

Other situations developed that now engaged the attention of Stone and others. Robert Marshall became "convinced of the truth of the Baptists' view on the subject of baptism and ceased from the practice of pedobaptism; and it was believed he was on the eve of uniting with the Baptists. Alarmed lest he should join them, Stone wrote him a lengthy letter on the subject, laboring to convince him of error." It turned out that Marshall wrote so convincingly in favor of believer's immersion, that Stone was convinced that he needed to be baptized scripturally. Too, in their search for truth, they concluded that the purpose of baptism was the remission of sins. Stone said: "Into the Spirit of the doctrine I was never fully led, until it was revived by Brother Alexander Campbell some years after." We must remember that this was a period when Stone was searching for the Truth. It did not come immediately. In 1807, Stone and most of his congregation were immersed in Stoner's Creek, near Paris, Kentucky.

The life of the Stone Movement was threatened by a strange delusion. Three men, Benjamin Youngs, Isaachar Bates and John Meacham had come to Kentucky from New York. They were Shakers and their purpose was to get converts at any cost. Shaker doctrine was a mixture of Communism and Asceticism. The group had its beginning in England in the eighteenth century. Shaker doctrine was that Christ appeared first as a male and then as a woman — Ann Lee, who was now the Christ. Shakers claimed to have revelations from God, superior to the Scriptures. They did not believe in marriage and the perpetuation of the human race. Their worship consisted partly in voluntary dancing among themselves. They flourished for only a short time. It was a blow to Stone when Richard McNemar and John Dunlavy renounced their marriage relationship and joined the Shakers.[18] But Stone's greatest blow, perhaps, was the return of Marshall and Thompson to the Presyterians. With a note of sadness Stone wrote, "Of all the five of us that left the Presbyterian church, I only was left, and they sought my life."[19] Only David Parviance (1766-1847) stood firm with Stone. His influence was widespread. He was a strong advocate for the principles enunciated in "The Last Will and Testament of The Springfield Presbytery."

On May 30, 1810 Stone's beloved wife, Eliza, was taken by death. Their only son died in infancy. He broke up housekeeping and boarded his four little daughters with brethren. At this particular time, Reuben Dooley (1773-1822) joined Stone in evangelistic work, which proved effective. Several churches were established in Ohio, Kentucky and Tennessee. Stone referred to Dooley as "my companion and fellow-laborer." They worked together effectively.

On October 31, 1811, Stone married Celia Bowen, who lived near Nashville, Tennessee. They went to Bourbon County to the old home place and remained there for one year. His wife's widowed mother persuaded them to return to Tennessee. This arrangement did not work out and they returned to Kentucky and conducted a school in Lexington until 1819. He preached once each month at Cane Ridge, and studied Hebrew under a Prussian doctor, a Jew of great learning. He then moved to Georgetown, where he served as principal of Rittenhouse Academy.

Barton W. Stone was a man of indomitable courage and unflinching faith. In spite of reverses and persecutions by enemies of the Truth, he continued to forge ahead with his New Testament message of hope and salvation. Aristotle defined eloquence as "persuasive speaking." If we accept that definition, we must conclude that Stone was a man of true eloquence. With his invincible logic flowing from a heart of love he influenced a number of outstanding men to become a part of "the good cause." Among those stalwarts that he enlisted were John Allen Gano (1805-1887), John Rogers (1800-1867). J.T. Johnson (1788-1856), Reuben Dooley (1773-1822), Robert Milligan (1814-1875), and B.F. Hall (1803-1873).

Stone was unexcelled as a preacher, teacher, writer and editor. At Georgetown, Kentucky, in 1826, Stone began editing and publishing a monthly religious journal called *The Christian Messenger*, that had a tremendous impact on the development of the Christian church in Kentucky. The paper proved to be a powerful evangelistic force, and continued to be such until the death of Stone in 1844.

The pages of the *Christian Messenger* breathed the great spirit of Stone and his intense desire to restore pure, unadulterated Christianity. His emphasis was always on the supreme importance of restoring the spirit of New Testament Christianity. In an 1828 article on "Christian Union" Stone stated: "The union of Christians is confessed to be the most desirable of objects. All Christians of every order and name, acknowledge it right and important, and therefore are they earnestly engaged in praying for it. We have in former numbers stated our convictions that this desirable object can never be obtained, while the various parties are tenacious of their creeds and names. The reasons by which our convictions have been produced are, we think, irrefutable. On no other foundation can the parties ever meet, than on the Bible alone, without note or comment; and in no other name will they ever unite, but in that given to the disciples at Antioch—CHRISTIAN. But should all the professors of Christianity reject all their various creeds and names, and agree to receive the Bible alone, and be called by no other name than Christian, will this unite them? No, we are fully convinced that unless they all possess the spirit of that book and name they are far, very far, from Christian union."

In 1841, after being attacked for allegedly renouncing views he had held at the beginning of his Christian Movement he replied: "Why boast of the Bible alone, if we must believe no more of it than what were our former views? In fact, did we all agree in our first views? And have we all, or any, remained in them all, without renouncing some? Except such as are afraid to think, lest they should think wrong; and such as may be too lazy to read or think at all. For the sake of such, must we be kept back from receiving further truths; or if we do, must we be denounced as departing from former truths?"

In 1835, Stone severely chided those in the Movement who dogmatically made their own notions into terms of Christian fellowship. "The scriptures will never keep together in union, and fellowship members not in the spirit of the scriptures, which spirit is love, peace, unity, forebearance, and cheerful obedience. This is the spirit of the great Head of the body. I blush for my fellows, who hold up the Bible as the bond of union, yet make their opinions of it tests of fellowship; who plead for union of all Christians; yet refuse fellowship with such as dissent from their notions. Vain men! Their zeal is not according to knowledge, nor is their spirit that of Christ. There is a day not far ahead which will declare it. Such antisectarian-sectarians are doing more mischief to the cause and advancement of truth, the unity of Christians, and the salvation of the world, than all the skeptics in the world. In fact, they make skeptics."

In 1841 Stone spoke again on the subject of Christian union, and warned his brethren that unwritten creeds were just as divisive as those written. Many in the present century have seen, and many begin to see, that creeds are in the way of christian union; and that to support them is to support a limb of anti-christ. Thousands from this conviction have abandoned them all, and cast them to the moles, and to the bats, and have taken the Bible alone as the sole rule of faith, and practice. This is commendable, and a long stride from Babylon. But will this affect Christian union? Alas! we have to acknowledge the reverse. Thousands in this day have made this public profession, and are as much disunited in Christian love and cooperation as other sects—They have no written creeds, but they make their unwritten opinions of the Bible truths the tests of union. As long as opinions of truth are made tests of union all our boasting that the Bible alone is our religion is vain. The Bible alone in heart believed, and in the spirit obeyed, is doubtless the means of Christian union.

In 1824, Alexander Campbell (1788-1866) made an extended tour of Kentucky. It was on this trip that he and Stone met for the first time in Georgetown. The meeting was pleasant for both men. Here are Stone's own words concerning Campbell:

> When he came to Kentucky, I heard him often in public and private. I was pleased with his manners and matter. I saw no distinctive feature between the doctrine he preached and that which we had preached for many years, except on baptism for the remission of sins. Even this I had once received and taught, as before stated, but had strangely let it go by my mind till Brother Campbell revived it afresh. I thought, then, he was not sufficiently explicit on the influences of the Spirit, which led many honest Christians to think he denied them. Had he been as explicit then, as since, many honest souls would have still been with us and would have greatly aided the good Cause. In a few things I have dissented from him but was agreed to disagree.
>
> 'I will not say there are no faults in Brother Campbell but that there are fewer, perhaps, in him than any man I know on earth. Over these few my love would throw a veil and hide them from view forever. I am constrained, and willingly constrained, to acknowledge him the greatest promoter of this reformation of any man living. The Lord reward him![20]

In Georgetown, Stone had come to know J. T. Johnson (1788-1856), a former Baptist preacher, but now a "Reformer." Under their leadership, two congregations - one "Reformers" the other "Christian" - agreed to merge and work together. This greatly strengthened "the good Cause" in and around Georgetown. Johnson was educated at Transylvania University; he studied law and was admitted to the bar when he was twenty years old. He served in the state legislature for a time. In 1820, he was elected to Congress where he served two full terms. But his first love was preaching. These are his words:

> During the years '29 and '30, I had more leisure. The public mind was much excited in regard to what was vulgarly called 'Campbellism' and I resolved to examine it in the light of the Bible. I was won over and contended for it with all my might in the private circle. I was astonished at the ignorance and perversity of learned men who were reputed pious and otherwise esteemed honorable. My eyes were opened, and I was made perfectly free by the truth. The debt of gratitude I owe to this man of God, Alexander Campbell, no language can tell.[21]

J.T. Johnson was one of the shining lights in the nineteenth century reformation. Boles said of him: "He labored incessantly as an evangelist for seventeen years and became known as *The Evangelist of Kentucky.*[22] As an evangelist, Samuel Rogers referred to him as "the best model I have ever known."[23]–

There was a consuming desire on the part of both Stone and Johnson to build upon the Bible alone. Both were opposed to creeds as terms of communion, and both desired the spread of the primitive gospel. The "Christians" of Georgetown and the "Reformers" of nearby Great Crossings, where Johnson was a member, agreed to meet together for worship. The results were so pleasant they desired to meet in Georgetown for a four day conference, beginning on Sunday, December 24, 1831, for the purpose of considering the complete union between the two groups. Many of the leading preachers on both sides attended the various sessions, "and so much evidence was afforded of mutual Christian love and confidence, and such undoubted assurances were given of a firm determination on the part of all to have nothing to do with doctrinal speculations, but to accept as conclusive upon all subjects the simple teaching of the Bible, that there seemed to be no longer anything in the way of the most earnest and hearty cooperation."[24] So much enthusiasm was manifested that another meeting was called for January 1, 1832, in Lexington. The meeting place was the Hill Street church building, used by the "Christians." At a very early hour, the house was filled to overflowing. B.W. Stone, Samuel Rogers (1793-1877), G.W. Elley, (1801-1884), J.T. Johnson,(1788-1856), Jacob Creath, Sr., (1777-1854), "Raccoon" John Smith, (1784-1868), and other noted men were present. Excitement was in the air! It was decided that Smith would represent the "Reformers" and Stone the "Christians." Even though Alexander Campbell was not present, he gave editorial endorsement of this unity effort.[25]

The inimitable "Raccoon" John Smith made the first speech. As he mounted the podium, people sat on the edges of their seats, leaning forward in order to hear every word spoken. Smith stood in silence for a few moments. He broke the silence with these words:

> God has but one people on the earth. He has given to them but one Book, and therein exhorts and commands them to be one family, a union such as we plead for - a union of God's people on that one Book - must then be practical. Every Christian desires to stand complete in the whole will of God. The prayer of the Savior, and the whole tenor of his teaching clearly show that it is God's will that his children should be united. To the Christian, then, such a union must be desirable.... For several years past, I have tried to speak on such subjects only in language of inspiration, for it can offend no one to say about those things just what the Lord, himself, has said. In this scriptural style of speech all Christians should be agreed. It cannot be wrong, it cannot do harm.
>
> The gospel is a system of facts, commands, and promises; and no deduction or inferences from them, however logical or true, forms any part of the gospel of Christ...While there is but one faith, there may be ten thousand opinions; and hence, if Christians are ever to be one, they must be one in faith, and not in opinion...
>
> For several years past I have stood pledged to meet the religious world, or any part of it, on the ancient gospel and order of things as presented in the words of the Book. This is the foundation on which Christians once stood, and on it they can and ought to stand again....Let us, then, my brethren, be no longer Campbellites, or Stoneites, New Lights, or Old Lights, or any other kind of lights, but let us all come to the Bible and to the Bible alone, as the only Book in the world that can give us all the light we need.[26]

This speech captured the hearts of the people who heard it. B. W. Stone made his way to the podium, and with his heart filled with love said:

> I will not attempt to introduce any new topic, but say a few things on the subject presented by my beloved brother....After we had given up all creeds and taken the Bible, and the Bible alone, as our rule of faith and practice, we met with so much opposition that I was led to deliver some speculative discourses upon these subjects. But I never preached a sermon of that kind that really feasted my heart; I always felt a barrenness of soul afterward....I have not one objection to the ground laid down by him as the true scriptural basis on union among the people of God, and I am willing to give him now and here my hand.[27]

As he spoke these words he extended his trembling hand to John Smith, which was warmly clasped with the hearty approval of the emotionally stirred congregation. It was then proposed that all who approved this union to give each other the right hand of fellowship, which was joyfully done. Stone was elated at what had taken place and wrote: "This union, I view as the noblest act of my life."[28] Alexander Campbell looked upon the union as desirable, but it was Stone who actually brought it about.

The editors of the *Christian Messenger* of January, 1832, wrote: "We, the elders and brethren, have separated two elders, John Smith and John Rogers, the first known formerly by the name Reformer, the latter by the name of Christian. These brethren are to ride together through all the churches, and to be equally supported by the united contributions of the churches of both descriptions, which contributions are to be deposited together with Brother John T. Johnson as treasurer and distributor. We are glad to say that all the churches, so far as we hear, are highly pleased and are determined to co-operate in the work."[29] After the first few months, the union made rapid progress throughout the land. There were differences, to be sure, but the people were willing to test every sentiment by the infallible word of God. Considerable time was required to bring about a complete union between the Reformers and Christians, but in time it was done. T. M. Allen suggested for the merger in Lexington the designation of "the Church of Christ."[30]

Peter Cartwright took note of the new church and had this to say: "They established no standard of doctrine; everyone was to take the New Testament, read it, and abide his own construction of it. They adopted the mode of immersion, the water God of all exclusive errorists; and directly there was a controversy about the way to heaven, whether it was by water or by land. . . .B.W. Stone stuck to his new Lightism, and fought many bloodless battles till he grew old and feeble, and the mighty Alexander Campbell, the great, arose and poured such flood of regenerating water about the old man's cranium that he formed a union with this giant errorist and finally died not much lamented out of the circle of a few friends." (Peter Cartwright, Autobiography, p. 32)

It is interesting to note that throughout the fourteen year history of *The Christian Messenger* B.W. Stone and other editors of the paper were always listed as "Elders in the Church of Christ." B. W. Stone was devoid of any sectarian spirit as is clearly seen in his "Address to the Church of Christ" which was published in *The Christian Messenger* of September, 1832.

Stone moved from Georgetown, Kentucky, to Jacksonville, Illinois, in 1834. There he found "Reformers" and "Christians" meeting in different locations. He urged them to unite and when this was done, he became a member of the new congregation.[31] In 1835, *The Disciples' Hymn Book* was published by B. W. Stone, Alexander Campbell, Walter Scott and J. T. Johnson. There was considerable objection to the title of the Hymn Book. It was felt by some of the Stone people that the name "Christian" should be used and not "Disciples" to identify God's people. Subsequently, the song books were simply titled *Christian Hymns.*

In August of 1841, Stone was stricken with paralysis. He was incapacitated for some months and never fully recovered but, in the fall of 1843, accompanied by his son Barton and his youngest daughter, began his last preaching tour. This tour took him to Indiana, Ohio, Kentucky and Missouri. Seeing old friends from whom he had been separated for a number of years was an emotional drain. The scene at Cane Ridge "baffles our description."[32] As Stone read the twentieth chapter of Acts "tears started down his furrowed cheeks. The effect was overwhelming."[33]

On October 19, 1844, he reached Bear Creek, Missouri, where the brethren were assembled for the annual meeting. Being quite feeble, he left the meeting house and did not return until the 21st at which time, laboring under affliction, he preached his last sermon. T. M . Allen gives this record: "His great age, his whittened locks, his feeble frame, his deep and ardent piety, his pure morality and unblemished character. . . .all conspired to make this last sermon solemn. Thirteen additions were obtained."[34] Stone spent a day or so with his son, Dr. Stone, and left for Illinois an enfeebled man. He could go no farther than Hannabal where his son-in-law, Captain S. S. Bowen, lived. He was taken to his bed, and after more than a week of intense suffering, he passed away on November 9, 1844.

A short time before he passed on, his physician, Dr. D. T. Morton, said to him: "Father Stone, you have been much persecuted on account of the peculiarities of your teaching. Are you willing to die in the faith you have so long taught to others?" He replied: "I am. During my long life I may have had some errors on minor points but, in the main, I conscientiously believe I have taught the truth, and have tried to live what I have preached to others". . . .There was then sung a favorite song, which he had so often sung with J.T. Johnson,

> Farewell vain world, I'm going home,
> My Savior smiles and bids me come;
> Bright angels beckon me away
> To sing God's praise in endless days.[35]

On the night that Barton W. Stone died, he was lucid to the very end. He wanted to talk about the love of God. Having been placed in an arm chair, he called for his clay pipe. His son, Barton, came and sat by the side of his father, who leaned his head on the son's shoulder and quietly breathed his last breath without a struggle.

The next day, his body was taken in a wagon "to the locust grove, west of his cabin home on Diamond Grove Prairie, where he was buried." In 1846, his remains were removed to Jacksonville, Illinois, and interred seven miles east of the city. Then, in the spring of 1847, at the insistence of friends in Kentucky, his remains were carried to Cane Ridge to await the resurrection.[36]

In the *Millennial Harbinger* of 1832, Mr. Campbell refers to a letter that he had received from Georgetown, Kentucky, under date of November 13, informing him "that the good cause still advances." Campbell noted that Brother John Smith conducted a meeting at Great Crossing, where J. T. Johnson preached. After a powerful sermon by Smith, "four were immersed by the latter into the death of Christ." A congregation of more than forty members had grown up within a few months. Campbell expressed joy at the unity that existed between the "Disciples" and "Christians," "notwithstanding the sparring between us editors." "These brethren," he asserted, "are endeavoring every Lord's Day to keep the ordinances as they were delivered to the holy apostles. Hence, they commemorate the Lord's death as often as his resurrection. . . ."[37]

Stone differed radically from Alexander Campbell. Although the latter repudiated Calvinism as a basis of Christian fellowship he never did repudiate it as a type of thought. In this respect, he remained a Calvinist to the end. For this reason, he was never able to understand and appreciate Stone without reservation. Stone lived in a new order of life generated by American conditions and experiences in which Calvinism had become obsolete."[38]

Endnotes

1. McAllister-Tucker, *Journey In Faith*, p. 63.
2. Barton W. Stone, *Biography of Barton W. Stone*, p. 1.
3. Ibid, p. 8.
4. Ibid, p. 22.
5. Ibid.
6. Ibid, p. 30; Although some Restoration historians have maintained that these proceedings were unusual, actually they were quite normal. In the early 1700's when the Presbyterian church in America was in its formative years, a heated dispute arose over whether ministers should be required to subscribe to the Westminster Confession of Faith. A synod was held in 1709 to deal with that and other problems and its decision was set forth in the so-called 'Adopting Act.' The measure required ministers to subscribe, but it made a distinction between essential articles, and allowed local Presbyterians to decide whether a candidate's reservations about any part of the confession violated its intent. Sidney E. Ahlstrom, *A Religious History of the American People* (1972), pp. 268-9.
7. Stone, *Biography*, pp. 33-34.
8. McAllister-Tucker, p. 71.
9. West, (Vol. 1) p. 23; cf. Stone, *Biography* pp. 39-42.
10. A. W. Fortune, *The Disciples in Kentucky* p. 36.
11. Ibid., p. 37.

12. The full text of the *Apology* is reprinted in The Biography of Barton W. Stone, pp. 147-191; It is also found in *The Cane Ridge Reader* by Hoke Dickson, pp. 147-191.

13. Stone, *Biography*, p. 137.

14. The full title of this pamphlet published in 1804: *An Address to the Different Religious Societies on the Import of the Christian Name*. Though the pamphlet was written anonymously, John W. Neth, Jr. through research proves that it was written by Haggard. For a thorough study of Haggard and the name *Christian* consult Max Ward Randall, *The Great Awakening and the Restoration Movement* pp. 73-98. It is interesting to note that Haggard suggested the name *Christian* to the O'Kelley Movement, 1794, in Virginia.

15. F. L. Rowe, *Pioneer Sermons and Addresses*, pp. 7-10.

16. F. D. Kersner, *The Restoration Handbook* (Series 1), p. 24.

17. F. W. Shepherd, *The Church, The Falling Away and The Restoration*, p. 163.

18. Max Ward Randall, *The Great Awakening*, pp. 68-69.

19. B. W. Stone, *Biography*, pp. 66-67.

20. Ibid, pp. 75-76.

21. John Rogers, *Biography of J. T. Johnson*, p. 21.

22. H. Leo Boles, *Biographical Sketches of Gospel Preachers*, p. 45.

23. Samuel Rogers, *Autobiography*, p. 200.

24. Robert Richardson, *Memoirs* (Vol. 2), p. 383.

25. Alexander Campbell, *Millennial Harbinger, Religious News* (Jan. 2, 1832), p. 29.

26. John P. Williams, *Life of Elder John Smith*, pp. 378-380.

27. Ibid, p. 380.

28. Barton W. Stone, *Biography*, p. 79.

29. *Christian Messenger* (1832), pp. 6-7.

30. Robert Richardson, *Memoirs* (Vol. 2), p. 384.

31. Barton W. Stone, *Biography*, p. 79.

32. Ibid, p. 84.

33. Ibid, p. 85.

34. Ibid, pp. 100-101.

35. Ibid, pp. 103, 104. The song that was sung is found in Rice Haggard's *A Selection of Christian Hymns* (1818), reprint ed., 1983, p. 323.

36. C. C. Ware, *Barton W. Stone*, p. 323; B. W. Stone Jr., *The Bible Advocate* (1846), p. 112; *Christian Messenger* (1844), pp. 231-232; See letters, Dr. D. T. Morton and T. M. Allen, Ibid, pp. 241-244; Discourse on death of B. W. Stone, Ibid, pp. 290-319; July 22, 1845. John Allen Gano delivered an eloquent discourse occasioned by Stone's death. See Biography of B. W. Stone, pp.

130-146.

37.   Alexander Campbell, *Millennial Harbinger* (1832), p. 29.

38.   C. C. Ware, *Barton W. Stone*, p. 13.

Chapter 5

Thomas Campbell, Man of the Book

Unless we are very careful we will underestimate the genius of Thomas Campbell. This is due to the fact that his son had such an overshadowing personality. To be sure, Alexander was a gifted son, "richly endowed with powers of argument and oratory. But in intellectual insight and originality he was not superior to his illustrious father."[1] Thomas Campbell blazed the trail over which Alexander traveled to fame. I like to think of Thomas Campbell as being the architect of The Restoration Movement and Alexander, his son, as the builder.

Together, these two men, father and son, brought about conditions that changed the world of religion. Who was this man, Thomas Campbell? He was a natural born teacher and a profound scholar. He was one of the most highly educated preachers in America. F. D. Kershner said that he was the best trained man academically in the restoration movement of the nineteenth century.

Thomas Campbell was born February 1, 1763, in County Down, North Ireland. The Campbells were a distinguished family that immigrated to North Ireland from western Scotland generations before the subject of this sketch was born. They claimed kinship with "the Campbells of Argyleshire," which the Duke of Argle headed.[2] We know very little about the mother of Thomas, but a great deal about his father, Archibald.

Archibald grew up as a member of the Catholic church. As a young man, he served in the British army in America under General Wolf. After the battle of Quebec, he returned to his home in Ireland - at which time he gave up Catholicism and became a member of the Church of England. He died in his eighty eighth year. He used to say that he worshipped God according to an act of Parliment. Archibald had four daughters, each of whom was given the name Mary, but each died in infancy. He had four sons, Thomas, James,

Archibald, and Enos. He gave to each an excellent English education at a military school near by.

In his early youth, Thomas, who possessed a deep religious character, developed a love for the Scriptures. Family worship was encouraged in the Campbell home. It is related that when preparing himself for the ministry, Thomas had been permitted to conduct worship and that on one occasion, when he had prayed unusually long, the old man, whose kneeling posture had become painful to him on account of his rheumatism, was no sooner upon his feet than, in a sudden gust of passion, he began greatly to belabor poor Thomas with his cane because he had kept them so long upon their knees.[3]

The rigid formalities of the Anglican church did not appeal to Thomas. He found more congenial, spiritual alignment among the "warm-hearted and zealous Seceders. . .a branch of the Presbyterian church."[4]

After much prayer, study and soul-searching he cast his lot with the Seceders, much to the displeasure of his father. Even before joining the Seceders, he was filled with an ardent desire to be helpful to others. He traveled to a point in South Ireland and established an English academy, which he operated with signal success. But at the insistence of his father, Thomas returned to the North and, with the help of one John Kinley, obtained a good school at Sheepbridge, near Newry. Kinley had such high regards for the ability of Thomas that he urged him to enroll as a student at Glascow University, offered financial support.[5] It should be noted that the brothers of Thomas - James, Archibald and Enos, also joined the Seceder church.

Thomas Campbell, at the age of twenty, in 1783, enrolled at Glasgow University as a freshman. The University, at the time, was more than three hundred years old. The course for divinity students required three years. Thomas also attended the medical lectures which qualified him to practice medicine, had he chosen to do so. He wanted to be in a position to render medical as well as spiritual aid to his parishioners.

After graduating with honors from the University, he enrolled in a theological school operated by the Anti-Burger branch of the Presbyterian church. At that time, Dr. Archibald Bruce, who was living at Whitburn, was the sole professor of the establishment. It was the custom to transfer Divinity Hall to the place where the appointed professor was preaching.[6]

The course of study at Whitburn consisted of five annual sessions of eight weeks each. It was required by the Synod that he should be examined as to his proficiency in Latin and Greek. In addition, he was examined in the various branches of Philosophy that he had studied at the University. His sessions lasted five years—from 1786 to 1792. Between the annual sessions at Divinity Hall, he evidently spent his time in North Ireland, preaching and teaching.

It was during the first of these vacation periods that he met Jane Corneigle (1763-1835). They married in June 1787. Jane was a descendant of the French Huguenots, who fled from France in 1681.[7] At the time of their marriage she was twenty-four and he was twenty-five. Their home was in Ballymena, in County Antrim. Alexander, their first child, was born September 12, 1788. Thomas finished his theological studies in 1792 and, for several years, he taught and preached as opportunities presented themselves. After some time, the Campbells moved to Market Hill, near Armagh. Still on probation, Thomas preached for small congregations in the area. During this period, Dorothea was born (July 27, 1793) and on September 18, 1795, Nancy was born. The family was increasing along with the corresponding responsibilities.

In 1798, Thomas accepted a call from a recently established Seceder church at Ahorey, in the open country. The family moved to Rich Hill on a farm, about three miles from the Ahorey church. "Here the family resided until their great adventure to America."[8]

Because of the influence upon Thomas Campbell (and later upon his son, Alexander) it is important that note be taken of the religious conditions in North Ireland at the time. The National church (church of Scotland), was having internal strife over whether congregations had the right to choose their ministers. After much discussion, Alexander Erskine and others formally seceded in 1733 and formed the Associate Presbytery, which became a new party called Seceders.[9] This secession was the first great schism in the Church of Scotland.

The Seceder church continued in a prosperous condition until 1747, when it divided into two parties. The division was over the question of certain oaths required by the burgesses of towns, binding people to support "the religion presently professed within the realm." Those who considered the Oath unlawful were called Anti-Burghers, and the others Burghers.[10]

In 1795, a question arose among the "Burghers" as to the power of civil magistrates in religion. This controversy brought about a division in both the "Burghers" and the "Anti-Burghers" who were divided into "Old Lights" and "New Lights." The "Old Light" party was led by Dr. Archibald Bruce, who had been the teacher of Thomas at the Theological School at Whitburn. When Thomas began preaching at Ahorey, he found himself identified as a minister in the Seceder, Anti-Burgher, Old Light Presbyterian church.

These divisions which had splintered the Presbyterian church proved to be an almost unbearable burden for this Godly man who had a passion for unity on a Biblical basis. He made strong efforts to bring about unity, at least among the Seceders. All parties were saturated with a sectarian spirit, hence, efforts to unite were futile.

From his university days at Glascow, Thomas Campbell had become familiar with the Independent churches, which had resulted from the efforts of such men as John Glas, Robert Sandeman, the Haldane brothers and others. While he was preaching at Ahorey, Thomas would frequently attend the Independent church in Rich Hill. The Seceders were a dogmatic and narrow sect, who would tolerate no views other than their own. By way of contrast, Mr. Campbell saw a different attitude that greatly influenced him and helped prepare him for the work that he would later perform in America.

In the year of 1805, it seems that Mr. Campbell was deputed to travel from his home in North Ireland to Glascow to lay the matter of Unity before the General Synod. A man who heard the debate among the Seceders, made the following comment to Alexander Campbell some four years later: "I listened to your father in our General Assembly in the city pleading for a union between the Burghers and the Anti-Burghers. But, sir, while in my opinion he out argued them, they out voted him."[11]

But Mr. Campbell's experience with this volatile sectarian spirit—"fraught with the awful consequences of distracting, disturbing and dividing the flock of the Lord's heritage, and sowing discord among the brethren," as he said in his address to the Anti-Burgher Synod of Ireland. This incident, according to Garrison and DeGroot, turned his mind permanently toward Christian unity. Campbell's passion for unity, on a Biblical basis, might well summarize his life.

Back in Ahorey and Rich Hill, Thomas continued to hear James and Robert Haldane, Alexander Carson and Roland Hill when, on occasion, they preached at Rich Hill. He would hear them at night when he was not preaching at Ahorey. They were much pleased to see him at their meeting. They esteemed him as a learned and pious minister.[12]

The Campbell family continued to grow. In addition to Alexander, Dorothea and Nancy, there followed Jane, James, Archibald and Alicia. Mr. Campbell personally supervised the training and education of his children, and he was a strict disciplinarian. For example, he drilled his oldest son in Latin and Greek classics, French/English literature and other branches of learning. He made him like them as well as learn them. Every morning and evening, there was family worship, where Scripture was read, memorized and recited. There were prayers and singing of Psalms. These kinds of activities created strong spiritual ties in the Campbell family.

Often though, young Alexander was more occupied with sports than with his studies. One warm, sunny spring day when Alexander was about nine years old, his father assigned him a French lesson in *The Adventures of Telemacus*. He went out and sat under the shade of a tree to study, and fell asleep. A cow, grazing nearby, came up and ate the book. When Thomas learned of the incident, he reprimanded Alexander, saying: "That cow has more French in her stomach than you have in your head."

It was becoming more and more difficult for Thomas to make a living for his large family. The church at Ahorey never paid him more than two hundred and forty dollars per annum. And his attempts at farming met with little or no success. He was not a man of the soil, he was a man of intellectual pursuits. His private school at Rich Hill brought very little revenue for it was difficult for him to turn away a student, even though he was unable to pay. His health had begun to deteriorate at the age of forty-four. His doctor advised a sea voyage in order for his health to improve, but this advice was extremely distasteful to him. He could scarcely endure the thought of leaving his family. Yielding at length to the encouragement of his family and close friends, he decided to go to the United States in view of his wife and children following at a later date.

Accordingly, on April 1, 1807, he stood before his weeping congregation and bade them farewell. On April 8, at Londonderry, he boarded the sailing vessel Brutus, bound for Philadelphia. After a voyage of thirty five days, the vessel landed safely at its destination. Upon his arrival, Thomas wrote a letter dated May 27, 1807, to his precious family. Among other things he said:

> My dear Jane, let nothing discourage you. Turn to God; make his Word and will your constant study and rely upon it . . . so the Lord will make you glad and satisfy you with his tender mercies. . . my dear children . . . if you have any sympathy, any sincere affection for a father who cannot cease to love you and pray for you so long as his heart shall beat or tongue be able to articulate, see that you follow the directions that I gave you at parting . . . Be a comfort to your mother; love, cherish and pity one another. Love the Lord your God; love his son Jesus Christ and pray to the Lord . . . for me your poor father, who longs after you all . . .[13]

It so happened that at the time that Campbell arrived in Philadelphia, the Associate Synod of North America was in session. This Synod represented Seceder Presbyterians in America. Mr. Campbell went before this body and his credentials were such that he was warmly received and given an assignment in the Chartiers Presbytery at Washington, Pennsylvania, a village not far from Pittsburgh. He made the three hundred mile journey by stage and was delighted to find a number of people he had known in Ireland, some of whom had been members of his church. Hence, he had a very favorable beginning in his new charge in America.

Mr. Campbell at once received a warm welcome from the people. His natural ability, his scholarship and literary culture made him head and shoulders above the preachers in that region. His deep religious fervor and zeal, along with his rare courtesy of manner, won the hearts of the people.

Thomas Campbell had not been long in America before he ran into a serious problem. He was asked to visit Cannamaugh, just north of Pittsburgh, to preach and serve communion to the Anti-Burghers in the area. In the community there were some who belonged to other segments of the Presbyterian church. He invited them all to take communion. A young Seceder preacher, William Wilson, accompanied Mr. Campbell on this trip. Wilson said nothing at the time, but later, back home at the regular meeting of the Presbytery, which met October 27, 1807, Wilson reported Mr. Campbell's "heresy." This deviation from Orthodoxy loomed large as an ecclesiastical blunder of the most iniquitous kind.

The Presbytery, already dissatisfied with Campbell's liberal views, quickly accepted the charges that were made by Mr. Wilson. Mr. Campbell was brought before the Presbytery and was severely rebuked. He freely acknowledged what he had done, but pleaded for Christian liberty. His efforts were in vain. He then appealed to the Synod, which acquitted him, however, he was again rebuked. Feeling against him was so high that, through the medium of a letter addressed to the Synod, he declined "all ministerial connection with, or subjection to, the Associate Synod of North America." Thus, he found himself in a strange land without any official ministerial connection. This, however, only increased his zeal to extend the Lord's kingdom as directed by the Holy Scriptures.

After almost two years of controversy, Campbell felt that the time was ripe for some kind of constructive movement. The consuming ambition of his heart was to go forward with the Bible as his guide. He continued to preach regularly to people like himself, who yearned to be free from sectarian bitterness and narrowness. He continued to preach, but church houses were closed to him. He preached in private homes and in the open. Great throngs of people gladly heard this preacher who was searching for truth.

Consequently, in the early summer of 1809, a meeting was called at the home of Abram Alters. The purpose of the meeting was to discuss the future of those who had decided to take the Bible as their only rule of faith. Scores of eager people were present and Thomas Campbell was urged to speak. Mr. Campbell, in his quiet way, talked about the horrid evils of division among God's people. He insisted that the people read the Bible and follow its teaching, and abandon everything in religion not authorized by Scripture. He reached the climax of his sermon by saying, "That rule, my highly respected hearers, is this, that where the Scriptures speak, we speak; and where the Scriptures are silent, we are silent."

Andrew Munro, a Scotch Seceder, arose and said, "Mr. Campbell, if we adopt that as a basis, then there is an end to infant baptism." This observation somewhat stunned Campbell. He stood in silence for some moments and then said, "Of course, if infant baptism is not in the Scripture, we can have nothing to do with it." Upon this, Thomas Acheson of nearby Washington arose, greatly excited, laying his hand on his heart exclaimed, "I hope I may never see the day when my heart will renounce the blessed saying of the Scripture, 'Suffer little children to come unto me, and forbid them not, for of such is the Kingdom of heaven.'" He was so much affected that he burst into tears, and was about to leave the crowded room when James Foster cried out, "Mr. Acheson, I would remark that in that portion of Scripture you have quoted there is no reference whatever to infant baptism."

The rule which Mr. Campbell had announced seemed to cover the whole ground, and to be so obviously just and proper, that after further discussion and conference, it was adopted with apparent uninimity, no valid objection being urged against it.[14] They had thus a clear and well-defined basis of action, and the hearts of all who were truly interested re-echoed the resolve: "Where the Scriptures are silent, we are silent." Dr. Robert Richardson says: "It was from the moment when these significant words were uttered and accepted that the more intelligent ever after dated the formal and actual commencement of The Reformation, which was subsequently carried on with so much success, and which has already produced such important change in religious society over a large portion of the world."[15]

In order to expedite the efforts of Campbell and his associates, a meeting was set for August 17, 1809. At this meeting, they formed themselves into what they called "The Christian Association of Washington." They then appointed a committee of twenty one to meet and confer together and, with the assistance of Thomas Campbell, to determine upon the means to carry into effect the important ends of the Association.[16] It appears that Thomas Campbell was elected to write a document spelling out the objectives of the Association. In the home of Mr. Welch, a local farmer, Mr. Campbell was supplied with a small apartment in which to work.

By September 7, 1809, the now famous "Declaration and Address" had been written, approved by the committee, and ordered printed. It is one of the classic documents of church history. M. M. Davis referred to it as "The Magna Charta of the great Restoration Movement. . .and a Declaration of Independence" for the Christian man.[17] A. S. Hayden declared, "It is a remarkable production for its catholicity, its supreme exaltation of the word of God, its clear, unequivocal statement of the true and practical ground of union, and its enunciation of all the principles of this rising religious movement."[18] N. B. Hardeman called it "The most wonderful document of its kind in all the world."[19] David Lipscomb said it was "The beginning of the present effort to restore the Apostolic Order."[20] Just a short time before his death, Alexander Campbell referred to it in this way: "The Declaration and Address contains what may be called the embryo, or the rudiments, of a great and rapidly increasing community. It virtually contains the elements of a great movement of vital interest to every citizen of Christ's kingdom.[21]

In its published form, the document was a pamphlet of fifty six pages, small print, involving some thirty thousand words. It consisted of four parts: first, a declaration, stating its central ideas and purposes; second, an address giving thirteen propositions that would produce unity among God's people; third, an appendix, the largest part of the document, explaining in detail the things written in the address; fourth, a postscript, written some time later, suggesting how the enterprise might be promoted.

The Declaration involves four important matters in embryo: (1) The right of private judgment is proclaimed. Every one has the right to read the Bible for himself. (2) The sole authority of the Scriptures in matters of faith is boldly asserted. (3) The horrid evils of sectarianism is pointed out. (4) That unity among Christians can be achieved and maintained by conforming exactly to Scripture. The thirteen propositions of the Address are so vital that they are here given in full.

Let none imagine that the subjoined propositions are at all intended as an overture toward a new creed or standard for the Church, or as in any wise designed to be made a term of communion; nothing can be further from our intention. They are merely designed for opening up the way, that we may come fairly and firmly to original ground upon clear and certain premises, and take up things just as the apostles left them; that thus disentangled from the accruing embarassments of intervening ages, we may stand with evidence upon the same ground on which the Church stood at the beginning. Having said so much to solicit attention and prevent mistake, we submit as follows:

Prop. 1. That the Church of Christ upon earth is essentially, intentionally, and constitutionally one; consisting of all those in every place that profess their faith in Christ and obedience to him in all things according to the Scriptures, and that manifest same by their tempers and conduct, and of none else; as none else can be truly and properly called Christians.

2. That although the Church of Christ upon earth must necessarily exist in particular and distinct societies, locally separate one from another, yet there ought to be no schisms, no uncharitable divisions among them. They ought to receive each other as Christ Jesus hath also received them, to the glory of God. And for this purpose they ought all to walk by the same rule, to mind and speak the same thing; and to be perfectly joined together in the same mind, and in the same judgment.

3. That in order to do this, nothing to be inculcated upon Christians as articles of faith; nor required of them as terms of communion, but what is expressly taught and enjoined upon them in the Word of God. Nor ought anything to be admitted, as of Divine obligation, in their Church constitution and managements, but what is expressly enjoined by the authority of our Lord Jesus Christ and his apostles upon the New Testament Church; either in express terms or by approved precedent.

4. That although Scriptures of the Old and New Testaments are inseparably connected, making together but one perfect and entire revelation of the Divine will, for the edification and salvation of the Church, and therefore in that respect cannot be separated; yet as to what directly and properly belongs to their immediate object, the New Testament is as perfect a constitution for the worship, discipline, and government of the New Testament Church, and as perfect a rule for the particular duties of its members, as the Old Testament was for the worship, discipline and government

of the Old Testament Church, and the particular duties of its members.

5. That with respect to the commands and ordinances of our Lord Jesus Christ, where the Scriptures are silent as to the express time or manner of performance, if any such there be, no human authority has power to interfere, in order to supply the supposed deficiency by making laws for the Church; nor can anything more be required of Christians in such cases, but only that they so observe these commands and ordinances as will evidently answer the declared and obvious end of their institution. Much less has any human authority power to impose new commands or ordinances upon the Church, which our Lord Jesus Christ has not enjoined. Nothing ought to be received into the faith or worship of the Church, or be made a term of communion among Christians, that is not as old as the New Testament.

6. That although inferences and deductions from Scripture premises, when fairly inferred, may be truly called the doctrine of God's Holy Word, yet are they not formally binding upon the consciences of Christians farther than they perceive the connection, and evidently see that they are so: for their faith must not stand in the wisdom of men, but in the power and veracity of God. Therefore, no such deductions can be made terms of communion, but do properly belong to the after and progressive edification of the Church. Hence, it is evident that no such deductions or inferential truths ought to have any place in the Church's confession.

7. That although doctrinal exhibitions of the great system of Divine truths, and defensive testimonies in opposition to prevailing errors, be highly expedient, and the more full and explicit they be for those purposes, the better; yet, as these must be in a great measure the effect of human reasoning, and of course must contain many inferential truths, they ought not to be made terms of Christian communion; unless we suppose, what is contrary to fact, that none have a right to the communion of the Church, but such as possess a very clear and decisive judgment, or are come to a very high degree of doctrinal information; whereas the Church from the beginning did, and ever will, consist of little children and young men, as well as fathers.

8. That as it is not necessary that persons should have a particular knowledge or distinct apprehension of all Divinely revealed truths in order to entitle them to a place in the Church; neither should they, for this purpose, be required to make a profession more extensive than their knowledge; but that, on the contrary, their having a due measure of Scriptural self-knowledge respecting their lost and perishing condition by nature and practice, and

of the way of salvation through Jesus Christ, accompanied with a profession of their faith in and obedience to him, in all things, according to his Word, is all that is absolutely necessary to qualify them for admission into his Church.

9. That all that are enabled through grace to make such a profession, and to manifest the reality of it in their tempers and conduct, should consider each other as the precious saints of God, should love each other as brethren, children of the same family and Father, temples of the same Spirit, members of the same body, subjects of the same grace, objects of the same Divine love, bought with the same price, and joint-heirs of the same inheritance. Whom God hath thus joined together no man should dare to put asunder.

10. That division among the Christians is a horrid evil, fraught with many evils. It is antichristian, as it destroys the visible unity of the body of Christ; as if he were divided against himself, excluding and excommunicating a part of himself. It is antiscriptural, as being strictly prohibited by his sovereign authority; a direct violation of his express command. It is antinatural, as it excites Christians to condemn, to hate, and oppose one another, who are bound by the highest and most endearing obligations to love each other as brethren, even as Christ has loved them. In a word, it is productive of confusion and of every evil work.

11. That (in some instances) a partial neglect of the expressly revealed will of God, and (in others) an assumed authority for making the approbation of human opinions and human inventions a term of communion, by introducing them into the constitution, faith, or worship of the Church, are, and have been, the immediate, obvious, and universally acknowledged causes, of all the corruptions and divisions that ever have taken place in the Church of Cod.

12. That all that is necessary to the highest state of perfection and purity of the Church upon earth is, first, that none be received as members but such as having that due measure of Scriptural self-knowledge described above, do profess their faith in Christ and obedience to him in all things according to the Scriptures; nor, secondly, that any be retained in her communion longer than they continue to manifest the reality of their profession by their temper and their conduct. Thirdly, that her ministers, duly and Scripturally qualified, inculcate none other things than those very articles of faith and holiness expressly revealed and enjoined in the word of God. Lastly, that in all their administrations they keep close by the observance of all Divine ordinances, after the example of the primitive Church, exhibited in the New Testament; without any additions whatsoever of human opinions or inventions of men.

13. Lastly, That if any circumstantials indispensably necessary

to the observance of Divine ordinances be not found upon the page of express revelation, such, and such only, as are absolutely necessary for this purpose should be adopted under the title of human expedients, without any pretense to a more sacred origin, so that any subsequent alteration or difference in the observance of these things might produce no contention nor division in the Church.

From the nature and construction of these propositions, it will evidently appear, that they are laid in a designed subserviency to the declared end of our association; and are exhibited for the express purpose of performing a duty of previous necessity, a duty loudly called for in existing circumstances at the hand of every one that would desire to promote the interests of Zion; a duty not only enjoined, as has been already observed from Isaiah 57:14, but which is also there predicted of the faithful remnant as a thing in which they would voluntarily engage. "He that putteth his trust in me shall possess the land, and shall inherit my holy mountain; and shall say, Cast ye up, cast ye up, prepare the way; take up the stumbling-block out of the way of my people." To prepare the way for a permanent Scriptural unity among Christians, by calling up to their consideration fundamental truths, directing their attention to first principles, clearing the way before them by removing the stumbling-blocks—the rubbish of ages, which has been thrown upon it, and fencing it on each side, that in advancing toward the desired object they may not miss the way through mistake or inadvertency, by turning aside to the right hand or to the left, is, at least, the sincere intention of the above propositions.[22]

F. D. Kershner has condensed the thirteen propositions under the following brief headings:

1. The unity of the Church of Christ.
2. Congregational diversity.
3. The Bible the only rule of faith and practice.
4. The New Testament the supreme authority for Christians.
5. All human authority disallowed in the church.
6. Deductions from the Bible are not binding upon Christians.
7. Opinions cannot be made tests of fellowship.
8. The only creed of the church is faith in the divine Christ.
9. All who accept this creed and live by it are brothers in Christ.
10. Sectarian divisions among Christians are unchristian.
11. The cause of such divisions is the neglect of God's word and the introduction of human innovations.
12. The cure for such divisions is the restoration of the New Testament church.
13. Human expedients in the Church, when permissible, are not to usurp the authority granted in the Scriptures.[23]

This remarkable address was signed by Thomas Campbell and Thomas Acheson. It will be remembered that this was the same Thomas Acheson who became so emotionally upset at Campbell's statement, "We speak where the Bible speaks; we are silent where the Bible is silent," because it would eliminate infant baptism.

Thomas Campbell and his close associates were sorely disappointed that the religious leaders of Western Pennsylvania took so little note of the Declaration and Address. All the ministers in the area received a copy of the document, and "if they bothered to read it, they said nothing about it." Although little notice was given the Declaration and Address, the Christian Association itself was watched with much interest. Nevertheless, the Christian Association accomplished none of the things it set out to do, and within two years it ceased to exist in its original form.

In the Declaration and Address, Mr. Campbell was convinced "that he had discovered an infallible formula for Christian union. . . He was willing to stake his entire case for union on this platform."[24]

Richardson points out that: "So fully and so kindly was every possible objection considered and refuted, that no attempt was ever made by the opposers of the proposed movement to controvert directly a single position which it contained.."[25]

In telling the story of Thomas Campbell, a number of interesting matters have been omitted here that will be told in a later chapter in connection with Alexander Campbell.

The travels of Thomas Campbell were very extensive and his labors abundant. In 1813, he moved to Cambridge, Ohio, and opened a school there. After two years, he moved to Pittsburgh, Pennsylvania. His next move was to Newport, Kentucky, where he also taught. He made frequent preaching tours to Ohio, Pennsylvania, Kentucky, North Carolina, and Indiana. His beloved wife, Jane, died in 1835 at the age of seventy one. She was buried in the Campbell cemetery at Bethany.

Thomas Campbell moved about quite a bit after publication of The Declaration and Address. Alexander took note of this and other things in a letter dated December 28, 1815, to his uncle Archibald at Newry, North Ireland.

> Dear Uncle: More than seven years have elapsed since I bade farewell to you and my native country. During this period of time, my mind and circumstances have undergone many resolutions. . . no consideration that I can conceive of, would induce me to exchange all that I enjoy in this country, climate, soil, government, for any situation which your country can afford. I would not exchange the honor and privilege of being an American citizen for the position of your king.
>
> My father still resembles one of our planets in immigrating from place to place. . . As to our religious state, news, progress and

attainment I expect my father has written you. . . I have, through clear convictions of truth and duty, renounced much of the traditions and errors of my early education. I am now an independent in church government. . .what I am in religion, I am from examination, reflection, conviction, not from 'ipsi dixit', tradition or human authority, and having halted, and faltered, and stumbled, I have explored every inch of the way hitherto, and I trust through grace, I am what I am. Though my father and I acede in sentiment, neither of us are dictators or imitators. Neither of us lead; neither of us follow.[26]

At the earnest entreaty of his friends, Mr. Thomas Campbell preached his farewell sermon on June 1, 1851, at Bethany, to a large audience. His subject was "The Two Great Commandments," love to God and love to man. At the time, he was totally blind and in his eighty ninth year. It has been said by Robert Richardson, who heard him, that his mental faculties were still active and vigorous.

This farewell sermon is given in full in *The Millennial Harbinger*, (Vol. 4, 1854) pp 133-145. From it, the reader will gain an insight into the character and the complete dedication of this man of great soul. He says, for example, "But you ask, who is our neighbor? Our blessed Lord has beautifully and feelingly answered this question in the parable of the good Samaritan, recorded in Luke. I am sorry I cannot read to you for it has pleased my merciful heavenly Father—ever blessed be his name—in the wisdom of his providence, to take from me my eyesight; but I trust you have your Bibles and consult them continually, night and day, that you may know the will of him who has so graciously condescended to enlighten us; and that knowing it, you may be found continually walking in his commandments, for they are holy, just and good. . . In conclusion my dear brethren, I can say no more to you, as the last words of a public ministry. . .protracted for more than three score years, in this my farewell exhortation to you on earth—I can say no more than what I have already urged upon you, 'Love the Lord thy God with all thy heart, and all thy soul, and all thy mind, and all thy strength, and thy neighbor as thy self,' for in so doing, the powers of hell shall not prevail against you."[27]

Mr. Campbell's health continued to be good until some three weeks before his death. He declined rapidly and died on January 4, 1854, in his ninety first year. He died in the Campbell mansion where he had lived for the last years of his life.

After the death of his father, Alexander asked his sister, Dorothea, (Mrs. Joseph Bryant) to write Walter Scott, requesting from him any facts or documents connected with the life and labors of Father Thomas Campbell during his association with him. He printed the request that he had made to Dorothea in *The Millennial Harbinger*, and he added: "Will not our friends and the friends of the cause we plead, favor us in like manner."

A number of letters were received; of the many I will notice a few. Walter Scott wrote from his home in Mayslick, Kentucky: "I always regarded your father as a man of fine intellectual parts. . .It was impossible to look upon his lofty brows and facial lines of thought without reading in these exterior symbols intellectual greatness—reason, robust common sense, capacity, skill, wisdom. . .I once heard him in my Academy, which was large, deliver a current commentary on James, first chapter, and can say in regard to it, that I have not since that time listened to anything in the way of teaching more beautiful in expression or in thought and reason, more delightful and ravishing. Touching his practical nature, its basis seemed moral rather than sentient. His affections were, therefore, stirred from within rather than from without, and shone forth in respect for the rights of others, rather than in excitability for their faults.

He had, as a scholar, mingled with the aristocracy of his own native land; and without contracting any of their luxurious habits, had come off victorious from the contact impressed only with the grace and elegance of their lordly address. He was one of the best bred men of his day.

Touching his religion, he was the most devout man I ever knew. He loved God and adored him for the gift of his Son in our great redemption. . .He was the most exemplary man I ever saw. . ."[28]

Jacob Creath, Jr., wrote from Western Missouri: "We preached together in Maysville, Kentucky, before the meeting in Mayslick, and I was struck with the extensive and accurate acquaintance which your father manifested with the Hebrew prophets, and the sacred writings of the Old Testament Scriptures. He seemed to me to have memorized a great portion of the prophets, and to quote them more readily than any man I ever heard. With the New Testament he was perfectly familiar, and seemed always delighted to dwell on the love of God to men, and our love to him and one another, and on holiness and purity of life. . .I venerate your father as one of the most apostolic and noble Christian spirits I ever saw. . .He was the most perfectly polite Christian gentleman I ever knew."[29]

John R. Frame, writing from Milfordton, Ohio, said: "I never knew a more pious and godly man. My father used to say he reminded him of the Apostle John. His piety and sweetness of manner reminded him of the character one would form, from reading history, of that lovely apostle."[30]

An affinity existed between Thomas Campbell and his son, Alexander, perhaps without parallel in American history. They thought alike. Even though they studied independently, they nearly always reached the same conclusions. It comes as no surprise that Alexander spoke so highly of his deceased father. In a letter addressed to "Brother Dungan" of Baltimore, he wrote: "I never knew a man, in all my acquaintances with men, of whom it could have been said with more assurance that he 'walked with God.'"[31] In his *Memoirs of Thomas Campbell*, Alexander talked about a number of things in the life of his father as they flooded through his mind. He spoke of his unfeigned piety and his constant, free and familiar communion with God, and how superlatively adverse he was to evil speaking. His great passion was to unite Christians on a Biblical basis. This was the consuming ambition of his life, and to this end he wrote the *Declaration and Address*. His family discipline was the most perfect that Alexander had ever seen. He always honored his own word; what he promised he performed, and what he threatened he carried out to the letter. The Bible was not only always on the table, but daily in the hands of his family, including the servants. The Bible was read daily in the family worship, and a portion of it was memorized and repeated on Sunday evenings." Alexander said, "If permitted to speak of one's self, we must say that to Father Campbell we are more indebted than to all other teachers and instructors for such a command of attention as enables me even yet...to recollect that material of any lecture or sermon...without the loss of a prominent idea."

Alexander remembered as a boy entering his father's study which was well stocked with books, yet with few exceptions he would note only the Bible and Concordance on the table. Alexander was grateful that his father constrained him to memorize, in early life, much of the sacred writings, especially Proverbs, Ecclesiastes, many of the Psalms of David, as well as much of the New Testament. Alexander concluded his remarks by saying, "Among all my acquaintance, in the Christian ministry or out of it, I know no man that so uniformly, so understandingly, practiced what he taught."[32]

There is a story told by Richardson in *Memoirs of Alexander Campbell* (Vol. 1, p 494f), that reveals a great deal about the character of Thomas Campbell. He was operating a flourishing Seminary in Burlington, Kentucky. Pupils from some of the best families in the state were sent there to receive instruction from the distinguished pedagogue. On a Lord's Day in 1819, in the afternoon Mr. Campbell noticed a large number of slaves amusing themselves in a nearby grove. The heart of the great man went out to them. He invited them to come into his room that he might read to them from the Bible. They immediately assembled, and were happy to receive instructions from the Word of God. He spent considerable time teaching them to sing, and they sang with sweet melodious voices. He dismissed them in view of repeating the activities at the first favorable opportunity. However, the next day he was informed that what he had done was unlawful in Kentucky. He was advised not to allow this to happen again. At this announcement, Thomas Campbell was thunderstruck. He had been totally unaware of such a law. "Is it possible for me to remain in a place where I am forbidden to preach a crucified Savior to my perishing fellow-beings?" He made up his mind quickly as to what he should do. He would leave Kentucky and go where the preaching of the gospel was untrammeled.

He wrote Alexander informing him of his intentions. Alexander replied with haste, urging him to come immediately, and assist him in operating Buffalo Seminary. Thomas took up his residence near West Middleton, Pennsylvania, mid-way between Washington and Wellsburg. Buffalo Seminary was seven miles away. There he spent his time teaching the classics with which he was so familiar. He preached at Brush Run church to which he was so strongly attached.

Once again, Thomas was happily situated, doing the things which were close to his heart—teaching and preaching.

There was a uniqueness about the preaching methods of Thomas Campbell that captured the imagination of his hearers. In 1828, Mr. Campbell was scheduled to preach on the Western Reserve. A. S. Hayden wrote that "The venerable preacher read the first two chapters of Genesis and the last chapter of Revelation—chapters which give the history of the creation of man, and an account of the New Jerusalem. He then remarked—holding the intervening portion of the Bible between his thin hands—that had it not been for sin there would have been no need for any other revelation than the three chapters he had read; all the rest was to unfold the scheme of redemption. He said that in his earlier years he had often wished he had lived in the days of the Jews, that he might offer his sacrifice at the altar, and know by the direct assurance of God that his offering was accepted. Then, quoting from the sixth of Jeremiah the words: 'Stand ye in the ways, and see, and ask for the old paths, where is the good way, and walk therein, and ye shall find rest for your souls,' he proceeded to unfold the law of pardon as taught in the gospel, and concluded with an invitation to sinners to obey."[33] In response to the invitation a number came to be baptized for the remission of their sins.

J. W. McGarvey, who graduated from Bethany College in 1850, reveals that several years before Thomas Campbell died he was totally blind, and his memory was treacherous, though his hearing was acute. "But his cheerfulness, politeness and thankfulness for every favor were unfailing, and this made everybody solicitous to do him a favor. Young and old, wherever he was, were eager to serve him with quick feet and ready hands.

> After his eyesight became so dim that he couldn't read, it was his custom to sit in an arm chair in one corner of the large family room, and to spend as much time as he could in reciting hymns, Psalms, and chapters in the New Testament, with some one holding the book to correct his mistakes, if he made any. He called to the service any young member of the family or any visitor who could spare him a few moments. Once, when I was crossing the room (I forget the occasion of my being there) he heard my footsteps and said, 'My dear, can you spare time to hold the book a few minutes for grandfather?' Of course I consented, took a seat by his side. He handed me his hymn book, and said, 'Now that I can no longer read for myself, I don't wish to forget the good hymns and Scripture passages which I memorized in my earlier days. Please turn to page— and look on while I recite; and if I miscall a word, please correct me.' He recited hymn after hymn without

missing a word; and then, handing his well-worn Bible, he recited in the same way a number of the most devotional of the Psalms.[34]

J. W. McGarvey continued his narrative by relating a rather unusual incident in the later years of Thomas Campbell when his memory was fading. "His oldest daughter, Mrs. McKeever, was on a visit to him and, in the course of the conversation, he inquired of her respecting the present circumstances of his brothers. After having called their names and learning something of them, he said, 'Well daughter, there was one of us, I think, named Thomas; what has become of him?' She laughed and said, 'Why father, that is your name.' 'Yes, yes.' he said, 'My memory is failing me.' McGarvey added, "Blessed man—forgetting his own name, but careful not to forget the Word of the Lord and the hymns of devotion which he had learned and loved." McGarvey's concluding remarks were: "It has been my privilege to know only one other man between whom and Thomas Campbell I am not able to decide as to which appeared to me to be the most devout."[35] The other man that McGarvey had in mind was the celebrated Robert Milligan.

Endnotes

1. M. M. Davis, *Restoration Movement of The Nineteenth Century*, p. 69.
2. Robert Richardson, *Memoirs of Alexander Campbell*, p. 21.
3. Ibid, p. 22.
4. A. S. Hayden, *A History of the Disciples on the Western Reserve*, p. 41.
5. Richardson, *Memoirs*, Vol. 1, pp. 24, 25.
6. Ibid.
7. Alexander Campbell, *Memoirs of Thomas Campbell*, p. 309.
8. James DeForrest Murch, *Christians Only*, p. 36.
9. W. W. Jennings, *Origin and Early History of The Disciples of Christ*, p. 83. In this connection, consult Richardson, *Memoirs*, Vol. 1, pp. 53-55.
10. Ibid.
11. Richardson, *Memoirs*, Vol. 1, p. 58.
12. Ibid, p. 60.
13. Ibid.
14. Ibid, pp. 235-239.
15. Ibid, p. 237.
16. Ibid. p. 241.
17. M. M. Davis, *The Restoration Movement of the Nineteenth Century*, p. 100.

18. A. S. Hayden, *A History of the Disciples on The Western Reserve*, p. 45.
19. N. B. Hardeman, *Tabernacle Sermons*, Vol. 3, p. 117.
20. David Lipscomb, *Christian Unity*, p. 19.
21. A. Campbell, *Memoirs of Thomas Campbell*, p. 109.
22. C. A. Young, *Historical Documents Advocating Christian Union*, pp. 107-114.
23. F. D. Kershner, *The Restoration Handbook*, Series 1, p. 15, 16.
24. Lester McAllister, *Thomas Campbell*, p. 139.
25. Richardson, *Memoirs*, Vol. 1, p. 273.
26. Ibid, pp. 466-67.
27. Robert Richardson, 'Thomas Campbell', *Millennial Harbinger* (1854), pp. 117, 118.
28. Walter Scott, 'Letter', *Millennial Harbinger,* 1860, pp. 396-399. Alexander Campbell, *Memoirs of Elder Thomas Campbell*, pp. 275-279.
29. *Millennial Harbinger*, 1860, pp. 499-500.
30. Ibid, p. 346.
31. Richardson, *Memoirs*, Vol. 2, p. 606.
32. Alexander Campbell, *Memoirs*, pp. 265-274.
33. A. S. Hayden, *History of Disciples*, pp. 248, 249.
34. J. W. McGarvey, *Christian Standard* (January 4, 1905), p. 58.
35. Ibid.

Chapter 6

Alexander Campbell—"Noblest Roman of Them All"

Part I: *Early Life*

Thomas Campbell left his home in Ireland and came to America in the spring of 1807. He left his wife, Jane, and their seven children behind in view of their following him after a few months. Alexander, who was nineteen at the time, was left in charge of the school at Rich Hill.

At this point, we need to say more about the ancestry of Alexander Campbell, who was born in County Antrim, September 12, 1788. His maternal ancestors, as we have observed, were Huguenots who were driven from France after Louis XIV had revoked the edict of Nantes and had sought refuge among the Presbyterian population of North Ireland. The blood of these intelligent, God-fearing, but man-defying and courageous Frenchmen was no slight legacy. On his father's side, Alexander was of Highland Scotch descent. No Highland clan has played more important and respectable a part in the history of the world than has the Campbells of Argyle.

With such an illustrious heritage we are not surprised at the rich contributions that Alexander Campbell made to society, especially the world of religion.

After about one year in the new world, Thomas Campbell wrote a letter to his family urging them to make speedy preparation to join him in America.

Passage was secured on the ship Hibernia, which departed Londonderry, October 1, 1808. After a few days at sea, the vessel was grounded on the isle of Islay, off the western coast of Scotland. Fortunately, the Campbells and their meager belongings were rescued.

The ship wreck proved to be a blessing. "It's an ill wind that blows no good." This unhappy incident proved to be a turning point in the life of Alexander, who, at the time, was twenty years of age. As a result of this shipwreck, Alexander's previous thoughts about entering the Christian ministry crystalised into a firm resolution. It was his determination to spend the remainder of his life as a proclaimer of the word of God.

The Campbells were for some days on the island, where they were treated with much kindness. Finally, they went into Glasgow, where Alexander found an apartment for the family. There, Alexander made the momentous decision that he would enroll as a student in the University of Glasgow. Some of his professors had taught his father twenty five years before. During his year at the University, Alexander applied himself diligently. He became proficient in Greek, Latin, Hebrew, French and English literature, Philosophy, Logic and Church History. He developed study habits that served him well through life. Retiring at 10:00 p.m., he rose regularly at four in the morning. At six, he attended a class in French, from seven to eight, a class in the Greek New Testament; from eight to ten, he studied Latin. In the afternoon he studied Advanced Greek, plus a class in Logic. He attended several lectures each week, delivered by Dr. Ure. He also studied under Professors Young and Jardine, who had been his father's professors years before.[1]

In Glasgow, the Campbells attended a Seceder Presbyterian church, usually on Sunday mornings. On Sunday evening, they would attend an Independent church where Greville Ewing (1767-1841), one of the most popular preachers in the city, was the pastor. Audiences numbering from one to two thousand would come to hear the gifted preacher each week. Alexander was intrigued with this Independent church, and its adherence to Bible teaching. While attending this Independent church, Alexander had opportunity to hear such distinguished preachers as Robert and James Haldane, Alexander Carson (1776-1844) Roland Hill (1744-1833), and John Walker (1768-1833). These men had in common the idea that religious unity could be achieved by adhering strictly to Bible teaching.

Greville Ewing was very popular with the university students. He often had groups of students at his home for what was called "discussion groups." It was in these discussion groups that Alexander became acquainted with the works of such men as John Glas, Robert Sandeman, and other reformers.

The Independent church, where Ewing preached, observed the Lord's Supper every first day of the week. They proposed to take the Bible as their only guide in matters of faith. They believed in the possibility of restoring the church of the New Testament by using the Bible as a blue print. It was during his stay in Glasgow that Alexander "received his first impulse as a religious reformer, and which may be justly regarded, indeed, as the first phase of that religious reformation which he subsequently carried out so successfully to its legitimate issues."[2]

Even though Alexander was impressed with the teaching of Greville Ewing, he did not feel himself at liberty, at the time, to abandon rashly the cherished religious views of his youth and the Seceder church, to which all the Campbells belonged and in which he thought it was his duty to be a regular communicant. It was during this period of uncertainty that the annual communion period of the Seceder church approached. Alexander had begun to have considerable misgivings about his connections with the Seceder church. But as a matter of principle and habit, he decided to appear before the elders and get the metalic token which every one had to obtain who wished to take the Lord's Supper. He was questioned, not only by the elders, but was sent to the session to be further examined, after which he received the token. There were some eight hundred communicants on communion day. He decided to wait until the very last, in hopes of overcoming his doubts about the Seceder church and its practices. When the time came for him to take the communion, "he threw his token upon the plate handed round, and when the elements were passed along the table, declined to partake with the rest." Robert Richardson said, "It was at this moment that the struggle in his mind was completed, and the ring of the token, falling upon the plate, announced the instant at which he renounced Presbyterianism forever."[3]

During the year that the twenty-year-old Alexander was a student at Glasgow University, he kept a notebook, in which he entered a number of statements advocating religious reforms. For example: "I see as many marks of wisdom in what is omitted in the Bible as in what is included."[4] Thomas Campbell had something like this in mind when he said, "Where the Bible speaks, we speak; where the Bible is silent, we are silent." On Party names he wrote: "I observe that the Scriptures positively testify against the practice of Christians calling themselves by their earthly leaders."[5]

John Walker had made a strong impression on the mind of the young Alexander in Glasgow and perhaps North Ireland, where Alexander had become acquainted with his tenets. Mr. Walker had resigned his work in Ireland and had become an Independent. In his notebook at the University, Alexander had written extracts from "John Walker's Address to the Methodists in Ireland." For example: "The writer who takes the sacred scriptures *alone* for the standard of his faith and takes the *whole*" of them must expect opposition and dislike, more or less, from all sects and parties." "The more clearly we maintain and exhibit the simplicity of the real Gospel of Christ, the more we shall be disliked and despised by the world."

"What are we to understand by being sanctified, or made holy? I answer in a word—'separated unto God.' Successfully brought into a particular relation unto him, appropriated to his use and service."

It was time for the Campbells to resume their journey to the New World. Accordingly, Alexander made all the necessary arrangements for the voyage on the ship Latonia. On August 3, 1809, the vessel departed from Greenock, near Glasgow, and landed in New York city Friday, September 29. They had been on the high seas for fifty seven eventful days.

On the following Sunday, Alexander made it a point to hear Dr. John M. Mason preach. Mason was the son of Dr. John Mason who had been sent, in 1761, by the Anti-Burgher Synod as a missionary to America. Dr. John M. Mason was an eloquent and popular preacher with a rich and varied scholarship.[6] After two days of sight-seeing in the city, the Campbells travelled by stage coach to Philadelphia, a trip which required three days. In Philadelphia, Alexander hired a wagon and team to convey the family to Washington. On Monday morning, October 9, they started on their long trip of some three hundred and fifty miles.

Thomas Campbell was so eager to see his family, from whom he had been separated for more than two years, that he started on horse back to meet them, accompanied by his good friend, John McElroy. After travelling three days, there was a happy reunion between Thomas and his family. Everybody was eager to talk and each took his or her turn. Mrs. Campbell related to her husband the various incidents which had occurred in the family since he had been in the United States. Thomas detailed the religious trials and the many persecutions he had suffered at the hands of the Seceder clergy, due to his efforts to promote unity on a Bible basis. He believed strongly that unity could be achieved by adhering strictly to the Scriptures.[7]

As the happy family journeyed toward the village of Washington, father and son had opportunity to talk about the changes that had taken place in their respective thinking. Thomas Campbell had in his saddle bags the proof sheets of a document that he had recently written with the title of "Declaration and Address." The elder Campbell was eager for his son to read the document and tell him what he thought of it. Alexander devoured every word and heartily approved of the principles it set forth. Back in Scotland, Alexander had independently reached the same conclusions that his father had set forth in the "Declaration and Address." Alexander indicated that he was going to preach these wonderful principles for the rest of his life, without any remuneration whatsoever; to which his father replied: "Son, if you do this, I fear that you will wear many a ragged coat."[8] It was a happy surprise when each learned that the other no longer held to the old religious party in which they had been reared. The circumstances under which they reached their conclusions were wholly different. Independent study of God's Word brought them together in their thinking. Thomas Campbell was more than pleased at his son's decision to preach and urged him to make an intensive study of the Bible for at least six months.

After settling down in their two-story log house on Strawberry Alley in Washington, Pennsylvania, Alexander began his systematic study, under the tuteledge of his scholarly father.

Studies for the Winter of 1810
One hour to read Greek - from 8 to 9 a.m.
One hour to read Latin-from 11 to 12 a.m.
One hour to read Hebrew-from 12 to 1 p.m.
Commit ten verses of the Scriptures to memory each day, and read the same in the original languages, with Henry and Scott's notes and practical observations. For this exercise, we shall allow two hours. These exercises, being intended for every day, will not be dispensed with. Other reading and studies as occasion may serve. These studies in all require four and one half hours. Church history and divers other studies, are intended to constitute the principle part of my other literary pursuits.[9]

Not long after the family was settled in their two-story log house on Strawberry Alley, Thomas Campbell preached a sermon at a nearby farm house. After the sermon had been delivered, Thomas asked Alexander to give an exhortation. Thomas was so well pleased with the efforts of his son that he was heard to say in an undertone, "Very well, very well."[10]

Alexander preached his first full sermon on July 15, 1810. He was in his twenty second year. The sermon was based on Matthew 7:24-27, the thrust of "which was a call to the world to heed the words of Jesus." This effort was successful beyond the expectations of the people who heard him. Some even said, "he can preach better than his father." This sermon was preached at Buffalo, in the home of Major Templeton, who was greatly pleased at the emphasis on the Bible as expressed by the Campbells. This was something new in this community, which was largely Calvinistic in its theology.[11]

In his ledger, Alexander noted that "this sermon was written out in full and committed to memory." His second sermon was preached July 22, 1810, at the "Cross-roads" from Galatians 3:28-29, on the subject of Christian Unity.[12] During his first year as a preacher, Alexander preached one hundred and six times.

It was the custom of Thomas Campbell, as a Seceder preacher, to visit the homes of people for miles around Washington, not only to promote the interests of religion, but also to see the friends with whom he had formed affectionate attachments. He had come to know, in a very favorable way, Mr. John Brown and his family who lived on a farm near Buffalo Creek. The Brown home is described as a "comfortable and capacious dwelling, two stories high, weather-boarded, painted white, with green venetian shutters." Mr. Brown was a member of the Presbyterian church, but somewhat independent in his thinking. A warm friendship existed between him and Mr. Campbell. On one occasion, Thomas had promised his friend, Mr. Brown, some books; Alexander was asked to deliver them. This was the young Campbell's first visit to that part of the country, and the acquaintance which he then formed with the Brown family had some far-reaching results.[13] Here, Alexander met Margaret Brown, who was eighteen years of age. A warm friendship developed with Mr. and Mrs. Brown and their talented daughter, Margaret. After this first visit, Alexander often found it convenient to be in those parts, always stopping for a visit at the "Brown mansion." Alexander and Margaret became very attracted to each other, which eventually led to a proposal of marriage. This being entirely agreeable to the relatives on both sides, the date for the marriage was set.

On March 10, two days before the wedding, Alexander preached twice at Brush Run, and on the following two Lord's Days, he preached at Washington. The term "Brush Run" (as used here) is somewhat clouded in mystery. The Brush Run church was not organized until May 4, 1811, and the Brush Run meeting house was not completed until after June 16, 1811. We must conclude that when Alexander preached at Brush Run on March 10, 1811, he preached in a private home or even in the open, at the place where the church building was later constructed. Some think it was the church building in near-by Mt. Pleasant.

Alexander and Margaret were married at the Brown home on March 12, 1811, by "Rev. Mr. Hughes, pastor of the Presbyterian church at the town of West Liberty, four miles distant, and of which Mr. Brown and his family were members."[14] On the day after the wedding, Alexander took his bride to Washington to meet the Campbell family.

On March 25, Alexander returned with his wife to live with the Brown family.[15]

A short time later, the Browns moved to their new home in Wellsburgh on the Ohio River, some eight miles away. Eventually, the "Brown Mansion" came to be known as the "Campbell Mansion," as it is known to this day. It is interesting to note that the community known as "Buffalo" where the mansion was located, was changed to "Bethany." Bethany became the center of Campbell's printing and publishing activities. Alexander became the postmaster of Bethany and served in that capacity for thirty years.

Due to the hostile attitude of the religious bodies toward his efforts, Thomas Campbell thought it wise to form an independent church from the nucleus of the Washington Association. The question was considered and agreed to at the next meeting of the Association, and on Saturday May 4, 1811, another meeting was held for the purpose of organizing a church. At this meeting, Thomas Campbell was appointed elder, and Alexander was licensed to "preach the gospel."[16] Four men were selected as deacons. At the next meeting, May 5, 1811, which was the Lord's Day, the church held its first communion service, and Alexander preached on the subject, "I Am The Bread of Life." It was observed that Joseph Bryant, Margaret Fullerton, and Abram Alters did not commune. When asked why, they replied that they had never been baptized. Some weeks later, they were immersed by Thomas Campbell.

Thomas had serious misgivings about baptizing those who had already been recognized as members of the church. However, he had no problem with the present instance, since none of the three had received baptism at all in any of its so-called forms.[17] Neither did he have any doubts or objection with reference to immersion. Campbell agreed that it "was evident that in the primitive age they went down into the water and were buried in it..." Mr. Campbell consented, therefore, to perform the ceremony, which took place on July 4, 1811, in a pool in Buffalo Creek, about two miles from Brush Run. The pool was narrow, and so deep that the water came up to the shoulders of the candidates when they entered it. Thomas Campbell, without going into the water, "stood on a root that projected over the edge of the pool and bent down their heads until they were buried in the liquid grave."[18] Mr. Campbell was the first to introduce immersion in the "reformatory movement" as espoused by the Campbells. Stone had introduced it in his work some years before in Kentucky.

On March 13, 1812, a little girl was born to the young Campbell couple. The child was given the name of Jane, in honor of Alexander's mother, Jane Corneigle Campbell. Soon after this happy event, Alexander's thoughts turned to Baptism. His wife, Margaret, and her parents, as well as Alexander and his parents, were members of the Presbyterian church. The question arose as to whether the infant should be baptized according to regular Presbyterian practice. Desiring to maintain "a conscience void of offence," and aware of the responsibilities resting upon him as a father, Alexander decided to set aside a period for special study to determine what constituted Biblical baptism. Up to this time, Alexander had given little thought to the subject. As a matter of fact, on February 3, 1810, May 19, 1811, and June 5, 1811, he had delivered sermons on texts relating to baptism in which he stated, "As I am sure it is unscriptural to make this matter a term of communion, I let it slip. I wish to think and let others think on these matters."[19]

Now, with a consuming ambition to know the will of God, he abandoned all uninspired authorities, and applied himself diligently to the Scriptures, searching out critically the significance of the words rendered "baptism" and "baptize," in the original Greek. He soon became satisfied that they could only mean "immersion" and "immerse." He also discovered that only believing penitents were fit subjects for baptism. In addition, he discovered that the "simple acknowledgement of the Messiahship of Jesus was the only divinely required prerequisite to baptism."[20]

To summarize, Alexander, in his studies, discovered three New Testament truths hitherto unclear to him:

(1) Only penitent believers are fit subjects for Christian Baptism. (2) The baptism of the New Testament was immersion. His conclusion was that the sprinkling of infants did not constitute baptism, because it was the application of an unauthorized form to an incompetent subject. This answered negatively the question about baptizing his little daughter, and also swept away the concept of "rebaptism." To immerse those who had been sprinkled was not "rebaptism," but baptism itself.[21] (3) Only a simple confession of faith that Jesus Christ

is God's Son is required of one prior to baptism. This simple little confession eliminated the unscriptural Baptist requirement of relating an "experience" as evidence of salvation.

The design of baptism was yet to come in Campbell's understanding and teaching. This was developed in the Campbell-McCalla debate in 1823 and Walter Scott's evangelism which began on a large scale in 1827.

Alexander was now fully convinced that the rite of sprinkling, to which he had been subjected in infancy, was wholly unauthorized, and that he was an unbaptized person. He concluded that he could not consistently preach a baptism to others of which he had never been a subject himself. After discussing the matter with his wife, Margaret, she agreed with Alexander's Biblical reasoning. Thomas Campbell and his wife, Jane, along with their daughter, Dorothea, reached the same conclusions on baptism that Alexander had reached after their own independent study of the matter.

To find a preacher in the community who would baptize the Campbells on a simple confession of faith without having to relate an "experience" was no little task. Having formed the acquaintance of a Baptist preacher by the name of Matthias Luce, who lived some distance from Washington, Alexander decided to ask him to perform the baptisms. Alexander stipulated with Elder Luce that the ceremony should be performed precisely according to the pattern given in the New Testament, and that, as there was no account of any of the first converts being called upon to give what is called a "religious experience" this modern custom should be omitted, and that the candidates should be admitted on the simple confession that 'Jesus is the Son of God'. . . .Elder Luce had, at first, objected to these changes as being contrary to "Baptist usage," but finally consented, remarking that he believed they were right, and he would run the risk of censure.[22]

Wednesday June 12, 1812, was fixed as the day for the baptizing. Buffalo Creek, where the three members of the association had been baptized a few days before, was selected as the place. Because of the prominence of the Campbells and the novelty of the scene, a large crowd assembled on the day appointed. Matthias Luce and Henry Spears, along with David Jones, another Baptist preacher, were present. It was observed that these three were the only Baptists who showed up. Thomas Campbell made an elaborate address, in which he reviewed the entire ground which he had occupied, and the struggles that he had undergone in reference to the subject of baptism. He explained that he had earnestly desired to dispose of the topic in such a manner that it might be no hindrance in the attainment of that Christian unity which he had labored to establish upon the Bible alone. Alexander folllowed with an extended defense of their proceedings, urging the necessity of submitting implicitly to all that God commands "and showing that baptism of believers only was authorized by the Word of God."[23] Father and son spoke for a total of seven hours.[24]

Concerning this event, Robert Richardson relates the following story: "Before the service commenced, Joseph Bryant had to leave in order to attend a muster of volunteers for the war against Great Britain which, it was reported, Congress had declared on the fourth day of the same month, June, although the declaration was not formally made until the 18th. After attending the muster, he returned in time to hear an hour's preaching and to witness the baptisms."[25]

The following people were immersed by Matthias Luce upon a simple confession of their faith in the Messiahship of Jesus: Thomas Campbell and his wife, Alexander Campbell and his wife, Dorothea Campbell, sister of Alexander, James Hanen and his wife. These seven persons had two things in common: All had emigrated to America from Ireland, and all had been members of the Seceder Presbyterian church.

Alexander Campbell, in writing of this eventful occasion said: "This company, as far as I am yet informed, was the first community in the country that was immersed into that primitive, simple, and most significant confession of faith in the divine person and mission of the Lord Jesus Christ, without being brought before a church to answer certain doctrinal questions, or to give a history of all their feelings and emotions, in those days falsely called "Christian Experience," as if a man could have Christian experience before he was a Christian."[26]

The adoption of immersion as an essential item in the Campbell's plan of Christian union radically changed the direction which they were to take from this time forward. No longer was it simply a matter of persuading churches to unite on beliefs which all Christians already held. It would now be necessary to persuade them also to accept immersion which, at the time, only Baptists believed to be essential. It now seemed more important to seek first the restoration of the New Testament church, and then to work for Christian unity.[27]

There were now ten immersed members of the Brush Run church; the three immersed earlier by Thomas Campbell, and the seven immersed by Matthias Luce. On the following Lord's Day, June 16, 1811, the first service was conducted in the new meeting house of the Brush Run church. Though the building was unfinished and the seats were crude, a large crowd was present. Alexander preached, using as a text Galatians 1:4. Thomas Campbell immersed thirteen people. In a matter of time, most of the Brush Run people were immersed, along with some in the community. The total number of immersed soon came to be thirty three. Those of the original Brush Run church who did not submit to immersion moved away.

This New Testament teaching and practice of immersion brought the Brush Run church into closer and more friendly relationship with the Baptists. Yet, Alexander made it known that he "had no idea of uniting with the Baptists more than with the Moravians or the mere Independents. I had, unfortunately, formed a very unfavorable opinion of the Baptist preachers as then introduced to my acquaintance, as narrow, contracted, illiberal, and uneducated men. This, I am sorry to say, is still my opinion of the ministry of that Association at that day; and whether they are yet much improved, I am without satisfactory evidence."[28] Campbell went on to say that the Baptists "pressed me from every quarter to visit their churches, and though not a member, to preach for them. I consented through much importunity, and during that year I often spoke to the Baptist congregations for sixty miles around. They all pressed me to join their Redstone Association."[29]

The matter of joining the Redstone Baptist Association was put before the Brush Run church in the fall of 1813. After much discussion, it was decided to seek admission to the Association with the stipulation that they "be allowed to preach and teach whatever we learned from the Holy Scriptures, regardless of any creed or formula in Christendom." This proposition was discussed at the next meeting of the Association. There was some opposition on the part of Elder Pritchard, of Cross Creek, Virginia; Elder Brownfield, of Uniontown, Pennsylvania, and Elder Stone of Ohio. These three Baptist preachers united in their opposition to Alexander Campbell and the things for which he stood. As I write these lines I have before me a copy of the "Minutes of the Redstone Baptist Association, Held by Appointment, at Big Redstone, Fayette County (Penn.) September 1, 2, 3, 1815." The minutes indicate that on Saturday, September 2, "a letter from a church in Washington was read, requesting union to this Association, which was unanimously granted. Likewise, a letter was received, making a similar request from a church at Brush Run; which was also granted." Thomas Campbell, A. Campbell and J. Foster were listed as ministers and messengers of the Brush Run church.[30]

Shortly after the Brush Run church had been received into the Redstone Association, Alexander expressed the idea that a church should be started in Charlestown, later named Wellsburg. The town was without a church house of any kind. Alexander was wise enough to know that his teaching of reform would likely create controversy, and he was correct.

He volunteered his services to solicit funds for a meeting house in Wellsburg, and left home on December 12, 1815. He arrived in Pittsburgh on the 14th. Here he visited his parents and also Nathaniel Richardson, who gave twenty dollars, this being the first contribution to the building fund. On December 15, he journeyed to Philadelphia. He then went to Trenton and other towns in New Jersey and on to New York, where he called upon a number of wealthy Baptists. In New York, he visited William Colgate, who had just begun to establish himself in business. Later, he headed the famous Colgate Company, now known around the world. Being impressed with Alexander Campbell's appeal, Mr. Colgate made a generous gift to the building project. Campbell then went on to Washington City, where he met many influential people.[31] He succeeded in obtaining one thousand dollars, a rather large sum for that time. With this money and additional assistance in Wellsburg and its vicinity, a lot was obtained at the upper end of the main street of the town, and a neat brick meeting house was soon constructed, whose curtains and cushions were prepared and carefully arranged by Miss Selina Bakewell. Elder Pritchard, who preached at the Cross Creek Baptist church three miles away, who had already signaled his hostility to Alexander Campbell, was not at all happy with this church in Wellsburg. He seemed to think that it was designed to weaken and to diminish his congregation. This personal jealousy became more manifest at a later time of which we will have more to say.[32] Because of his heterodoxy, Alexander Campbell suffered "a seven year persecution" at the hands of Elder Pritchard.[33]

A number of things were then taking place that are of interest to students of the restoration. For one thing, Alexander Campbell had become a naturalized citizen of the United States. Mr. and Mrs. John Brown had been immersed and were active workers in the Wellsburg church. John Brown had given Alexander a deed to the "Brown Mansion" along with three hundred acres of rich land. The deed read as follows: "Know all men by these presents that I, John Brown, of the County of Brooke and state of Virginia; for and in consideration of the natural love and affection which I bear to Alexander Campbell, my son-in-law of the county and state aforesaid, as well as for the further consideration of one dollar to me in hand paid by the said Alexander Campbell at or before the unsealing and delivery of these presents to give and grant unto said Alexander and his executors, administrators and assigns, a tract or parcel of land supposed to contain three hundred acres."[34] The real leader of the Restoration Movement was no longer Thomas Campbell but his son, Alexander.

The next Redstone Association convened at Cross Creek, August 30, 1816. Mr. Campbell, who well knew the spirit of the Baptist preachers' coalition against him, headed by Elder Pritchard, said to his wife on the way to the meeting, "I do not think they will let me preach at this Association at all." However, some of the preachers were favorable to Campbell, and the people in general wanted to hear him preach. On Saturday, August 29, when preachers were being chosen for the following day, Alexander was immediately nominated, along with several others. Elder Pritchard objected, saying that the people wanted to hear a man from a distance, rather than one from the neighborhood. Elder Stone from Ohio was then selected by the Association. However, due to illness, Elder Stone was unable to speak. After considerable discussion, Alexander was invited to speak. Not having a subject at his command, Alexander asked to be the second speaker. At the impulse of the moment, he decided to draw a clear line between the law and the gospel, the old dispensation and the new, Moses and Christ. He used as his text Romans 8:3. This turned out to be his famous "Sermon on the Law," which created tremendous excitement in the Baptist fold. More than one thousand people heard this sermon. Alexander was no sooner under way than Elder Pritchard called out two or three of the preachers supposedly to attend to a lady suddenly taken sick. Whatever the reason, a disturbance was created which interrupted Campbell's sermon. Finally, however, Alexander was able to proceed without further interruption. He later learned that the reason Elder Pritchard had called out the preachers was for the purpose of suggesting that Alexander be condemned before the people because he was not preaching "Baptist Doctrine." The Baptist preachers decided it was better to say nothing publicly about the sermon.

This sermon, without question, is one of the greatest sermons ever preached in America and, for that matter, in any part of the world since the days of the apostles. It is published in full in *The Millennial Harbinger* of 1846. It can be found in other places as well, such as in *Historical Documents Advocating Christian Union*, by Charles Alexander Young. The sermon on The Law was the entering wedge which led to the separation between Campbell and the Baptists. The sermon led to a heresy trial, but Alexander was acquitted.[35] The railing accusations against Mr. Campbell, for the most part, fell on deaf ears. Alexander Campbell himself believed that this Sermon on The Law was the springboard that was needed to put The Reformation he advocated before the world of religion.

As was his father, Alexander Campbell was a natural-born teacher. He wanted to do something for the youth of the neighborhood by giving them a better education than they could otherwise obtain. More importantly, he wanted to prepare young men to become effective preachers of the Word. He felt this could be done by boarding them in his own home and exposing them daily to Bible instruction. In January of 1818, he opened "Buffalo Seminary," where the languages and sciences were taught. Though the school was well supported, he closed it after some four years. It seems that most of the young men went into law and medicine, rather than into the Christian ministry.

Endnotes

1. Robert Richardson, *Memoirs* (Vol. 1), p. 131.
2. Ibid, p. 149.
3. Ibid, pp. 189, 190.
4. Alexander Campbell, *Glasgow University*, Transcribed by Lester G. McAllister), p. 93.
5. Ibid, pp. 89, 92.
6. Richardson, *Memoirs*, Vol. 1, p. 205.
7. Ibid, pp. 215-219.
8. Ibid, p. 275.
9. Ibid, pp. 278, 279.
10. Richardson, *Memoirs*, Vol. 1, p. 312.
11. Ibid, p. 317f.
12. Ibid.
13. Ibid, p. 357.
14. Ibid, p. 363.
15. Ibid, p. 365.
16. Ibid, p. 367.
17. Ibid, p. 372.

18. Ibid, pp. 372, 373.
19. Ibid, p. 392.
20. Ibid. p. 410.
21. Garrison-DeGroot, *The Disciples of Christ*, p. 160.
22. Richardson, *Memoirs,* Vol. 1, p. 398.
23. Ibid, p. 397.
24. Ibid, p. 398.
25. Ibid, p. 398.
26. Alexander Campbell, *Millennial Harbinger* (1848), p. 283.
27. McAllister and Tucker, *Journey In Faith*, p. 119.
28. Alexander Campbell, *Millennial Harbinger*, (1848), p. 345.
29. Ibid, p. 346.
30. Minutes of Redstone Association.
31. Richardson, *Memoirs,* Vol. 1, pp. 467, 469.
32. Ibid, p. 469.
33. Alexander Campbell, *Millennial Harbinger*, (1848), p. 347.
34. Discipliana (May 1963), p. 347
35. Richardson, *Memoirs,* (vol. 1) pp. 470-481; Alexander Campbell, *Millennial Harbinger* (1848), pp. 347-349.

Chapter 7

Alexander Campbell—"Noblest Roman of Them All"

Part Two: *Middle Years*

Though Alexander was controversial in many of the things he taught, he at first disliked public debates. Both he and his father believed that such engendered partyism and ill-will. In the spring of 1820, Alexander Campbell was urged to engage in a public debate with a Seceder Presbyterian preacher by the name of John Walker. At first he declined, suggesting that such was not "the proper method of proceeding in contending for the faith once delivered to the saints." In the fall of 1819, John Birch, a Baptist preacher near Mt. Pleasant, Ohio, had baptized a large number of people. This induced John Walker to preach a series of sermons in favor of infant baptism. Birch wrote Campbell twice to consider debating Mr. Walker, but Campbell answered neither letter. Somewhat in desperation, Mr. Birch wrote a third letter to Campbell:

> Dear Brother: I once more undertake to address you by letter. As we are commanded not to be weary in well-doing, I am disposed to persevere. I am coming this third time unto you. I cannot persuade myself that you will refuse to attend to the dispute with Mr. Walker; therefore, I do not feel disposed to complain because you have sent me no answer. True, I have expected an answer, signifying your acceptance of the same. I am, as yet, disappointed but am not offended nor discouraged. I can truly say it is the

unanimous wish of all the church to which I belong that you should be the disputant. It is Brother Nathaniel Skinner's desire; it is the wish of all the brethren with whom I have conversed that you should be the man. You will, I hope, send me an answer by Brother Jesse Martin, who has promised to bear this unto you. Come, brother; come over into Macedonia and help us.

Yours in the best of bonds,

John Birch[1]

With that exhortation, Campbell agreed to debate Walker. The debate was held at Mt. Pleasant, Ohio, beginning June 9, 1820. Alexander Campbell was accompanied by his father and a few special friends. The place of debate was only twenty three miles from Bethany. Alexander was thirty two years of age at the time of this debate on the "subject and mode" of baptism.

According to the rules of the debate, Walker made the first speech and Campbell the last. Walker's first speech lasted but two minutes in which he asserted that baptism came "in the room of circumcision." Here is his speech in full:

> My friends—I don't intend to speak long at one time, perhaps not more than five or ten minutes, and will, therefore, come to the point at once: I maintain that baptism comes in the room of circumcision—that the covenant on which the Jewish church was built, and to which circumcision is the seal, is the same with the covenant on which the Christian church is built, and to which baptism is the seal—that the Jews and the Christians are the same body politic, under the same lawgiver and husband; hence, the Jews were called the congregation of the Lord—and the bridegroom of the church says, 'My love, my undefiled is one; consequently the infants of believers have a right to baptism.'

Campbell arose and after introductory remarks said: "I cannot persuade myself to believe that they who affirm that baptism comes in the room of circumcision really think so: for if they thought so, they would certainly act more consistently than they do." He then named five things: (1) They would baptize none but males; (2) They would baptize precisely upon the eighth day; (3) They would baptize all the slaves or servants that the master or householder possessed, upon his faith, for the Jews circumcised all their slaves, all in their house or bought with money, on the footing of their covenant relation to Abraham; (4) They would not confine the administration of baptism to the clerical order, for both men and women circumcised their own children; (5) They would not confine baptism to the infants of professed believers only, for the most wicked Jews had the same privileges to circumcision that the most faithful had. Campbell went on to say, Baptism is connected with the promise of remission of sins, and the gift of the Holy Spirit—circumcision had only temporal blessings promised.

In his last speech, Campbell issued the challenge: "I, this day, publish to all present that I feel disposed to meet Paedobaptist ministers of any denomination, of good standing in his party, and I engage to prove with the pen that infant sprinkling is a human tradition and injurious to the well being of society, religious and political."

The debate was soon put in book form, and was widely distributed and favorably received. Mr. Campbell was then convinced that public discussion of religious questions had real merit in promoting "the reformation we plead." The printed page also began to loom large in Campbell's thinking.

In the summer of 1821, Alexander was sitting on his front porch resting. He had just finished his noon day meal and was waiting until it was time to return to the class room at Buffalo Seminary. Two strangers on horseback rode up to the gate, dismounted and hitched their horses, then walked the cinder path that led to the Campbell mansion. As they approached, Mr. Campbell arose and greeted them. The older of the two men said, "Mr. Campbell, my name is Adamson Bentley and this is my brother-in-law, Sidney Rigdon. We are Baptist preachers who live in Warren, Ohio." Bentley continued by saying, "We have read your debate with Mr. John Walker. We would like to talk to you about matters introduced in that debate." Campbell assured them that when his afternoon duties at his Seminary had been taken care of it would be a pleasure to talk with them.

After the evening meal, the discussion began and continued until the next morning. In this discussion Campbell said, "Beginning with the baptism that John preached, we went back to Adam, and forward to the final judgment. The dispensations, or covenants—Adamic, Abrahamic, Jewish and Christian, passed and repassed before us. Mount Zion, Mount Calvary, Mount Tabor— the Red Sea, and the Jordan—the Passover and the Pentecosts—the law and the gospel; but especially the ancient order of things. . .engaged our attention."

On the next morning, Sidney Rigdon said, "If I have within the past year taught and promulgated from the pulpit one error, I have a thousand." At that time, he was the great orator of the Mahoning Association—though in authority with the people, he was second to Adamson Bentley.

Bentley and Rigdon left Bethany, completely and thoroughly converted to the principles advocated by Campbell. Campbell had cautioned them "not to begin to pull down anything they had builded until they had reviewed again and again what they had heard nor, even then, rashly and without consideration."[2]

We now notice three important events of 1823. In the early part of the spring of that year, Alexander Campbell sent out a prospectus for a religious journal to be named *The Christian Baptist,* a name suggested by Walter Scott. The objectives of the journal were set forth as follows: "The Christian Baptist shall espouse the cause of no religious sect, excepting the ancient sect 'called Christians first at Antioch.' Its sole object shall be the eviction of truth, and the exposure of error in doctrine and practice. The editor acknowledging no standard of religious faith or works, other than the Old and the New Testaments, and the latter as the only standard of the religion of Jesus Christ will, intentionally at least, oppose nothing which it contains and recommend nothing which it does not enjoin. Having no worldly interest at stake from the adoption or reproduction of any article of faith or religious practice—having no gift nor religious involvement to blind his eye or to pervert his judgment, he hopes to manifest that he is an impartial advocate of truth."

The first issue of *The Christian Baptist* came from the press July 4, 1823. It appeared at a time when opposition to Alexander Campbell was at a new high. From the first issue to the last, seven years later, Campbell was the iconoclast. "Restoration of the ancient order of things" became the slogan and was applied with skill and diligence. More than thirty editorials were written under the above caption. He pleaded for the return of the church of the New Testament and the destruction of denominationalism. Alexander was determined to expose the pretentions of the clergy. He attacked, with remorseless zeal, their unscriptural organizations. He set out to destroy the creeds which were tests of fellowship.

Alexander Campbell grew up in a religious atmosphere dominated by human creeds but, as he began to study the Bible, he developed a strong aversion to them. He reached the point in life where he boldly attacked them as "misnomers." He said they were "not confessions of faith, but of opinions." He suggested that "creeds, clergy and councils" rob people of their liberty in Christ. With boldness, he urged that the Bible should be accepted as the rule of faith and not the creeds of men.

In the October, 1826, issue of *The Christian Baptist,* he published "The Parable of the Bedstead." "In the days of the Abcedarian Popes, it was decreed that a good Christian just measured three feet, and for the peace and happiness of the church it was ordained that an iron bedstead, with a wheel at one end and a knife at the other, should be placed at the threshold of the church, on which the Christian should be laid. The bedstead was just three feet long. Every Christian was laid on this bedstead; if less than the standard, he was stretched; if too tall, the knife was applied to his extremities. In this way, they kept Christians, for nearly a thousand years all of one stature."

Mr. Campbell continued his satire by saying Luther used a four foot stature, Calvin added six inches, and the Baptists added another six more inches. Campbell, of course, urged that the iron bedstead be discarded and that the New Testament be used as the standard of faith and practice. Campbell never lost sight of the all-sufficiency of the Word of God. He never failed to hold it up as the only safe guide in spiritual matters. It was his contention that the Bible alone must always decide every question involving the nature, the character, or the design of the Christian institution."

In *The Christian System* (page 114) Mr. Campbell wrote, "Let the Bible be substituted for all human creeds; facts, for definitions; things, for words; faith, for speculation; unity of faith, for the unity of opinion; the positive command-ments of God, for human legislation and tradition; piety, for ceremony; morality, for partisan zeal; the practice of religion, for the mere profession of it; and the work is done."

In the *Christian Baptist* Alexander Campbell made it crystal clear that he had "no idea of adding to the catalogue of new sects. This game has been played too long. I labor to see sectarianism abolished, and all Christians of every name united upon the one foundation on which the apostolic church was founded. To bring Baptist and Paedobaptist to this is my supreme end. But to connect myself with any people who would require me to sacrifice one item of revealed truth, to subscribe any creed of human device, or to restrain me from publishing my sentiments as discretion and conscience direct is now and, I hope, ever shall be the fartherest from my desires and the most incom-patible with my views."[3]

Campbell was hard on professional denominational ministers, calling them "The Kingdom of the Clergy." In referring to them he used such uncomplimen-tary terms as "scrap doctors," "textuary divines," and "hireling priests."

Like Jonathan Swift (1667-1745) Alexander Campbell was a master in the use of satire. In his day, Swift wrote, among other things, a satire on corrup-tion in religion that he called "A Tale of a Tub." Campbell's satire on the clergy is called "The Third Epistle of Peter." It was addressed to "Preachers and Rulers of Congregations—a Looking Glass for the Clergy." This article was pure satire. It contained many points that deserve the attention of preachers today. It is so rich in content that it is here given in full:

THE THIRD EPISTLE OF PETER

To The Preachers and Rulers of Congregations

A Looking Glass for the Clergy

One of the best proofs that a prophecy is what it purports to be is its exact fulfillment. If this rule be adopted in relation to the "Third Epistle of Peter," there can be no doubt that it was written in the true spirit of prophecy. We thought it worthy of being preserv-ed and have, therefore, given it a place in this work. Ed. C.B.

Preface

How the following epistle came to be overlooked by the early saints of Christendom and by all the Fathers, or whether it was purposely suppressed by the Council of Nicea, and why it was at

Robert Sandeman

Early Leaders of the Scottish Restoration Movement

John Glas

Elias Smith

Leaders of the New England Restoration Movement

Abner Jones

Barton W. Stone

Cane Ridge Meeting House

Thomas Campbell

Church house in Ahory, Northern Ireland where Thomas Campbell was preaching when he came to America in 1807.

Alexander Campbell

Walter Scott

Hill Street Meeting House, Lexington, Kentucky. Here on January 1, 1832, the followers of Stone (Christians) and the followers of Campbell (Disciples or Reformers) united into one body of "Christians only."

"Raccoon" John Smith

Tolbert Fanning

David Lipscomb

N. B. Hardeman

Benton Cordell Goodpasture

last destined to be found with other old manuscripts among the ruins of an ancient city by a miserable wandering monk, are all circumstances which my limited knowledge of these subjects does not enable me to explain. I am answerable only for the accuracy of the translation from a French copy presented by the monk himself. Neither can I prove the authenticity of the original, unless it be on the strict correspondence of the actual state of the church with the injunctions contained in the epistle, a correspondence which seems to hold as much veracity as that which is found in the fulfillment of any prophecy with the prediction itself. Translator

Chapter I

The Style and Manner of Living

Now ye who are called and chosen to go forth to all nations and among all people, in time present and time to come, to preach the word, see ye take unto yourselves marks, nay many outward marks, whereby ye shall be known of men. Be ye not called as men are called; but be ye called Pope, Archbishop, Archdeacon, or Divine, or Reverend, and Right Reverend, or some like holy name; so may you show forth your honor and your calling.

And let your dwelling places be houses of splendor and edifices of cost; and let your doors be decked with plates of brass, and let your names, even your reverend titles be graven thereon; so shall it be as a sign.

Let your garments in which you minister be garments not as the garments of men, neither let them be "seamless garments woven throughout" but let them be robes of richest silk and robes of fine linen, of curious device and of costly workmanship; and have ye robes of black and robes of white, that ye may change the one for the other; so shall ye show forth your wisdom and humility.

Let your fare be sumptuous, not plain and frugal as the fare of the husbandman who tilleth the ground; but live ye on the fat of the land, taking "good heed for the morrow and wherewithal ye shall be fed."

And drink ye of the vines of the vintage brought from afar, and wines of great price; then shall the light of your spirits be the light of your countenances, and your faces shall be bright, even as the morning sun shall your faces glow in brightness; thus shall ye show forth your moderation and your temperance in all things.

Let the houses in which you preach be called churches, and let them be built in manner of great ornament without, and adorned with much cost within; with rich pillars and paints, and with fine altars and pedestals, and urns of precious stones, and cloths and velvet of scarlet, and vessels of silver.

And let there be rooms for the changing of robes, and places for the precious metals and mitres.

And let the houses be divided into seats for the congregation, and let every man know his own seat; and let the first seats in front of the altar be for the rich that pay by thousands; and the next for the poorer that pay by the hundreds; and the last for those that pay by tens. And let the poor man sit behind the door.

And let the seats be garnished with cushions and crimson cloth and with fine velvet; for if the houses of players and vain people who deal in idle sayings and shows of mockery, be rich and gorgeous, how much more so should be the houses that are dedicated to him "that is meek and lowly of spirit."

Chapter II

The Choosing of Ministers

When ye go out to choose holy ones to be of your brethren and to minister at the altar, choose ye from among the youth, even those whose judgments are not yet ripe, and whose hearts know not yet whether they incline to God or Mammon.

But ye are wise, and ye shall know the inclining of their future spirits, and ye shall make them incline to the good things which the church hath in store for them that are called, even those that shall be called of you.

Then shall ye have them taught exceeding many things. They shall not be as "ignorant fishermen," or husbandmen, or men speaking one tongue, and serving God only by the knowledge of his law. Nay, ye shall make them wise in the things of your wisdom; yea, exceedingly cunning in many mysteries, even the mysteries which you teach. Then shall they be fitted for the "laying on of hands," and when the bishop hath done his office then shall they be reverend divines.

But if any man believe that he is called of God to speak to his brethren "without money and without price," though his soul be bowed to the will of the Father, and though he work all righteousness, and "speak as with the tongue of an angel"—if he be not made a Divine by your rulers and by the hands of a bishop, then he is not a Divine, nor shall he preach.

He that is chosen of you shall give you honor, and shall be honored of men, and honored of women, and verily he expects his reward.

Chapter III

The Performance of Preaching

When ye go to the church to preach, go not by the retired way where go those who would shun the crowd, but go in the highway where go the multitude, and see that ye have on the robes of black, and take heed that your pace be measured well, and that your march be stately. Then shall your "hearts be lifted up," even as the hearts of mighty men shall they be lifted up. And ye shall be gazed upon by the multitude, and they shall honor you; and the men shall praise you, and the women shall glorify you, even by the women shall ye be glorified.

And when ye go in, go not as the ordained, prepared only with a soul to God and with a heart to men, and a spirit filled with the Holy Ghost; but go ye with your pockets full of papers and full of divine words; even in your pockets shall your divinity be.

And let your sermon be full of "the enticing words of man's wisdom," and let it be beautified with just divisions, with tropes, and with metaphors, and with hyperbole, and apostrophe, and with interrogation, and with acclamation, and with syllogisms, and with sophisms, and throughout let declamation be.

And take heed to your attitudes and your gestures, knowing when to bend and when to erect, when to lift your right hand and when your left, and let your motions be graceful, even in your attitudes and in your gestures let your grace be. Thus shall ye be pleasing in the eyes of the people and graceful in their sight.

Let your voice at times be smooth as the stream of the valley, and soft as the breeze that waves not the bough on its bank; and at times let it swell like the wave of the ocean, or like the whirl-wind on the mountain top. Then shall ye charm the ears of your hearers and their hearts shall be softened, and their minds shall be astounded, and their souls shall incline unto you; and the men shall incline unto you, and likewise the women; yea, unto your sayings and unto your persons shall they be inclined.

And be ye mindful not to offend people; rebuke ye not their sins; but when ye rebuke sin, rebuke it at a distance; and let no man apply your sayings to his own case; so shall he not be offended.

If a brother raise up the banner of war against brother, and Christians against Christians, rebuke them not; but be some of you on the one side and some on the other, and tell the one host that

God is on their side, and the other host that God is on their side; so make them bold to kill. And even among swords and lancets let your black robes be seen.

Preach ye not "Peace on earth and good will to men," but preach ye glory to the victor, and victory to the brave. If any man go into a foreign land and seize upon his fellow man, and put irons on his feet and irons on his hands, and bring him across the great deep into bondage; nay, if he tear asunder the dearest ties of nature, the tenderest leagues of the human heart; if he tear the wife from the husband, and force the struggling infant from its mother's bleeding breast, rebuke him not!

And although he sell them in foreign slavery to toil beneath the lash all their days, tell him not that his doings are of Antichrist; for lo! he is rich and giveth unto the church, and is esteemed pious, so shall ye not offend him, lest peradventure he withdraw himself from your flock.

Teach them to believe that you have the care of their souls, and that the saving mysteries are for your explaining; and when you explain your mysteries, encompass them round about with words as with a bright veil, so bright that through it no man can see. And lo! ye shall bind the judgments of men, (and more especially of women) as with a band of iron; and ye shall make them blind in the midst of light, even as the owl is blind in the noon day sun, and behold ye shall lead them captive to your reverend wills.

Chapter IV

The Clergy's Reward

In all your gettings get money! Now, therefore, when ye go forth on your ministerial journey, go where there is silver and gold, and where each man will pay according to his measure. For verily I say ye must get your reward. Go ye not forth as those that have been sent, "without two coats, without gold or silver, or brass in their purses; without scrip for their journey, or shoes, or staves," but go ye forth in the good things of this world. And when ye shall hear of a church that is vacant and hath no one to preach therein, then be that a call unto you, and be ye mindful of the call, and take ye charge of the flock thereof and of the fleece thereof, even the golden fleece. And when ye shall have fleeced your flock, and shall know of another call, and if the flock be greater, or rather if the fleece be greater, then greater be also unto you the call. Then shall ye leave your old flock, and of the new flock ye shall take the charge.

Those who have 'freely received' let them 'freely give,' and let not men have your words "without price," but bargain ye for hundreds and bargain for thousands, even for thousands of silver and gold shall ye bargain. And over and above the price for which ye have sold your service, take ye also gifts, and be ye mindful to refuse none, saying, 'Lo! I have enough!' but receive gifts from them that go in chariots, and from them that feed flocks, and from them that earn their morsel by the sweat of their brow. Yea, take ye gifts of all, and take them in gold and in silver, and in bread; and in wine and in oil; in raiment and in fine linen.

And the more that the people give you the more will they honor you; for they shall believe that "in giving to you they are giving to the Lord;" for behold their sight shall be taken from them, and they shall be blind as bats, and "shall know not what they do." And ye shall wax richer and richer, and grow greater and greater, and you shall be lifted up in your own sight, and exalted in the eyes of the multitude; and lucre shall be no longer filthy in your sight. And verily ye have your reward.

In doing these things ye shall never fail. And may abundance of gold and silver and bank notes, and corn, and wool, and flax, and spirits and wine, and land be multiplied unto you, both now and hereafter. Amen.

Mr. Campbell was so often caustic in his editorials that Robert Semple, who used the pseudonym of Robert Cautious, wrote the editor a letter: "Sir, Having read with considerable attention the numbers of the *Christian Baptist* already published, and approving of the general spirit and tendency of your work, I take the liberty of suggesting to you the necessity of avoiding extremes." He went on to warn that in his haste to get out of Babylon, he might go past Jerusalem.[4]

The editor of the *Northern Whig* of Belfast said concerning the *Christian Baptist*, "It might do good provided it were written with less bitterness. It is a mixture of pepper, salt, and vinegar, served with a dash of genuine Irish wit—but with a great deal of instruction."[5] Another has referred to the *Christian Baptist* as "a peppery periodical."

Walter Scott was a frequent writer for the *Christian Baptist* using the pseudonym of "Philip." Scott looked upon himself as sustaining the same relationship with Alexander Campbell that Philip Melanchton had with Martin Luther. Moses E. Lard looked upon the *Christian Baptist* as being the "Masterpiece" of Campbell's life. "In polish and completeness of thought, it cannot be pronounced equal to some volumes of his Harbinger; but in originality and utility he has written nothing to excel it."[6]

In the last issue of the *Christian Baptist* Mr. Campbell wrote: "I have commenced a new work and taken a new name for it on various accounts. Hating sects and sectarian names, I resolved to prevent the name of Christian Baptist from being fixed upon us; to do which, efforts were making. It is true men's tongues are their own, and they may use them as they please; but I am resolved to give them no just occasion for nicknaming advocates for the ancient order of things. My sheet admonishes me that I must close and, as usual on such occasions, I ought to return thanks to all those who have aided in the circulation of this work, and patronized it...I have found myself blessed in this undertaking—my heart has been enlarged and no reader of the *Christian Baptist* I think will ever derive more advantage from it than I have from the writing and conducting of it. To Jesus Christ my Lord be everlasting praise."[7]

Some of the great preachers in the Restoration Movement of the nineteenth century were directly influenced by the *Christian Baptist*. I mention Racoon John Smith, J. T. Johnson, Philip S. Fall, Jacob Creath, Jr., and the parents of David Lipscomb, et al.

Opposition to Alexander Campbell was steadily mounting. Elder Pritchard and his associates of the Redstone Association were out to get him. They planned a public ex-communication of Campbell at the next meeting of Redstone, which was only days away. Alexander found out about this devious plan, however, and on August 31, 1823, he appeared before the Brush Run church and asked for a letter of dismissal for himself and thirty one others in order to organize a church at Wellsburg, where a meeting house had been previously constructed. The Wellsburg church was promptly received into the fellowship of the Mahoning Association at the instigation of Adamson Bentley.

Campbell went to the Redstone Association as an observer and not a messenger from Brush Run. When his enemies demanded to know why he was not there as a messenger, Mr. Campbell stated that the church of which he was a member did not belong to the Redstone Association. In describing the chagrin of his enemies Mr. Campbell said: "Never did hunters, on seeing the game unexpectedly escape their toils at the moment when its capture was sure, glare upon each other a more mortifying disappointment than that indicated by my pursuers at that instant on hearing that I was out of their bailiwick and, consequently, out of their jurisdiction. A solemn stillness ensued and, for a time, all parties seemed to have nothing to say."[8]

At the close of the debate with Walker, Mr. Campbell had issued a general challenge for a public debate with any reputable Pedobaptist. W. L. McCalla, a Presbyterian preacher of Augusta, Kentucky, accepted the challenge. Arrangements were made for the debate to be held in Washington, Kentucky, October 1823. Several days before the debate was to begin, Mr. Campbell set out on horseback to make the three hundred mile trip. Sidney Rigdon accompanied him to take notes. Reaching Washington on October 11, Alexander wrote home:

My dear Margaret: Through the mercy and kindness of our heavenly Father we have arrived in safety and in health at the grounds of the debate. . . .This is a healthy and fine country, and everything is cheerful and animating. . . .I have no news relative to the debate. . . .I hope and pray that the Lord will enable me to speak as I ought to speak, and cause the truth to be glorified. . . .Remember me to the children—to Joseph Freeman, James Anderson, and all inquiring friends. May grace, mercy and peace be multiplied unto you! Your loving husband, A. Campbell.

On the 14th, Campbell met Mr. McCalla and found him to be very obstinate and a difficult person with whom to have friendly relations. The rules for the debate were made according to his thinking. Mr. Campbell had selected for his moderator the most popular Baptist preacher in Kentucky, Jeremiah Vardeman. Vardeman related that on his way to the debate, traveling in a gig, he overtook a man on foot who told him he was on his way to Washington to hear the debate which was to begin on the 15th. Vardeman took him to be a zealous Baptist and, affecting to be on the other side, said, "Is not our man likely to whip your man Campbell?" The man gave him a searching look and asked, "Can you tell me if this is the same Mr. Campbell who debated with Mr. Walker at Mt. Pleasant, Ohio?" Vardeman said he believed he was. The stranger said, "I heard that debate and all I have to say is that all creation cannot whip that Mr. Campbell."[9]

Though William McCalla was trained as a lawyer, he had been preaching for a number of years for the Presbyterian church. He was looked upon as a man of great polemical power. The subject of baptism was discussed from every angle in this debate.

Alexander Campbell announced that he would proceed as follows: (1) "We will go to the New Testament, and not to the Old Testament, to ascertain the nature, design, and subject of baptism. (2) We shall appeal to the words of Jesus Christ for the institution of baptism. He set forth three propositions that he would prove: (a) "I will first prove that a believer is the only subject of baptism. (b) that immersion is the only baptism. (c) that infant baptism, or infant sprinkling, is injurious to society, religious and political."[10]

On the second day, Campbell said: "Our third argument is deduced from the design, or import, of baptism. . . .I will first merely refer to the oracles of God, which show that baptism is an ordinance of greatest importance and of momentous significance. Never was there an ordinance of so great import or design. . . .Its great significance can be seen from the following testimonies:" Mr. Campbell then cites a number of scriptures with appropriate comments, including Mark 16:16; John 3:5; Acts 2:38, 22:16; Titus 3:5 and I Peter 3:21.

Campbell reflects that "On the evening of the fourth day, having secured the special favor and attention of the Baptist ministry and of the uncommitted public, while I had in one room at the residence of my kind host Major Davis of Washington, all the principal Baptist preachers of the state, I thought it expedient to introduce myself more fully to their acquaintance. This I did in the following manner: 'Brethren, I fear that if you knew me better you would esteem and love me less. For, let me tell you in all candor, I have almost as much against you Baptists as I have against the Presbyterians. They err in one thing and you in another; and probably you are each nearly equidistant from original apostolic Christianity.' I paused and such a silence ensued, accompanied with a piercing look from all sides of the room, I seldom before witnessed.

"Elder Vardeman, at length, broke silence saying, 'Well, sir, we want to know our errors in your heterodoxy. Do let us hear it. Keep nothing back.'

"I replied, 'I know not where to begin. . . .'But,' said I, 'I am commencing a publication called the *Christian Baptist* to be devoted to all such matters, a few copies of which are in my portmanteau and, with your permission, I will read a few specimens of my heterodoxy.' They said, 'Let us hear—let us hear the worst error you have against us.' I went upstairs and unwrapped the three first numbers—(July, August and September numbers) of the *Christian Baptist*, that ever saw the light in Kentucky. I had just ten copies of the three first numbers. I carried them into the parlor and, sitting down, I read as a sample the first essay on the clergy—so much of it as respected the 'call to the ministry,' as then taught 'in the kingdom of the clergy,' and especially amongst the Baptists. . . .This was the first essay ever read from that work in Kentucky. After a sigh and a long silence, Elder Vardeman said, 'Is that your worst error—your chief heterodoxy? I don't care so much about that, as you admit we may have a providential call, without a voice from heaven, or a special visit from an angel or spirit. If you have any thing worse, for my part, I wish to hear it.' The cry was, 'Let us hear something more. . . .' I then distributed my ten copies amongst the ten most distinguished and advanced elders in the room—requesting them to read those numbers during the recess of the debate, and to communicate freely to me their objections. We separated. So the matter ended at that time."[11]

As a result of this debate with McCalla, Campbell became more favorable to public discussion than ever. "This," he said afterwards, "is, we are convinced, one of the best means of propagating the truth and exposing error in doctrine or practice. . . .and we are persuaded that a week's debating is worth a year's preaching." As to the effects of the debate on Mr. Campbell's reputation and influence, these were largely extended by it.[12]

In September, 1824, Campbell made an extended trip into Kentucky, which lasted for nearly three months. He was correct in thinking that the people in Kentucky would be receptive to the reformation he espoused. The *Christian Baptist* was widely distributed in the state and eagerly read. Campbell was warmly received wherever he preached. His method of discoursing was totally unlike that of other preachers of the time. In discussing the great themes of salvation, he manifested a breadth of view, a depth of Biblical knowledge, a freshness of thought, which both amazed and delighted his hearers.

Among the people he met on this trip was a Baptist preacher by the name of John Smith (1784-1868). Smith, though lacking a formal education, had raised himself by his extraordinary natural abilities to great and merited distinction. He possessed a largeness of heart and mind, along with a quickness and clearness of insight, such as are rarely found. He had a retentive memory, a remarkable talent for genial humor and unequaled skill at repartee that set him apart from others. Even though he had adopted the Calvinism held by the Baptists, he had a consuming ambition to know the truth of God. He was conversant with the various theories of religion and, at times, it was difficult for him to harmonize certain religious views with his understanding of the Scriptures.

On one occasion in 1822, while preaching at the Spencer Creek meeting house, Smith was suddenly struck with an inconsistency between the gospel and Calvinism. He stopped short, and to the surprise of his audience, he said, "Something is wrong among us, but how to get it right I know not." From this time onward, he devoted himself to a more careful study of the Bible. He had heard of Mr. Campbell's debate with Walker, and had desired to attend his debate with McCalla, but was hindered by sickness in the family. Through the recommendations of a friend in Mt. Sterling, he had subscribed to the *Christian Baptist* and read each issue with interest. When he read an essay on "Experimental Religion" he hardly knew what to think, as it was radically different from anything he had ever heard or read.

When Smith heard of Mr. Campbell's arrival in Kentucky in 1824, he made plans to visit the great reformer in Flemingsburg and to escort him back to Mt. Sterling, where Smith then lived and where Mr. Campbell was scheduled to preach. "Racoon" John Smith rode horseback to Flemingsburg, a distance of twenty miles, to hear Campbell preach. Upon entering the town, Smith met William Vaughan, who introduced him to Mr. Campbell. Smith noted that "Campbell's nose seemed to turn a little to the North." The meeting house where Campbell was to preach was found to be too small for the large crowd that had assembled and preparations were quickly made to have the service out side under the trees. At the proper time, Mr. Campbell arose to speak. He read from the fourth chapter of Galatians—the allegory of Sarah and Hagar. After giving a general outline of the whole epistle, and showing how it ought to be read in order to arrive at a proper understanding of what the apostle was saying, he took up the allegory itself and, in a simple, plain, and artless manner, leaning with one hand on the head of his cane, he preached his sermon. When the congregation was dismissed, Smith said to Vaughan: "Is it not hard, brother Billy, to ride twenty miles (as I have done) just to hear a man preach thirty minutes?" "Look at your watch, brother John, it has surely been longer than that." Smith looked at his watch and, to their surprise, observed that Mr. Campbell had spoken for two hours and thirty minutes. Holding up his watch, Smith remarked, "I have never been more deceived. Two hours of my life are gone, I know not how, though wide awake." Vaughan said, "Did you find out whether he was a Calvinist or an Armenian?" "No," Smith replied, "but be he saint or devil, he has thrown more light on that epistle and the whole Scripture than I have heard in all the sermons I ever listened to before."

It was arranged that Mr. Campbell should go a few miles that evening toward Mt. Sterling. As they drove along, Smith drew to his side and asked Campbell to tell his religious experience. His "experience" was simply reading the Scriptures, believing what he read, repenting of his sins and being immersed for the remission of sins. He learned from Campbell the necessity of depending upon the Word of God, rather than feelings, as a guide in matters of faith and life.[13]

For several days, Smith accompanied Mr. Campbell from place to place, listening intently to every sermon, and earnestly engaging him in conversation as they traveled. At last it became clear to Smith what his duty was, namely, to throw off the shackles of Calvinism and turn to the simplicity of the gospel and preach it to the best of his ability. John Smith was truly a unique person, a product of the age in which he lived. Alexander Campbell said of him, "John Smith is the only man that I ever knew who would have been spoiled by a college education." Smith was one of the great preachers of the Restoration Movement. He devoted himself faithfully to the preaching of the gospel, and his labors were not in vain. He was able to get entire congregations of the Baptist faith to turn away from their creeds and theories and accept the Bible way of doing things. His unique way of preaching reached the hearts of the people. On one occasion he was contrasting the different theories in religion with the gospel. He said that the gospel had this mark that was peculiar to it: "Whosoever does not believe it shall be damned." This could not be said of any of the theories of man. On another occasion, after he had shown the absurdities of the mourner's bench theory of getting religion, he was asked: "What is the difference between your baptism for the remission of sins and our mourner's bench?" He replied, "One is from heaven and the other is from the saw mill."[14]

It was on this trip to Kentucky, in 1824, that Mr. Campbell met Barton W. Stone. The meeting took place at Georgetown, where Stone then lived. A friendship, though strained at times, was then developed that lasted through life. Mr. Campbell had great respect for the Bible as the inspired Word of God. He was not exactly happy, however, with the King James Version of the Bible. In the early part of 1826, Campbell announced that he was publishing a new version of the New Testament. For his new version, which came to be known as *The Living Oracles*, he used the four gospels of George Campbell of Aberdeen Scotland; Acts and Revelation of Philip Doddridge, London; and the Epistles of James McKnight, of Edinburgh. Campbell made "various emendations" and added a preface of some one hundred pages. In the preface he told why it was important to bring out a new version: "A living language is continually changing. Like the fashions and customs in apparel, words and phrases, at one time current and fashionable, in the lapse of time become awkward and obsolete. . . .Many of them, in a century or two, come to have a signification very different from that which once was attached to them. Nay, some are known to convey ideas not only different from, but contrary to, their first signification."

In his version, Campbell resolved to translate every word of the Greek into clear English language. He, therefore, used "immerse" for "baptize" and "immersion" for "baptism." Moreover, instead of saying "John the Baptist," he said "John the Immerser." All the pronouns, "thee," "thou," "thine," and "thy," he changed to "you" except when applying to prayer.

Campbell's New Testament appeared in the spring of 1827, in one volume of five hundred and fifty pages. Richardson says that Campbell was "the first to furnish the English reader a version of the New Testament completely rendered into its own vernacular."[15] *The Living Oracles* went through a number of editions. It was well received by many, while others rejected it as a "Campbellite Bible." Among the Baptist preachers who approved it was the distinguished Andrew Broadus, of Virginia. Other Baptists disliked the version because it left the name "Baptist" out of the Bible. Some of the Baptists were so bitterly opposed to it that on two or three occasions copies of it were burned.

Since John Smith's meeting with Alexander Campbell in 1824, he had been preaching "the ancient gospel." He used Campbell's *Living Oracles* almost exclusively in his teaching. The North District Association met in July, 1828. At its meeting the previous year, the Lulbegrud church had brought a number of charges aimed at John Smith, but veiling the object of their charges under the designation, "one of their preachers." The accusations were: 1. That, while it is the custom of Baptists to use as the Word of God the King James Translation he had, on two or three occasions in public, and often privately in his family, read from Alexander Campbell's translation. 2. That, while it is the custom in the ceremony of baptism to pronounce, "I baptize you," he, on the contrary, is in the habit of saying, "I immerse you." 3. That in administering the Lord's Supper, while it is the custom to break the loaf into bits small enough to be readily taken into the mouth, yet he leaves the bread in large pieces, teaching that each communicant shall break it for himself.

Without waiting to be singled out, Smith arose and said, "I plead guilty to them all." After bitter debating and wrangling over the charges, it was finally voted that they be laid over for another year. At the meeting of 1828 these charges were brought up again to be acted on by the messengers. Smith had been unceasingly engaged in preaching, and marvelously successful in winning men to Christ during the year. Still, when the Association met he was in doubt, at first, as to which side had the majority of messengers. It was soon found, however, that the majority of messengers were in favor of him. Messengers from the five new churches he had established turned the scale in his behalf.

The debate with Robert Owen (1771-1858) of New Lanark, Scotland, in April of 1829, made Alexander Campbell an international celebrity. The debate was conducted in Cincinnati, Ohio, and people from all over the country attended. Robert Owen was a Socialist who traveled across America preaching a doctrine of godless communism. He insisted that in order for society to survive, private property, religion and marriage would all have to be abolished.

Whenever Mr. Owen lectured, he challenged the clergy to debate the issues with him. No one, however, had ever accepted the challenge. In January, 1828, in New Orleans, Owen once again challenged the clergy to debate. The challenge was published in the local press, and a copy was forwarded to Mr. Campbell at his home in Bethany. In the next issue of the *Christian Baptist* Mr. Campbell published the challenge.

To The Clergy of New Orleans

I propose to prove, as I have already attempted to do in my lectures, that all the religions in the world have been founded on the ignorance of mankind; that they are directly opposed to the never-changing laws of our nature; that they have been, and are, the real source of vice, disunion, and misery of every description; that they are now the only real bar to the formation of a society of virtue, of intelligence, of charity in the most extended sense, and of sincerity and kindness among the whole human family; and that they can be no longer maintained except through ignorance of the mass of the people, and the tyranny of the few over the mass. Robert Owen

Mr. Campbell replied,

Now, be it known to Mr. Owen, and all whom it may concern, that I, relying on the Author, the reasonableness, and the excellency of the Christian religion, will engage to meet Mr. Owen at any time within one year from this date, at any place. . . .and will then and there undertake to show that Mr. Owen is utterly incompetent to prove the positions he has assumed, in a public debate before all who may please to attend; to be moderated or controlled by proper tribunal, and to be conducted in perfect order from day to day, until the parties, or the moderators, or the congregation, or the majority of them are satisfied, as may afterwards be agreed upon.

Alexander Campbell
Bethany, VA
April 25, 1828[16]

A few weeks afterward, Mr. Owen made a trip to Bethany to make final arrangements with Mr. Campbell for the debate. A cordial relationship existed between the two men. One day, as they were walking around the farm, they came upon the Campbell family burying ground when Mr. Owen stopped and said, "There is one advantage I have over the Christian—I am not afraid to die. Most Christians have fear in death, but if some few items of my business were settled, I should be perfectly willing to die at any moment." "Well," answered Mr. Campbell, "you say you have no fear in death; have you any hope in death?" After a solemn pause, "No," said Mr. Owen. "Then," rejoined Mr. Campbell, pointing to an ox standing nearby, "you are on the level with that brute. He has fed till he is satisfied, and stands in the shade whisking off the flies, and has neither hope nor fear in death." At this Mr. Owen smiled and evinced some confusion, but was quite unable to deny the justness of Mr. Campbell's inference.[17]

The debate came off according to schedule with capacity crowds. Mr. Owen opened the discussion with a speech devoted largely to events leading up to the debate. He announced with a sense of pride that he had discovered certain fundamental laws of human nature that, if properly applied, would abolish such things as marriage, religion, and private property. This, in turn, would provide the good life for mortal man.

Campbell's first address was a prepared manuscript which he read. This was the only speech Campbell read during the debate. All other times he spoke extemporaneously.

In his second speech, Mr. Owen read a long manuscript in which he listed his twelve fundamental laws of human nature. He spent all of his time during the debate repeating and emphasizing these twelve laws, much to the amusement of the hearers. The twelve laws which represented the sum total of the arguments of Owen are here given:

> 1. That man, at his birth, is ignorant of everything relative to his own organization, and that he has not been permitted to create the slightest part of his natural propensities, faculties, or qualities, physical or mental.
>
> 2. That no two infants, at birth, have yet been known to possess precisely the same organization, while the physical, mental, and moral differences between all infants are formed without their knowledge or will.
>
> 3. That each individual is placed, at birth, without his knowledge or consent within circumstances, which, acting upon his peculiar organization, impress the general character of those circumstances upon the infant, child, and man. Yet the influence of those circumstances is to a certain degree modified by the peculiar natural organization of each individual.
>
> 4. That no infant has the power of deciding at what period of

time or in what part of the world he shall come into existence; of whom he shall be born, in what distinct religion he shall be trained to believe, or by what other circumstances he shall be surrounded from birth to death.

5. That each individual is so created that, when young, he may be made to receive impressions, to produce either true ideas or false notions, and beneficial or injurious habits, and to retain them with great tenacity.

6. That each individual is so created that he must believe according to the strongest impressions that are made on his feelings and other faculties, while his belief in no case depends upon his will.

7. That each individual is so created that he must like that which is pleasant to him, or that which produces agreeable sensations on his individual organization, and he must dislike that which creates in him unpleasant and disagreeable sensations; while he cannot discover, previous to experience, what those sensations should be.

8. That each individual is so created, that the sensations made upon his organization, although pleasant and delightful at their commencement and for some duration, generally become, when continued beyond a certain period without change, disagreeable and painful; while, on the contrary, when a too rapid change of sensations is made on his organization, it dissipates, weakens, and otherwise injures his physical, intellectual and moral powers and enjoyments.

9. That the highest health, the greatest progressive improvements, and the most permanent happiness of each individual depends, in a great degree, upon the proper cultivation of all his physical, intellectual and moral faculties and powers from infancy to maturity, and upon all these parts of his nature being duly called into action at their proper period, and temperately exercised according to the strength and capacity of the individual.

10. That the individual is made to possess and to acquire the worst character, when his organization at birth had been compounded of the most inferior propensities, faculties and qualities of our common nature, and when so organized, he has been placed, from birth to death, amid the most vicious or worst circumstances.

11. That the individual is made to possess and to acquire a medium character, when his original organization has been created superior, and when the circumstances which surround him from birth to death produce continued vicious or unfavorable impressions. Or when his organization has been formed of inferior

materials, and the circumstances in which he has been placed from birth to death are of a character to produce superior impressions only. Or when there has been some mixture of good and bad qualities, in the original organization, and when it has also been placed, through life, in various circumstances of good and evil. This last compound has been hitherto the common lot of mankind.

12. That the individual is made the most superior of his species when his original organization has been compounded of the best proportions of the best ingredients of which human nature is formed, and when the circumstances which surround him from birth to death are of a character to produce only superior impressions; or, in other words, when the circumstances, or laws, institutions, and customs, in which he is placed, are all in unison with his nature.

The most notable event of the debate was Mr. Campbell's famous twelve hour speech on the defense of the Christian religion. Eva Jean Wrather writes of this speech: . . . ."by the sixth day of the debate Robert Owen had really said all that he had to say about the twelve fundamental laws of human nature and society, and so suggested that Campbell take the rest of the time. So Campbell started to speak a half hour before lunch intermission on Friday; he returned and spoke all Friday afternoon; he started speaking again Saturday morning, and spoke until evening and then on Monday he resumed and spoke until 4 o'clock that afternoon. He did this without the use of notes of any kind."[18]

Of this speech Richardson said: "For cogency of argument, comprehensive reach of thought and eloquence, it has never been surpassed, if ever equaled."[19] Judge Jacob Burnet, a member of the Ohio Supreme Court, served as president moderator of the debate. Even though Burnet's sympathies separated him from Mr. Campbell religiously, he made the emphatic remark, "I have been listening to a man who seems as one who had lived in all ages."[20] In an interview, Mr. Campbell remarked that "of all his opponents in debate, the infidel, Robert Owen, was the most candid, fair, and gentlemanly disputant he had ever met."

After the debate with Owen, Mr. Campbell announced his candidacy for election to the Constitutional Convention of Virginia in 1829. Though he was criticized for turning to politics, he justified his actions by saying he wanted to do something to end slavery in Virginia. With reference to this matter he crossed swords with such illustrious Americans as two former presidents, James Monroe and James Madison, also John Randolph of Roanoke and John Marshall, Chief Justice of the Supreme Court of the United States. While in Richmond, Mr. Campbell preached every Sunday in one of the churches in the city. Many of his fellow delegates were in attendance to hear him.

W. K. Pendleton tells of this incident in 1830. "Ex-president Madison was returning from the convention, of which he had been a member, and spent the night at my father's house, which was just one day's journey from Richmond. The next morning Mr. Madison rose early and he found my father walking on the portico in the early sunlight, when the latter asked Mr. Madison his opinion of Alexander Campbell. After speaking in very high terms of his abilities as displayed in the convention, he said, "But it is as a theologian that Mr. Campbell must be known. It was my pleasure to hear him often as a preacher of the gospel, and I regard him as the ablest and most original and powerful expounder of the Scripture I have ever heard."[21]

The final and complete separation of The Reformers from the Baptists was becoming more and more inevitable. For approximately seventeen years the Reformation Movement had been within the Baptist churches, but now it was becoming a separate and independent movement.

Many within The Reformation were having serious doubts about the Scriptural authority of associations as the Red Stone, Mahoning, Beaver, and other such associations in the various states. Those who were searching for the truth felt that these associations were inconsistent with the principles they advocated.

In 1827, thirteen churches identified with the Redstone Association formed what they called The Washington Association, embracing the views of Alexander Campbell.

Two or three fragments of churches on the Western Reserve, as at Youngstown and Palmyra and the church at Salem, (which refused to go into The Reformation) had united with a small association on Beaver Creek, (Pennsylvania). Two preachers, who were violently opposed to Mr. Campbell, induced the association to publish a circular anathematizing the Mahoning Association, and "Mr. Campbell of disbelieving and denying many of the doctrines of the Holy Scriptures."[22]

The charges of the Beaver Association against the Reformers were as follows:

1. They, the Reformers, maintain that there is no promise of salvation without baptism;

2. That baptism should be administered to all without examination on any other point;

3. That there is no direct operation of the Holy Spirit on the mind prior to baptism;

4. That baptism procures the remission of sins and the gift of the Holy Spirit;

5. That the Scriptures are the only evidence of interest in Christ;

6. That obedience places it in God's power to elect to salvation;

7. That no creed is necessary for the church but the Scriptures as they stand; and

8. That all baptized persons have the right to administer the ordinance of baptism.[23]

The "Beaver Anathema" was scattered widely among the Baptist churches and caused no little stir. Other associations were quick to unite in an effort to purge the Baptist fold of "Campbellism." The phenomenal success of Walter Scott on the Western Reserve stimulated them to take drastic measures.

In the spring and summer of 1830, Thomas Campbell made a hurried trip to Kentucky and southern Ohio to take note of the efforts of the Baptists against the Campbell Movement. In June of that year ten of the twenty churches in the Tate's Association of Kentucky met to "consider not how they might reclaim, but how they might exclude their erring brethren," those who had adopted the views of the Campbells. They drew up a protest against the Campbell Movement that included not only the "Beaver Anathema," but four additional charges against the reformers:

1. That there is no special call to the ministry.
2. That the law given by Moses is abolished.
3. That experimental religion is enthusiasm.
4. That there is no mystery in the Scripture.

Sometime before his debate with Robert Owen, Mr. Campbell had decided to discontinue the *Christian Baptist*. He was fearful that the name "Christian Baptist" would be attached to the advocates of the Reformation. He wanted to commence a new periodical of larger size and of somewhat different character. Mr. Campbell greatly desired that the new periodical be called the *Millennial Harbinger* and that it should exhibit a milder tone than the *Christian Baptist*. He intended to embrace in this new work a wider range of subjects, and to show "the inadequacy of modern systems of education," and the injustice yet remaining, under even the best political governments, in regard to various matters connected with the public welfare."[24]

The first volume of the *Millennial Harbinger* came from the press January 4, 1830. Mr. Campbell's famous "Extra" on "Remission of Sins" was published in this volume, as well as his "Extra" on "The Breaking of the Loaf." These Extras are found at the close of the volume. From the title of the new periodical, some expected it to advocate some theory of the millennium. But such was not the case. In an article published ten years after the paper's introduction, the editor declared the meaning of the millennial character of the name, and incidentally, his own conception of the millennium:

> We have often rather jeeringly been asked, 'Wherein consists the millennial characteristics of the Harbinger?'— the querist imagining that a millennial harbinger must be always discovering or preaching millenniarian affairs. When we put to sea under this banner we had the port of Primitive Christianity, in letter and spirit, in profession and practice, in our eye; reasoning that all the millennium we could scripturally expect was not merely the restoration of the Jerusalem church in all its moral and religious characters,

but the extension of it through all nations and languages for one thousand years. To prepare the way for such a development of Christianity, several things are essential.

1) The annihilation of partyism.

2) The restoration of pure speech.

3) The preaching of the original gospel.

4. The restoration of the Christian ordinances.

5. Larger measures of the Holy Spirit, as promised to those who seek for it in the appointed way.[25]

Thus, Mr. Campbell proposed to continue the advancement of the reformation through the printed page, a less iconoclastic thrust. However, he was ready and prepared at anytime to use the polemic platform to defend and promote his views.

Mr. Campbell's next public discussion was in the city of Cincinnati, January, 1837. His opponent was Roman Catholic Bishop John Baptist Purcell. The discussion was the outgrowth of a lecture that Mr. Campbell gave on "Moral Culture" at the Teachers' College in Cincinnati. In this speech Campbell connected the rapid march of modern improvement with the spirit of inquiry produced by the Protestant Reformation. Bishop Purcell took exception to this argument and countered by saying, "the Protestant Reformation had been the cause of all the contention and infidelity in the world."[26] After an exchange of letters, Bishop Purcell agreed to meet Mr. Campbell in public debate. The propositions were arranged as follows:

1. "The Roman Catholic Institution, sometimes called the 'Holy, Apostolic, Catholic, Church,' is not now, nor was she ever, catholic, apostolic, or holy; but is a sect in the fair import of that word, older than any other sect now existing, not the "Mother and Mistress of all Churches," but an apostasy from the only true, holy, apostolic, and catholic church of Christ.

2. "Her notion of apostolic succession is without any foundation in the Bible, in reason, or in fact; an imposition of the most injurious consequences, built upon unscriptural and anti-scriptural traditions, resting wholly upon the opinions of interested and fallible men.

3. "She is not uniform in her faith, or united in her members; but mutable and fallible, as any other sect of philosophy or religion—Jewish, Turkish, or Christian—a consideration of sects with a politico-ecclesiastical head.

4. "She is the "Babylon" of John, the "Man of Sin" of Paul, and the Empire of the "Youngest Horn" of Daniel's Sea Monster.

5. "Her notion of purgatory, indulgences, auricular confession, remission of sins, transsubstantiation, supererogation, etc., essen-

tial elements of her system, are immoral in their tendency, and injurious to the well-being of society, religious and political.

6. "Notwithstanding her pretensions to have given us the Bible, and faith in it, we are perfectly independent of her for our knowledge of that book, its evidences of a divine original.

7. "The Roman Catholic religion, if infallible and unsusceptible of reformation, as alleged, is essentially anti-American, being opposed to the genius of all free institutions, and positively subversive of them, opposing the general reading of the scriptures, and the diffusion of useful knowledge among the whole community, so essential to liberty and the permanency of good government."

On Friday, January 13, 1837, the debate began. The audiences were large and enthusiastic from the beginning. An unusual incident occurred during the debate that is worthy of special attention. Mr. Campbell quoted from the *Moral Philosophy of Alphonsus de Liguori,* this passage:

"A bishop, however poor he may be, cannot appropriate to himself pecuniary fines without the license of the Apostolic See. But he ought to apply them to pious uses. Much less can he apply those fines to anything else than religious uses, which the Council of Trent has laid upon the non-resident clergymen, or upon those clergymen who keep concubines."

The object of this stinging quotation was to show that, among the Roman clergy, marriage was a greater sin than concubinage, because marriage brought excommunication, while concubinage was fined and winked at.

In reply to this, the Bishop insisted that no such doctrine was ever taught by the Catholic church, and no such passage was ever written by St. Liguori. The Bishop continued by saying, "I have examined these volumes (pointing to nine volumes of this author on the stand) from cover to cover and in none of them can be found the infamous charges." The Bishop then requested a classical scholar, who was present, to examine the works of Liguori and find, if possible, the statement in question. The next day, the classical scholar announced to the large and excited audience that he found no such passage. Things looked bad for Mr. Campbell. The quotation was not directly from Liguori, but from an English synopsis, made by a Mr. Smith, of New York. Campbell got in touch with Mr. Smith, who told him that he could find the passage in question on page 444 of Volume 8. Asking the loan of Volume 8, he turned to page 444 and found every word that he had quoted in the Bishop's own edition. He then took the original Latin and the synopsis of Mr. Smith to the classical scholar, who then certified that the version of Smith, as quoted, was a faithful translation of the passage. Mr. Campbell was vindicated and his prestige was elevated.[27]

It is noteworthy that after the debate, Campbell conducted a meeting in which there were forty baptisms. Years after the debate, Bishop Purcell had this to say about Alexander Campbell: "Campbell was decidedly the fairest man in debate I ever saw, as fair as you can possibly conceive. He never fought for victory, like Dr. Johnson. He seemed to be always fighting for the truth, or what he believed to be the truth. In this he differed from other men. He never misrepresented his case nor that of his opponent; never tried to hide a point; never quibbled. He would have made a very poor lawyer, in the ordinary understanding of the term lawyer. Like his great friend, Henry Clay, he excelled in the clear statement of the case at issue, no dodging with him. He came right out fairly and squarely."[28]

Endnotes

1.   Richardson, *Memoirs*, (Vol. 2) pp. 15, 16.
2.   Alexander Campbell, "Anecdotes, Incidents and Facts," (*Millennial Harbinger*, 1848), p. 523.
3.   Alexander Campbell, *Christian Baptist*, Vol. 3, p. 146.
4.   Robert Semple, *Christian Baptist*, Vol. 1, p. 100.
5.   "W. T." *Christian Baptist*, Vol. 7, p. 152.
6.   Moses E. Lard, *Lard's Quarterly*, Vol. 3, p. 254.
7.   Alexander Campbell, *Christian Baptist*, Vol. 7, p. 309.
8.   Richardson, *Memoirs*, Vol. 2, p. 70.
9.   Ibid, pp. 72, 73.
10. Campbell-McCalla Debate, p. 47f.
11. Alexander Campbell, "Anecdotes, Incidents and Facts," pp. 614, 615.
12. Richardson, *Memoirs*, Vol. 2, p. 90.
13. Ibid, pp. 103-113.
14. H. Leo Boles, *Biographical Sketches of Gospel Preachers*, pp. 37-41.
15. Richardson, *Memoirs*, Vol. 2, p. 147; Cecil K. Thomas, *Alexander Campbell and His New Version*, pp. 196, 197.
16. Alexander Campbell, *Christian Baptist*, Vol. 5, pp. 245-247.
17. Richardson, *Memoirs*, *Vol. 2*, p. 242.
18. Eva Jean Wrather, *Alexander Campbell and His Relevance for Today*, p. 9.
19. Richardson, *Memoirs*, Vol. 2, p. 274.
20. David Burnett, "Alexander Campbell," (*Millenial Harbinger* 1866), p. 312.
21. W. K. Pendleton, "Death of Alexander Campbell," (*Millennial Harbinger* 1866), p. 121.
22. Richardson, *Memoirs*, Vol. 2, p. 322.
23. John Augustus Williams, *Life of John Smith*, pp. 279, 317.
24. Richardson, *Memoirs*, Vol. 2, pp. 284-303.
25. *Millennial Harbinger* (1840), p. 561; Homer Hailey, *Attitudes and*

Consequences, p. 92.

26. Richardson, *Memoirs*, Vol. 2, p. 422.

27. Ibid, pp. 431, 432.

28. J. J. Haley, *Debates That Made History*, p. 248.

Chapter 8

Alexander Campbell—"Noblest Roman of Them All"

Part III: *Last Years*

An interesting facet in the life of Alexander Campbell is seen in a letter that he wrote his wife, Selina, from Louisville, Kentucky, March 12, 1839. Campbell's first marriage was to Margaret Brown on March 12, 1811. Eight children were born during the sixteen years they lived together. Margaret died in 1827, and the next year Alexander married Selina Bakewell, Margaret's best friend. On the anniversary of Alexander's marriage to Margaret he wrote:

> My dear Selina, This day, twenty eight years ago, I gave my hand, and my heart accompanied it, to your amiable and excellent predecessor in the holy bonds of matrimony. Heaven lent me that precious gift more than sixteen years, of the value of which I never did form an over-estimate. But more than eleven years since He called her to Himself from this land of cares and fears and griefs and woes unnumbered, and more than ten years ago appointed you to fill her place in my affections, and to be her successor in all the endearments and trials of conjugal and maternal relations.
>
> I have, dear Selina, found you worthy of all the affection and esteem which were due to her who desired to bless both you and me by nominating you to be her successor...though I have seen many an amiable and excellent woman since I gave you my heart and hand for life, I have never thought that I saw one more

deserving of my affection and esteem than yourself. . . .You are my fellow-soldier, my true yoke-fellow, my partner, and therefore, as you share in my toils and self-denials, I pray that we may equally partake in the eternal rewards and enjoyments. . . .

Meanwhile, my beloved Selina, constantly, as I know you do, pray to the Lord for me that I may be humble, spiritually-minded, wholly devoted to the Lord and that my labors may be accepted by him and blessed. . . . (Robert Richardson, *Memoirs of A. Campbell*, Vol. 2, pp. 460, 461)

Alexander and Selina lived together thirty nine years. They had six children of their own. Every year their wedding anniversary was celebrated on March 12, and Selina did not seem to mind.

One of the notable achievements of Alexander Campbell was the founding of Bethany College, which was chartered in 1840. Mr. Campbell was elected as president, in which capacity he served for twenty five years. The doors of the new school opened for students in 1841, with a first year enrollment of one hundred and two students who came from nine states and Canada. The bill of fare for the boarding students was "to be the same as that of the University of Virginia." The curriculum was to meet the highest academic standards. The institution opened favorably at the time announced with five highly qualified professors as faculty: A. F. Ross, Professor of Ancient Languages and Ancient History; Charles Stewart, Professor of Algebra and General Mathematics; Dr. Robert Richardson, Professor of Chemistry, Geology and the kindred sciences; W. K. Pendleton, Professor of Natural Philosophy, Astronomy, Geology, Zoology and Political Economy. In addition to being responsible for the general superintendency of the college, Campbell was assigned to teach Mental Philosophy, Evidences of Christianity, Moral and Political Economy. Later, a professor of English Literature, to whom was assigned Grammar, Logic, Rhetoric, and Elements of Criticism, was appointed. Twenty classes were formed, the first meeting at 6:30 a.m. Mr. Campbell walked one mile from his home to lecture to this class on Sacred History. Students in the school were required to converse in Hebrew, Latin and Greek, and they assembled for chapel as early as five o'clock each morning.

The school was unique in that it was founded on the Bible. "There is not a college in Christendom known to us," said Mr. Campbell, "which gives the same attention to religion and moral instruction given here, and without any sectarian bias whatsoever. The Bible is an everyday classic, publicly read by every student in rotation, accompanied with lectures and examinations on sacred history, chronology, geography, ancient manners and customs, and the literature of the Bible with its bearing upon men as individuals and upon society in all its development and destiny. The subjects receive one hour's attention in six working days in every week."[1] President Campbell further stated, "We make the Bible, the whole Bible and nothing but the Bible our creed, our standard of religion, and of all moral science. We have no hesitation in saying that this institution, from the nursery class upward to the church classes, shall make that volume a constant study. All science, all literature, all nature, all art, all attainments shall be made tributary to the Bible, and man's ultimate temporal and eternal destiny."[2]

That Mr. Campbell had a college that was unique in the realm of education was ever on his mind. In 1850 he wrote: "Bethany College is the only college known to us in the civilized world, founded on the Bible. . . .It is founded on the Bible in the following manner: The Bible is every day publicly read by one student in the hearing of all the other students. It is then lectured upon for nearly one hour, contemplated first historically; in which view of it, its facts of creation, providence, legislation and redemption, as developed in the writings of Moses, and other Jewish historians and prophets, and Christian apostles and evangelists are, in order, exhibited, investigated and classified under appropriate heads."[3]

Many of the great preachers of the past sat at the feet of the illustrious Alexander Campbell. Among the hundreds I name John W. McGarvey, J. M. Barnes, Moses E. Lard, and James A. Harding, co-founder of David Lipscomb College, in 1891, et al.

The Campbell-Rice debate, November 15-December 1, 1843, in Lexington, Kentucky, was not only Mr. Campbell's last public discussion, but perhaps his most significant one. In 1842, when Mr. Campbell was on a preaching tour of Kentucky, he learned from many sources that the Presbyterians were eager for another public debate with the "Reformers." Mr. Campbell had hoped to have for his opponent President Young of Center College, a gentleman distinguished not only for his scholarship but also for his urbanity and amiability. But, due to Dr. Young's health, he would not consider participating. The Presbytyrians next turned to Rev. J. R. Breckenridge to represent them, but he declined, saying: "No sir, I will never be Alexander Campbell's opponent. A man who has done what he has to defend Christianity against infidelity, to defend Protestantism against the delusions and usurpation of Catholicism, I will never oppose in public debate. I esteem him too highly." As a last resort, the Presbyterians selected N. L. Rice of Paris, Kentucky, to defend their cause. Mr. Campbell was not too pleased to have Mr. Rice as an opponent because of the reputation of the latter who always "manifested a prejudiced and hostile spirit, which Mr. Campbell thought quite unfavorable to a calm, Christian-like and satisfactory investigation of questions at issue."[4]

After much discussion, an agreement was reached and the debate began on Wednesday, November 15, 1843, in Lexington's Main Street Christian church. It is noteworthy that Henry Clay was selected as the president of the board of moderators, and president of the meetings.

The propositions discussed were as follows:

1. The immersion in water of a proper subject into the name of the Father, the Son, and the Holy Spirit is the one only apostolic or Christian baptism:

Mr. Campbell affirms,

2. The infant of a believing parent is a scriptural subject of baptism: Mr. Rice affirms,

3. Christian baptism is for the remission of past sins: Mr. Campbell affirms,

4. Baptism is to be administered only by a bishop or ordained Presbyter: Mr. Rice affirms,

5. In conversion and sanctification the spirit of God operates on persons only through the word of truth: Mr. Campbell affirms,

6. Human creeds are necessarily heretical and schismatical: Mr. Campbell affirms.

The debate lasted for sixteen days and created extraordinary interest. Feelings ran high at times, and gave rise to many amusing incidents. Two women in the balcony were heatedly engaged in maintaining the merits of their respective disputants. "Ah," said one of them to the other, "you can easily see that Mr. Rice is by far the most learned man. Just see how many books he has upon his table, while Mr. Campbell has hardly any." "But you don't appear to know," retorted the other, "that the books on Mr. Rice's table were written by Mr. Campbell."[5]

Robert Richardson points out that "Mr Campbell's opening address of an hour has been greatly and deservedly admired for its beauty of diction, its clearness of statement and its power of argument."[6]

It was said by Haley that this speech, "for rhetorical sublimity, literary finish, beauty and brilliancy of diction, to say nothing of the effects as an argumentative thunderbolt it equaled, if it did not surpass, the greatest effort of Daniel Webster, Patrick Henry, John Quincy Adams, or Wendell Phillips, in a different field."[7] It was remarked that Henry Clay, who had been very careful to avoid the slightest appearance of favoring either disputant, was so captivated by it as, for a time, to forget himself. It was observed that soon after Mr. Campbell began, Clay became unusually attentive, and that he leaned forward and nodded assent.

After the debate, the Presbyterians boasted of a complete victory. They seemed to have failed to notice the ominous fact that when Mr. Campbell preached during the period of discussion quite a number came forward to be baptized, including an intelligent Lutheran preacher, Mr. William McChesney.

Some time after the debate, Mr. McChesney communicated the following message to Mr. Campbell: "I could have sprinkled a child the day before the debate commenced with a good conscience. All my early education and associations were placed on a scale with Pedobaptism during the debate. I went there willing to ascertain the truth. I was a little prejudiced against you, and more than a little against the Reformation. I listened with candor and attention. After the whole ground had been gone over, I was satisfied that nothing but immersion would do, and that infant baptism could not be maintained from the Scriptures. I felt deeply interested in the whole matter. If Mr. Rice could have met all your arguments satisfactorily to my mind, and have sustained his own propositions, he would have received my warmest thanks. He failed, however, in my estimation—completely failed in both."[8]

In 1888, in Terre Haute, Indiana, Col. Thomas H. Nelson, formerly United States Minister to Mexico, and afterward to Chile, said, "I was a young lawyer at Lexington, Kentucky, and attended the Campbell-Rice debate. I was a Presbyterian. When I heard the debate I thought Mr. Rice got the better of Mr. Campbell; I purchased the debate when published, and have long since decided that Mr. Campbell was a giant beside the ordinary Mr. Rice. Even now, whenever I want an intellectual stimulus, I take down the Campbell-Rice debate and read Mr. Campbell's masterful arguments."[9]

The debate was published in 1844 in a large volume of 912 pages. It was widely distributed and eagerly read. Campbell's debate with Mr. N. L. Rice was "the most complete and adequate statement of the Restoration principles ever published. It was, in all probability, the greatest religious discussion ever recorded in human history."[10]

It has been reported on several occasions that Alexander Campbell spoke to a joint session of Congress in Washington. But here are the facts: In May of 1850, Mr. Campbell was in Baltimore giving a series of sermons at the recently erected church building. During the course of the meeting "Brother George E. Tingle of Washington City" brought Mr. Campbell a pressing invitation from "members of both houses of Congress" to deliver an address on Sunday, June 2. For a number of years it had been the custom to invite prominent ministers "of all denominations" to preach in the Hall of the House of Representatives..

An advertisement was placed in the May 30 Washington "Daily Globe" announcing:

Divine Service
Bishop Alexander Campbell of Bethany, Brook County, Virginia, will preach in the Hall of Representatives at eleven o'clock, a.m., on Sunday next, the 2nd of June.

At the appointed time, "Bishop Campbell" appeared at the House of Representatives and was introduced to those assembled by Congressman John S. Phelps of Missouri. Mr. Campbell found the Hall crowded to overflowing with representatives of the nation, of both branches of our Legislature, members of their families, and many citizens. He used as his text John 3:17. He spoke an hour and a half to an audience "as attentive, and apparently as interested and absorbed, as any congregation I have had the honor recently to address."[11]

On the 22nd of December, 1857, Campbell was again on the road; this time to raise money for Bethany College. The main structure of the college had burned the early part of December. In setting out on this mission, Mr. Campbell remarked: "Nothing but the absolute necessity which seems to be laid upon me by the burning of our college building, libraries, apparatus, etc., could induce me, at this season and at my time of life, with the many pressing demands calling for my presence at home, to undertake the arduous labors which are now placed before me. If I did not feel that it is the Lord's work and that He will be my helper, I would shrink from the task. I sometimes feel like asking to be relieved from further service, but it seems I cannot hope to rest from my labors till I am called also to rest with my fathers. Such as they are, or may be, therefore all my days shall be given to the Lord."

The first visits on this trip were to several eastern cities. At Washington City, he spoke in the Baptist church. President Buchanan, with some of his Cabinet and several from both Houses, was present. Among the prominent men present was Judge Jeremiah Black, Attorney General in President Buchanan's Cabinet. Several years before, Judge Black had been baptized by Mr. Campbell. After the sermon had been delivered, the President invited Mr. and Mrs. Campbell to come to the White House for dinner the following Tuesday night. Along with the Campbells were their daughters, Virginia and Decima, and Judge Black and "his pious and devoted Christian Lady." Writing about this occasion in the *Millennial Harbinger* W. K. Pendleton observed: "The manner of the President was exceedingly cordial and I could not but conclude that he was sincerely laboring, in his high and responsible position, for the greatest good to the greatest number, by the rigid faithfulness to the Constitution of our great republic, and an enlarged and conservative policy on the stormy questions of sectional differences that have ever been so perplexing to this distinguished patriot and his predecessors. In his personal friend and gifted Cabinet officer, Judge Black, sure we are he has at least one large minded and most competent counsellor, to whom, not alone in the department over which he presides, but in every question involving the national interest or honor, he can look with confidence and safety for advice."[12]

On this tour to raise money for Bethany College, Mr. Campbell arrived in Nashville, Tennessee, April 1, 1858. He stayed in the home of Philip S. Fall. This was Campbell's sixth, and last, visit to Nashville. (1) Campbell's first visit was in 1827. Philip S. Fall, a brilliant young preacher, had come the year before to preach for the Baptist church. Under the labors of Fall, the church was fully engaged in The Reformatory Movement.[13] (2) On his second visit in 1830, he debated Obadiah Jennings, pastor of First Presbyterian church. "Campbellism," observed a citizen, "is sweeping the city." (3) The third visit was made in 1835. Due to ill health, Philip Fall had resigned and returned to Kentucky. A young preacher, Tolbert Fanning, was preaching for the church on a part time basis. (4) His fourth visit to Nashville was in 1841. The church on Church Street had some five hundred members. Tolbert Fanning was growing in favor throughout middle Tennessee, having established the church in Franklin in 1833. Campbell preached at both Sunday services at "the Christian Church" on Church Street. In his audience on Sunday evening was teh distinguished editor of the *Nashville Whig*. On Monday he wrote: "We have rarely listened to a more finished or impressive argument from the pulpit. . . .The distinct enunciation and Scottish accent of Mr. Campbell renders his delivery eminently pleasing." It was on this visit that Mr. Campbell gave his famous lecture on "Demonology" at the "Popular Lecture Club." (5) Campbell's fifth visit was in 1854. He came at the instication of the congregation that was having problems with their polished and eloquent preacher, Jesse B. Ferguson. Ferguson had all but wrecked the church with his heretical teaching. Campbell watned to debate the questions, but Ferguson refused, saying that William Ellery Channing, who had been dead twenty years had appeared to him in a vision admonishing him to have nothing to do with Campbell.

On his first Sunday in the city, he preached both morning and evening at McKendree Methodist church. The following notice of his discourse appeared in The Methodist Christian Advocate: "The distinguished gentleman whose name heads this article is now on a visit to this city. We had an opportunity of hearing him on last Sabbath at the McKendree church. . . .The congregations were vast, filling the body and galleries of the spacious house. He ascended the pulpit at half past ten o'clock. . . .It was manifest to those who had seen Mr. Campbell in former years that his physical man is giving way under weight of years and labor. . . .His subject was Faith, founded on the eleventh chapter of Hebrews, and was listened to with profound attention. . . .

"The discourse was regarded as able and appropriate. . . .At the close of the sermon, Mr. Campbell was introduced to Bishop Soule, who was one of his auditors. The Bishop expressed his satisfaction at the exalted character Campbell had ascribed to Jesus Christ. At the evening hour, Mr. Campbell preached again at McKendree on the subject of Unity."

"The following five evenings he preached at the Cherry Street meeting house, which had only recently been constructed by the Christians. The thrust of these sermons was to warn his hearers against the pitfalls of "Fergusonian Neology." The celebrated J. T. Johnson was present at all the services.

On Saturday evening, at the invitation of Tolbert Fanning, Mr. Campbell preached at Franklin College on the theme of "Man as he was, man as he is, and man as he will and must hereafter be." After eight days in Nashville, it was back home to Bethany.

In his 1858 visit to Nashville, Campbell found a severely wounded, weakened and bleeding church. Its elegant building on Cherry Street had mysteriously burned. The aged Philip Fall had been recalled to Nashville to salvage the church, which was meeting in its original structure on Church Street.

Alexander Campbell was rapidly entering the sunset of life. His labors were abundant. The Reformation he pled was growing, but the robust health that he had so long enjoyed was declining. Because the re-building of the college and the completion of the endowment still demanded additional funds, Mr. Campbell continued to travel and address the public in various parts of the country. With the beginning of the war between the states, Mr. Campbell's labors abroad were, of necessity, considerably curtailed. The sudden decrease in the enrollment at Bethany and the departure of some of the faculty threatened to close the school. His many responsibilites were great, but due to ill health and advanced age it was necessary for him to rely heavily on W. K. Pendleton and others.

In 1862, owing to scarcity of paper, *The Harbinger* was reduced from sixty to forty eight pages per number. More and more, Mr. Pendleton was assuming editorial responsibility of *The Harbinger*, taking complete control at the beginning of the year 1865. The last article that Mr. Campbell ever wrote appeared in the November issue of The Harbinger, 1865. The subject was "The Gospel." Mr. Campbell wrote: "I have now before me a scrap of paper which furnishes me with seven texts, which, when I had noted down, I thought might suffice me for seven weeks. I will transcribe it by way of illustration. The preamble is in the following words: The word "gospel" occurs in the Christian Scriptures, in three forms, one hundred and thirty six times. We have "euaggelion," the gospel, "euaggelizoo," I preach the gospel, "euaggelistees," the evangelist, or he that preaches the gospel.

'We shall now propound or declare the seven facts that constitute the whole gospel. They are:

1.The birth of Christ; God being his Father and the Virgin Mary his mother. 2. The life of Christ; as the oracles of God and the ideal of human perfection. 3. The death of Christ; as a satisfactory sacrifice for the sin of the world. 4. The burial of Christ; as a prisoner of the grave. 5. The resurrection of Christ; 'O grave! I will be thy destruction.' 6. The ascension of Christ; 'He ascended up far above all heavens, that he might possess all things.' 7. The coronation of Christ, as Lord of the universe. God, His Father, constituted him the absolute sovereign of Creation."[16]

For the last two years of Mr. Campbell's life, his strength decreased, but he was ever cheerful, ever happy and knew what was approaching. He attended church services at Bethany for the last time in the middle of February, 1866. He passed away on the Lord's Day, March 4, the same year. The funeral service, in the presence of hundreds of friends, was conducted by Dr. Robert Richardson. C. L. Loos led the prayer. Burial took place in the Campbell family cemetery across the road from the Campbell home. Later, a tombstone was erected on which were carved the following words:

IN MEMORIAM
Alexander Campbell,
Defender of the faith,
Once delivered to the Saints,
Founder of
Bethany College
Who being dead yet speaketh
by his numerous writings
and holy example
Born in the county of Antrim, Ireland,

September 12, 1788
Died at Bethany, Virginia
March 4, 1866.

Alexander Campbell was no ordinary person. This was observable by all who came under his influence. It will be helpful to take note of what some of his contemporaries thought of him.

When Henry Clay learned that his friend, Alexander Campbell, was going abroad in 1847 he forwarded to him this letter:

> The Rev. Dr. A. Campbell, the bearer hereof, a citizen of the United States of America, residing in the Commonwealth of Virginia, being about to make a voyage to Europe and to travel particularly in Great Britain, Ireland and France, I take great satisfaction in strongly recommending him to the kind offices and friendly reception and treatment of all persons with whom he may meet and wherever he may go. Dr. Campbell is among the most eminent citizens of the United States, distinguished for his great learning and ability, for his successful devotion to the education of youth, for his piety and as the head and founder of one of the most important and respectable religious communities in the United States. Nor have his great talents been exclusively confined to the religious and literary walks in which he has principally moved; he was a distinguished member, about twenty years ago, of the convention called in the state of Virginia to remodel its civil constitution, in which, besides other eminent men, were ex-presidents Madison and Monroe, and John Marshall, the late Chief Justice of the United States.
>
> Dr. Campbell, whom I have the honor to regard personally as my friend, carries with him my wishes and prayer for his health and happiness whilst abroad, and for his safe return to his country, which justly appreciates him so highly.
> H. Clay[17]
> Ashland, KY., May, 1847

In January of 1854, Mr. Campbell delivered "An Address on Colleges" in Wheeling, Virginia, now West Virginia. It is published in full in the *Millennial Harbinger,* (1854) pp. 61-79. Some years later a copy of this address fell into the hands of Robert E. Lee who wrote: "I tender you many thanks for a copy of the address, and regard it as among the ablest productions I ever read. As Dr. Symonds said of the great Milton, so may I say of the late President of Bethany College, 'that he was a man in whom were illustriously combined all the qualities that could adorn or elevate the nature to which he belongs.' Knowledge—the most various and extended virtue that never loitered in her career, nor deviated from her course. A man who, if he had been delegated

as a representative of his species the one of the many superior worlds, would have suggested a grand idea of the human race. Such was President Campbell."
R. E. Lee[18]
Lexington, Virginia, Dec. 10, 1868

On his way home from Nashville in 1858, Mr. Campbell stopped over in Louisville and preached. The editor of "The Louisville Journal" had this to say:

> Alexander Campbell—this venerable and distinguished man is now in this city on business connected with his college at Bethany. . . .Alexander Campbell is unquestionably one of the most extraordinary men of our time. Putting wholly out of view his tenets, with which we of course have nothing to do, he claims by virtue of his intrinsic qualities, as manifested in his achievements, a place among the foremost spirits of the age. . . .His personal excellence is certainly without a stain or a shadow. His intellect, it is scarcely too much to say, is among the clearest, richest, profoundest ever vouchsafed to man. Indeed, it seems to us that in the faculty of abstract thinking—in so to say, the place of pure thought—he has few, if any, living rivals. . . .He grasps and handles the highest, subtlest, most comprehensive principles as if they were the liveliest impressions of the senses. No poet's soul is more crowded with imagery than his is with the ripest forms of thought. Surely, the life of a man thus excellent and gifted, is a part of the common treasure of society. In his essential character, he belongs to no sect or party, but to the world.[19]

In 1859, Campbell was again in Louisville, where he spoke several times. Dr. Heman Humphrey, former president of Amherst College, who was visiting in the city at that time, was one of his auditors. When the educator returned to the East, he published in the *New York Observer* an account of his visit to Kentucky, in which he had this to say about Alexander Campbell:

> Though the first evening I went an hour before the time, I found the house and aisles densely crowded from the porch to the pulpit. Very many, I am sure, must have gone away because they could find no room even to stand within hearing of the preacher's voice.
>
> At length, Dr. Campbell made his way up through the crowd and took his seat in the pulpit. . . .His voice is not strong, evidently owing, in part, to the indifferent state of his health, but it is clear and firmly modulated. His enunciation is distinct and as he uses no notes, his language is remarkably pure and select. . . .I think he is the most perfectly self-possessed, the most perfectly at ease in the pulpit, of any preacher I ever listened to except, perhaps, the celebrated Dr. John Mason of New York. . . .There were many

fine and truly eloquent passages in the two discourses I heard, but they seemed to cost him no effort or to betray no consciousness, on his part, that they were fine. In listening to him, you feel that you are in the presence of a great man.

Dr. Campbell's first discourse was an exceedingly fine eulogy. . .upon the Bible, glancing rapidly at some of the internal proofs of its divine origin. . . .dwelling upon its wonderful history, biography and prophecies, and following the sacred stream down through dispensations or, as he expressed it, 'the starlight and moonlight ages' of the patriarchs and of the Jewish commonwealth, till the glorious sun of righteousness rose upon the world and introduced the Christian era.

The text of the next evening was 'Great is the mystery of Godliness,' etc. . . .I cannot, in justice, refrain from acknowledging that I never remember to have listened to or to have read a more thrilling outburst of sacred eloquence than when he came to the scene of the coronation of Christ and quoted the sublime passage from the twenty fourth Psalm, beginning, 'Lift up your heads, O ye gates, and be ye filled up, ye everlasting doors, that the King of glory may come in'; when he represented all the angels, principalities and powers of Heaven as coming together to assist, as it were, in placing the crown upon the Redeemer's head."[20]

In March of 1866, the celebrated oil tycoon, Thomas W. Phillips (1855-1912), author of the best seller "The Church of Christ" was sitting in the lobby of a Philadelphia hotel. He overheard a stranger, who had picked up the morning paper, announcing the death of Alexander Campbell, remark "Alexander Campbell was the first man that ever tried to reconcile religion with common sense."[21]

No person ever had more reverence for the Bible as the Word of God and more respect for its authority than Alexander Campbell. No person ever studied this book more and lived daily by its precepts. In 1856, Mr. Campbell wrote: "I was led by parental authority to memorize much of the Christian Scriptures, and especially the Epistles of Paul; and pre-eminently, that of Romans and that of the Hebrews."

In 1837, during his debate with Robert Owen in Cincinnati, one of his auditors was Lyman Beecher, father of Henry Ward Beecher. Beecher was intrigued with Mr. Campbell's vast and ready knowledge, and his expert use of it in his speeches. He asked Mr. Campbell "how he possessed himself of such stores of methodized knowledge." He replied, "By studying sixteen hours per day."[22] These habits he maintained through life. But the secret of his triumphant success was his familiarity with the Bible, not only in the English language but in French, Latin, Greek and Hebrew. In his early twenties, Alexander could quote from memory most of the Psalms, Ecclesiastes, Proverbs, Song of

Solomon and much of the Law, and Prophetic books. In the New Testament, he memorized the four gospels, not only in English but in Greek, also.

> The finest passages in Greek, Roman, French and English literature, both in poetry and prose, were committed to memory and in his late years, it was his favorite recreation of his often overtaxed powers, to recite such of these as the incident of the occasion might suggest to the delight and admiration of his companions. Even on his death-bed rich passages that he had committed to memory when a boy, would often come to him by some hidden association of ideas, to illustrate with their golden beauty the subject of his discussion."[23] A few days before his death, upon some illusion to the creation, he quoted the first verse of Genesis, chapter one, in Hebrew, and then the first verse of John, chapter one, in Greek.[24]

The reputation of Alexander Campbell was without spot or blemish. His bitterest enemies failed to find a flaw in his character for truth, integrity and genuine goodness, and those who knew him well looked upon him as the personification of purity and piety.

In the first issue of the *Christian Standard*, published Saturday, April 7, 1866, there appeared on the first page an editorial by Isaac Errett, under the caption, "Alexander Campbell." Among other things Errett said: "It is not designed to enter here on a consideration of the peculiar features of Mr. Campbell's teaching. Briefly, they may be sketched thus:

> Christ the only Master invoking a rejection of all human names and leaderships in religion. The Bible the only authoritative book: necessitating a denial of the authority of all human creeds. The Church of Christ, as founded by Him, and built by the Apostles, for a habitation of the Spirit, the only divine institution for spiritual ends: logically leading to the repudiation of all sects in religion as unscriptural and dishonoring to the Head of the church. Faith in Jesus, as the Christ, the Son of God, and repentance toward God, the only scriptural pre-requisites to baptism and consequent church membership: thus dismissing all doctrinal speculation and all theological dogmata, whether true or false, as unworthy to be urged as tests of fitness for membership in the church of Christ. Obedience to the divine commandments, and not correctness of opinion, the test of Christian standing. The Gospel the essential channel of spiritual influence in conversion: thus ignoring all reliance on abstract and immediate influence of the Holy Spirit, and calling the attention of inquirers away from dreams, visions, and impressions, which are so liable to deceive, to the living and

powerful truths of the Gospel, which are reliable, immutable and eternal. The truth of the Gospel, to enlighten; the love of God in the Gospel, to persuade; the ordinances of the Gospel, as tests of submission to the divine will; the promises of the Gospel, as evidence of pardon and acceptance; and the Holy Spirit, in and through all these, accomplishing his work of enlightening, convincing of sin, guiding the penitent soul to pardon, and bearing witness to the penitent believer, of his adoption into the family of God.

On March 18, 1866, in a memorial service for Mr. Campbell at Allegheny City, Pennsylvania, Joseph King, a minister said: "I assert it without the fear of successful contradiction, that no man, since the time of Luther, has so honored the Word of God, and labored to restore it to its rightful but lost position in the Church as Alexander Campbell. Like Luther he fought, and like Luther he conquered, because he wielded the "sword of the Spirit, which is the Word of God."

I may simply mention, as particular tenets taught by him: 1st. The immersion of a penitent believer in water into the name of the Father, Son and Holy Spirit as the only apostolic and scriptural Baptism. Infant-sprinkling he regarded as a Papal corruption of the New Testament ordinance of immersion.

2. The rejection of all creeds and confessions of human device as necessarily schismatical—as promotive of divisions and sectarianisms—and as tending to lead the mind away from the simplicity of the Gospel and the oneness of the Christian faith. For three centuries there was no creed in the church except the God-given creed, the Bible. The church during these centuries was more united, and enjoyed a degree of peace, harmony and prosperity, which she has never since enjoyed. The introduction of creeds was the beginning of sects, divisions, and parties; and, therefore, as the union of Christians was destroyed by creeds, the church can be restored to her apostolic unity only by the destruction of every human creed, and accepting the Bible as in all things sufficient, perfect and infallible. "In matters of faith, unity; in opinion, liberty; in all things charity."

3. The Spirit of God operates only through the inspired Word in the conversion of sinners—that the Word is the "incorruptible seed" by which men are begotten—that the "Gospel is the power of God for salvation to every one that believes'—that "the Word of God is living and powerful'—that the Gospel is to be preached in its facts, commands and promises—that its facts are to be believed, its commands obeyed, and then its promises will be enjoyed, viz: the forgiveness of sins, the gift of the Holy Spirit, and the hope of eternal life; and that the Holy Spirit is given to dwell with, and to be in those who obey the Gospel.—He rejoiced in the indwelling and communion of the Holy Spirit. With regard to the action and subject of baptism, Mr. Campbell did not differ from the Baptists; but with regard to the specific design of baptism, he and

those associated with him have been considered peculiarly heretical, though he was always careful to show that the same view of the design of baptism which he took has been recognized and taught by leading authors in all past ages of the church. What is baptism for? What is the design of it? In the words of another, "The definite object of immersion was understood when it was recognized as the remitting ordinance of the Gospel, or the appointed means through which the penitent sinner obtained an assurance of that pardon, or remission of sins, procured for him by the sufferings and death of Christ." This view of baptism was founded on such passages as the following: Mark 16:16; Acts 2:38, 22:16; 1 Peter 3:21, etc., in all of which the promise of salvation follows faith, repentance and baptism.

4. The weekly observance of the Lord's Supper. This he regarded as a part of the regular Lord's Day worship of the primitive Christians, though he did not substitute this ordinance for personal sanctification, but accepted it as a divinely appointed means of obtaining a higher degree of sanctification.

5. The rejection of all unscriptural terms, and the necessity of speaking of Bible things in Bible language to avoid misconception and misunderstanding. In the full inspiration of the Holy Scriptures, the Divinity of our Savior, the atonement made by His death for sin, the influence of the Holy Spirit through the Truth in conversion and sanctification, the indwelling of the Holy Spirit, the resurrection of the dead, and the opposite destinies of the righteous and wicked, Mr. Campbell had full faith.

Of the personal character of Mr. Campbell, and his remarkable qualities of mind and heart I need not speak. Those who knew him best loved him most.

"'Twas only necessary to know him to love him. Acquaintance with him invariably removed prejudice. Like all truly great men, he was simple and engaging in his manners, humble, modest, courteous, condescending, as polite to the day laborer as to the greatest and noblest.

His qualities of heart and mind were of the highest order—the peer of the greatest and most cultivated of earth, and yet humble and condescending as a child.

There was a singular blending of opposite qualities in his nature. He had the strength and boldness of a lion, and the gentleness of a lamb. In public, in advocating what he believed to be the truth, he was perfectly bold, intrepid and fearless; he dealt heavy blows, but always kind and courteous; in private he was gentle, lively, cheerful, and as much as possible avoided controversy and dispute. He was a fine conversationalist, always instructive and entertaining. His intellect was of the highest order and well cultivated. This was evident to the most casual observer. When in Great Britain, he was walking the streets of London one day, and a man, not knowing who Mr. C. was, but impressed with his commanding presence and noble mien, said, "There goes a man who has brains enough to govern all Europe." His reverence for God and sacred things was equally great with his intellect. At the name of Jesus he ever bowed in deepest reverence and holiest adoration. I noticed, when a student at Bethany College, that Mr. Campbell, in time of public worship, if he himself was not in the pulpit conducting the services, always knelt during prayer. He never stood. He literally "bowed his knees to the Father of our Lord Jesus Christ." He was pre-eminently a religious man, pious, spiritual and devout at all times. Many, judging from his debates and writings of a controversial character, might suppose that he lacked piety, spirituality and prayerfulness: but personal acquaintance with him always reproved such supposition. His faith made him happy. He rejoiced in —*being a Christian.*[25]

It was thought that the following bit of information would be of interest to the readers of this book.

During his 1830 visit to Nashville, Alexander Campbell conducted a meeting at Spring Street church which had been established in 1826 by Philip S. Fall. In 1860, James Challen came to the Spring Street church to conduct a gospel meeting. During his stay in Nashville he wrote an informative and interesting letter to Mr. Campbell which was published in the *Millennial Harbinger.* The Nashville church had only recently been torn asunder by Jesse B. Ferguson. Philip Fall had been called back to undo the harm that had been done. Among other things Challen wrote: "A sad state of things had obtained in the Christian congregation here when Brother Fall consented to remove to the city. By his wise, prudent, and patient labors, it is rapidly rising from the dust, and regaining its former position and influence. . .

Brother Fall has been here now about two years; and the desert begins to look like a field that the Lord has blessed. He has enjoyed the hearty co-operation of the brethren and sisters, and their warmest sympathy in his efforts to re-construct the congregation. Last Lord's Day some two hundred broke the loaf together. Many have been immersed. . .A few adhere to the fallen fortunes of J. B. Ferguson—who has no church organization and no Christian influence. He speaks in the Theater without the exhibition of anything Christian, reformative or saving.

One of the modern day attractions of Nashville is the famous Bell Meade Mansion on the outskirts of the city. This mansion, with its formerly extensive plantation, was owned and operated by John Harding, one of the influential members of the Spring Street church. In his letter to Alexander Campbell in 1860, Challen writes about the justly famous John Harding.

Brother John Harding, whom you immersed with fifteen others on December 28, 1830, is a constant attendant at the church. He sits before the pulpit and, although he cannot hear a word, he watches intently the countenance of the speaker and catches his spirit as he proceeds. He is now 83 years old, and more grave, dignified, venerable or lovely disciple of Christ I have never seen.

On last Lord's Day night when three confessed the Lord, he was overwhelmed with joy, and tears ran freely down his furrowed cheeks. We have had four immersions, and most favorable hearing.

Yours in the Lord,

James Challen[26]

In this connection it is interesting to note that in August of 1833 Tolbert Fanning and Absalom Adams established the church in Franklin, Tennessee. Both of these men were members of the Nashville church. Fanning tells us that "we immersed seventeen for remission. And on Saturday morning some of the citizens of the town assembled with us at the Masonic Hall to see if it were possible for a church to be formed on the Word of God. There, for the first time, did they see sixteen intelligent disciples give themselves to each other to worship according to the Apostles' teachings. After we congratulated the saints we departed. They promised to meet the next day at the home of Brother Anderson to attend to the Ancient Order."[27] The church met in private homes and the Masonic Hall until a church building was constructed in 1851. A lot, on which the house was located, was purchased in 1836.

Conveyance was made in trust, nevertheless. to and for the following uses and trusts and none other, that is to say, that the party of the second part shall hold said premises in trust for the congregation of Christians who renounce all creeds and confessions and take the Holy Scriptures as their only rule of faith and practice, as and for a place of worship of Almighty God.[28]

The property was deeded to John Harding, Andrew Craig and Thomas Hardeman. This is the same John Harding who owned and operated the celebrated Bell Meade Plantation where he died in 1865.

Endnotes

1. F. D. Powers, *Life of W. K. Pendleton*, p. 84.
2. Ibid, p. 47.
3. Alexander Campbell, *Millennial Harbinger*, 1850, p. 291.
4. Richardson, *Memoirs*, Vol. 2, p. 502.

5. Ibid, p. 511.
6. Ibid, p. 513.
7. J. J. Haley, *Debates That Made History*, p. 211.
8. Richardson, *Memoirs*, Vol. 2, p. 525.
9. Benjamin Lyon Smith, *The Milennial Harbinger Abridged*, Vol. 2, P. 451.
10. F. D. Kershner, *The Restoration Handbook*, Series 1, p. 20.
11. Marvin D. Williams, "Alexander Campbell and Congress", *Discipliana*, (March 1965), p. 10; Richardson, *Memoirs*, Vol. 2, p. 587f.
12. W. K. Pendleton, *Millennial Harbinger*, (1858) p. 157f.
13. Richardson, *Memoirs*, Vol. 2, p. 168.
14. Alexander Campbell, *Millennial Harbinger*, 1835, pp. 277-282.
15. Alexander Campbell, *Millennial Harbinger*, 1855, pp. 96-107; Richardson, *Memoirs*, Vol. 2, pp. 603, 604; F. Garvin Davenport, *Cultural Life In Nashville*, pp. 100-107.
16. Alexander Campbell, *Millennial Harbinger*, 1865, p. 516.
17. Richardson, *Memoirs*, Vol. 2, p. 548.
18. Selina Campbell, *Home Life and Reminiscences of Alexander Campbell*, p. 118.
19. Richardson, *Memoirs*, Vol. 2, p. 548.
20. Ibid, pp. 581-583.
21. Thomas W. Phillips, *The Church of Christ (Biographical Sketch)*, p. 22.
22. D. S. Burnett, *Millennial Harbinger*, 1866, p. 319.
23. W. K. Pendleton, *Millennial Harbinger*, 1866, p. 122. 24. Ibid, p. 136.
25. Joseph King, *Millennial Harbinger*, (1866), pp. 203-204; See also *Millennial Harbinger*, 1846, p. 385; Campbell's *Christian System*.
26. *Millennial Harbinger*, 1860, pp. 215, 216.
27. Ibid, (1833), p. 526.
28. J. M. Powell, *History of The Franklin (Tennessee) Church of Christ*, p. 7.

Chapter 9

Walter Scott, Warm-hearted Evangelist

Walter Scott died April 23, 1861, at his home in Mayslick, Kentucky. His body was laid to rest in the cemetery across the road from his house. On his tombstone were carved the words taken from John 17:8: "The word which thou gavest me I have given unto them." This passage of Scripture sums up the life of Walter Scott, the warm-hearted evangelist.

J. J. Haley lists "the big four of the current reformation" as Thomas Campbell, Alexander Campbell, Barton W. Stone and Walter Scott. "The last named is fourth in enumeration, but by no means fourth in distinctive importance. In originality, enthusiasm, courage, boldness and eloquence, he comes near heading the list. He was not the initiator or representative of any organized movement within the church like his three illustrious comrades, but so far as the distinctiveness of his contributions to the New Movement was concerned, he stands first in historical and theological importance."[1]

Each of the "big four" did much to formulate the principles of The Restoration Movement, but it was Walter Scott who gave it popular appeal. Great men and great movements go together; the greater the men, the more successful the movements. By all standards, the "big four" were men of stature, and Scott was by no means the least.

Walter Scott was born into a strong Presbyterian family in Moffat, Dumfrieshire, Scotland, October 31, 1796. He was the sixth of ten children born to John and Mary Innis Scott, who were eager for him to become a minister in the "Kirk of Scotland." Walter was of the same family as his world-famous namesake, Sir Walter Scott, whose poems and novels have given him such a distinguished and permanent place among English authors.[2]

John and Mary Innis Scott, parents of Walter, were trained musicians, people of culture and refinement. In those days, a university education was usually limited to people with means. From birth, Walter gave such promise of superior talents that his parents were determined that he should enroll as a student at the University of Edinburgh. At the proper time, arrangements were made for Walter to live with an aunt who resided in Edinburgh. Not only did Walter receive a fine classical education at the university, he also became one of the best known flutists in the city.

A characteristic incident is related concerning the sensitive and tender-hearted nature of Walter. While pursuing his studies at the university, he walked one evening into the crowded streets of the city. When he did not return at the expected time James, an older brother, went out to search for him. James explored the city diligently, but failed to find him until after midnight. He found him in the midst of a crowd singing the popular Scottish airs, collecting money for a poor, blind beggar. He was not aware of the lateness of the hour, so completely was his benevolent heart interested in helping the blind beggar.[3]

After graduating with honors from the university, he received an invitation from his uncle, George Innis, who worked for the U. S. Customs in New York City, to come to "the land of opportunity." With high hopes, Walter accepted the invitation, little knowing what marvelous things lay ahead for him.

Accordingly, he sailed from Greenock, on the ship Glenthorn, arriving in New York, July 7, 1818. He was twenty two years of age at the time. He never again saw his parents. In June of 1821, his father went to a near-by city on business. While there, he suffered a heart attack and died immediately. When Scott's wife, Mary Innis, received the news, she was so overcome with shock that she, too, died immediately. They were buried in the same grave on the same day.

Walter was kindly welcomed by his uncle, through whose influence he secured a position as Latin instructor in a classical academy on Long Island. After the school year was over Walter had itching feet to go to the far West, which, in those days, was Pittsburgh, Pennsylvania. Having no funds, he and another young man took the "famous ankle bone express," walking all the way from New York to Pittsburgh. Reaching Pittsburgh on May 7, 1819, Walter began to seek employment. As fortune would have it, he came in contact with a fellow-countryman by the name of George Forrester. Forrester was the principal of a classical academy. Because of his superb credentials, Walter was immediately engaged as an instructor in the school. Forrester was also the preacher of a small group of Christians who met for worship in the courthouse. Back in Scotland, Forrester had come under the influence of Robert and James Haldane. Forrester, therefore, was attempting to reproduce New Testament Christianity. Walter was invited to attend the services of the small congregation. He liked what he saw and heard. He was deeply impressed with the simplicity of the worship and the reverence the people had for the Bible. By day, Walter and George taught in the academy. Each night, they studied the Word of God together. It was not long before Walter discovered that he had never been scripturally baptized. He was immersed by his friend, George Forrester.

Walter continued to search the Scriptures, "and the fresh insights awakened by them in a mind naturally inquisitive and greatly devoted to religious pursuits, gave him a powerful impulse to further scriptural investigations. He rapidly outstripped his teacher. He was not long in acquiring a wonderful store of knowledge of the Christian religion."[4]

There developed in the heart of Walter an earnest desire to know the Will of God, and a strong determination to follow wherever his word, the expression of his will, should lead. Walter entered enthusiastically into the work and worship of the small congregation that met in the courthouse. He proved to be a very valuable member; "his superior education, his gifts, zeal, and piety rendered him not only useful but causing him to be greatly beloved."[5] In this small group, Walter found a nearer approach to the purity and simplicity of the primitive church than ever he had seen or expected to find on earth. To him life was sweet and precious in every respect.[6]

A change in Forrester's plans made it necessary for him to give up his academy and, as Scott had proved himself to be eminently qualified, the management of the school fell into his hands. Walter continued to have unabated interest in his religious associations and with his trusted friend, George Forrester. But something occurred that terminated this pleasant and profitable relationship. Late on a warm summer afternoon July 7, 1820, Mr. Forrester went for a swim in the Allegheny River and was accidentally drowned. This sad event was a great affliction to one of Mr. Scott's affectionate and sympathetic nature, and upon him devolved the task of comforting and assisting the bereaved widow and orphans, as well as watching over and instructing the little church that Forrester had formed. Scott felt that he had lost his best friend in the world, which was no doubt true.

In the spring of 1821, Mrs. Forrester turned over to Scott the library of her late husband. In the small collection were works by John Glas, Robert Sandeman, Carson, Wardlaw, McKnight, the Haldanes and John Locke. There was also a pamphlet "On Baptism" by Henry Errett (1778-1825). Henry Errett was the father of Isaac Errett, (1820-1888). Mr. Errett preached for a small congregation of Scotch Baptists in New York city and had published a pamphlet on Baptism in 1820. In the publication, Errett emphasizes the fact that baptism is for the remission of sins. This tract, which fell into the hands of Walter Scott, played such a dramatic role in the Restoration Movement of the nineteenth century that a few excerpts from it will not be out of order.[7]

ON BAPTISM

It is not intended, in the article, to discuss the import of the term baptism, as that term is well known to mean, in the New Testament, when used literally, nothing else than immersion in water. But the intention is to ascertain what this immersion signifies, and what are the uses and purposes for which it was appointed. This can only be done by observing what is said concerning it in the holy scriptures.

One of the first things that strikes our attention in this inquiry is that the Lord Jesus entered upon his ministry by baptism, as he arose out of the water, that he was first publicly acknowledged as the Son of God (Matthew 3:15,17). This is very remarkable, and should be well remembered. The baptism of John is spoken of thus: 'John did baptize in the wilderness, and preach the baptism of repentance, for the remission of sins.' And of those who came to his baptism, it is said, they 'were all baptized of him in the river Jordan, confessing their sins.' Mark 1:4,5. John himself seems to connect this baptism with an escape from the divine wrath; for 'when he saw many of the Pharisees and Saduccees come to his baptism, he said unto them, O generation of vipers, who hath warned you to flee from the wrath to come,' Matthew 3:7.

The Lord Jesus discoursing with Nicodemus respecting the nature of his kingdom, and giving him to understand that no Jew would be taken into it in virtue of his having been born a descendant of Abraham, observed that 'except a man be born of water, and of the Spirit, he cannot enter into the kingdom of God,' John 3:5.

In the account given by Mark of the gracious message delivered to the apostles and to be by them conveyed to all nations it would seem, at first view, as if baptism was connected with salvation; 'He that believeth and is baptized shall be saved,' Mark 14:16. To the same effect was baptism spoken of in the discourse of the apostle Peter to the Jews, on the day of Pentecost. He seems to have viewed it as connected with the forgiveness of sins. 'Repent,' said he, 'and be baptized, every one of you, in the name of Jesus Christ, for the remission of sins.' Acts 2:38.

Paul, relating to the Jews how he had been brought to confess the Lord Jesus, and speaking of what had occurred after he went to Damascus, described Ananias as coming into his lodging and, among other things, saying to him, 'And now why tarriest thou? Arise and be baptized and wash away thy sins, calling on the name of the Lord.' Acts 22:16.

The same apostle writing to the church at Rome, and pointing out the efficacy of the doctrine of Christ, and the powerful motives which that doctrine furnished, for enabling the believers of it to walk in holiness and righteousness of life, speaks of baptism in the following manner: 'Know ye not that so many of us as were baptized into Jesus Christ, were baptized into his death? Therefore, we are buried with him by baptism into death; that, like as Christ was raised up from the dead by the glory of the Father, even so we also should walk in newness of life. For if we have been planted together in the likeness of his death, we shall also be in the likeness of his resurrection: knowing this, that our old man is crucified with him, that the body of sin might be destroyed, that henceforth we should not serve sin. For he that is dead is freed from sin. Now if we be dead with Christ, we believe that we shall also live with him; knowing that Christ, being raised from the dead, dieth no more; death hath no more dominion over him. For in that he died, he died unto sin once; but in that he liveth, he liveth unto God. Likewise reckon ye also yourselves to be dead indeed unto sin, but alive unto God, through Jesus Christ our Lord.' Romans 6:2,11.

In the epistle to the churches of Galatia, the apostle showing that men become sons of God, not by adhering to the law of Moses, but by the faith of Christ, drops the following remarks: 'For ye are all the children of God, by faith in Christ Jesus. For as many of you as have been baptized into Christ, have put on Christ. There is neither Jew nor Greek, there is neither bond nor free, there is neither male nor female: for ye are all one in Christ Jesus,' Galatians 3:26,28.

In some of the exhortations addressed to the church at Ephesus, we observe an allusion to baptism too striking to be passed over: 'Husbands, love your own wives, even as Christ also loved the church, and gave himself for her; that he might sanctify her, having cleansed her with a bath of water and with the word; that he might present her to himself, glorious, a church not having a spot, or wrinkle, or any such thing; but that she might be holy, and without blemish.' Ephesians 5:25,27.

In another part of the epistle to the same church, the apostle exhorting them to preserve 'the unity of the Spirit,' describes this unity as follows— 'One body and one Spirit even as ye are called in one hope of your calling—one Lord, one faith, one BAPTISM, one God and Father of all, who is above you all, and through you all, and in you all.' Ephesians 4:4,6. When we see a place so exalted as this assigned to baptism, we may infer that baptism is a matter of no inconsiderable moment.

The same apostle warning the church at Colossae against the crafty ways of the Judaizing teachers, and assuring them of the perfection of knowledge and of righteousness which they had by Christ Jesus, reminds the brethren of their baptism in the following manner—'Being buried with him in baptism, in which also ye have been raised with him through the belief of the strong working of God, who raised him from the dead. For you who were dead on account of trespasses and the uncircumcision of your flesh, he hath made alive together with him, having forgiven us all trespasses,' Colossians 2:12,13.

In the epistle to Titus, there seems to be an illusion to baptism, which deserves particular notice. The apostle desiring Titus to inculcate obedience to magistrates, and other excellent duties, says, 'For even we ourselves were formerly foolish, disobedient, erring, slavishly serving divers inordinate desires and pleasures, living in malice and envy, hated and hating one another. But when the goodness and the philanthropy of God our Savior shone forth, he saved us; not on account of works of righteousness which we had done, but according to his own mercy, through the bath of regeneration and the renewing of the Holy Ghost, which he poured out on us richly, through Jesus Christ our Savior.' Titus 3:3,6.

One other passage shall be noticed, where baptism is introduced and spoken of, by the apostle Peter, as the antitype of the water of the flood, whereby Noah and his family escaped death. 'To which water,' saith he, 'the antitype baptism, (not the putting away the filth of the flesh, but the answer of a good conscience toward God,) now saveth us also, through the resurrection of Jesus Christ,' etc. 1 Peter 3:21.

From these several passages we may learn how baptism was viewed in the beginning by those who were qualified to understand its meaning best. No one who has been in the habit of considering it merely as an ordinance, can read these passages with attention, without being surprised at the wonderful powers, and qualities, and effects, and uses, which are there apparently ascribed to it. If the language employed respecting it, in many of the passages, were to be taken literally, it would import that remission of sins is to be obtained by baptism, that an escape from the wrath to come is effected in baptism; that men are born the children of God by baptism; that salvation is connected with baptism; that men wash away their sins by baptism; that men become cleansed by baptism; that men are regenerated by baptism; and that the answer of a good conscience is obtained by baptism. All these things, if all the passages before us were construed literally, would be ascribed to baptism. And it was a literal construction of these passages which led professed Christians in the early ages to believe that baptism was necessary to salvation. Hence arose infant baptism, and other customs equally unauthorized. And from a like literal construction of the words of the Lord Jesus, at the Last Supper, arose the awful notion of transubstantiation.

But however much men may have erred in fixing a literal import upon these passages, still the very circumstances of their doing so, and the fact that the meaning which they imputed is the literal meaning, all go to show that baptism was appointed for ends and purposes far more important than those who think of it only as an ordinance, yet have seen.

It is for the churches of God, therefore, to consider well whether it does not clearly and forcibly appear from what is said of baptism in the passages before us, taken each in its proper connection, that this baptism was appointed as an institution strikingly significant of several of the most important things relating to the kingdom of God—Whether it was not in baptism that men professed, by deed, as they had already done by word, to have the remission of sins through the death of Jesus Christ, and to have a firm persuasion of being raised from the dead through him, and after his example—Whether it was not in baptism that they put off the ungodly character and its lusts and put on the new life of righteousness in Christ Jesus—Whether it was not in baptism that they professed to have their sins washed away, through the blood of the Lord and Savior—Whether it was not in baptism that they professed to be born from above and thereby fitted for an entrance into the kingdom of God, that is, the church of God here on earth—Whether it was not in baptism that they professed to be purified and cleansed from their defilement, and sanctified and separated to the service of God—Whether it was not in baptism that they passed, as it were, out of one state into another; out of the kingdom of darkness into the kingdom of God's Son—Whether if any were ever known or recognized as having put on Christ, who has thus been buried with Him in baptism—Whether, in fact, baptism was not a prominent part of the Christian profession or, in other words, that by which, in part, the Christian profession was made—And whether this one baptism was not essential to the keeping of the unity of the Spirit.

And if, on reflection, it should appear that these uses and purposes appertain to the one baptism, then it should be considered, how far any can now be known, or recognized, or acknowledged as disciples, as having made the Christian profession, as having put on Christ, as having passed from death to life, who have not been baptized as the disciples were.

The teaching of this Tract burned deeply into the heart and mind of Walter Scott. To him the views expressed were new and fascinating. In 1838, Scott gives details of how the Tract came to both him and Alexander Campbell.

The pamphlet containing the above piece was put into my hands in the spring of 1821. It only remains to be shown that Brother Campbell received it in the same year. The person who gave it to me was Mrs. Forrester, of the Church of Pittsburgh; and he who gave it to Brother Alexander Campbell was Brother John Tait, sen., now of Rising Sun, Indiana, who also received it from Sister Forrester. The very peculiar and, in my judgment, the very unwarrantable attitude in which the editor of the Harbinger has been pleased to place me before his readers and my fellow laborers, compelled me to seek the testimony of Brother Tait on this subject. It is as follows, and I trust that my beloved brother is perfectly able to supply all necessary explanation to such as need it:

Rising Sun, 25th October, 1838
My Dear Brother:
Yours of the 15th inst. came safe to hand, and I hasten to reply. You ask me to say "Where, and in what year, you (I) gave to brother Alexander Campbell the New York pamphlet published by the church in that city." Answer: It was at Bethany, in the later part of September, or early in October, in the year 1821. Of this I am positive, as I recollect the circumstances very well. I was called to Pittsburgh at the time stated above, and procured said pamphlet from our dearly beloved sister Forrester. On my way home I called at Bethany and showed the pamphlet to brother Campbell who was so highly pleased with it that I left it with him.
Believe me, my dear brother, respectfully and affectionately yours in the hope of eternity,
W.S.
JOHN TAIT

If, then, it is considered that we had all received the pamphlet and had read it, I conceive there was no impropriety in saying that we were acquainted with the import of baptism two years before the debate. Brother Alexander Campbell has quoted at length from it in the *Christian Baptist*; and father Campbell read from it, in my presence, before the Red-Stone Association in the very year of the debate, 1823.

I was at the residence of brother Campbell in the year 1824, and we journeyed together, and preached in Wheeling; but that I was there in 1823, I cannot, after the strictest and most assiduous inquiry, discover. He says he divulged the import of baptism to one of his students. As Rigdon, the now Mormonite, accompanied him to Kentucky, and to the debate, it is possible he divulged it to him also. I can apologize for him, therefore, by believing that he confounds things wholly distinct. I needed no such a disclosure, yet I urge not that these two brethren received their first impressions of baptism from me or from the piece referred to. I like not the lex talionis. Nor do I admire the morality that gratuitously, and in a manner altogether uncalled for, hazards the veracity of any man. Had I been challenged to measure obligations in this point I might not have shrunk from the task; but it would have been a most ungrateful one to me; for of all things on earth there is the least refined morality in that of conferring a benefit, and afterward speaking of it; father Campbell has never suggested to me that such a disclosure took place in 1823. affectionately, W.S.

Scott was so intrigued with this pamphlet on baptism that he wrote, "I took a journey into distant regions to increase my Christian learning and forward the cause of Reform." On account of the pamphlet, Walter walked all the way to New York and there "stayed with the church for three months." He was somewhat disillusioned with what he found in Errett's Scotch Baptist church. He felt that they stood in need of a mind to generalize their attainments, and for want of this their attempt at reformation was cramped, and finally abortive.[9]

Leaving New York, Walter Scott walked to Patterson, New Jersey, but he found the few disciples there in a state of disorganization. He pursued his journey to Baltimore, where he found a small church in "very low condition." Learning that there was a small group of worshippers in Washington City, he went thither, and found them "to be so sunken in the mire of Calvinism that they refused to reform," and finding no pleasure in them, he departed. He went to the capital, and climbing up to the top of its lofty dome, "I set myself down filled with sorrows at the miserable destitution of the church of God." Descending, he decided to return to Pittsburgh and "instruct the disciples in the great hope of the gospel element, that "Jesus is the Son of God."[10] This he referred to later as the "Golden Oracle."

In a spirit of dejection, and yet hope, he continued his travels on foot to Pittsburgh, a distance of about three hundred miles and reached there weary and travel worn. He was, however, cheered by the warmth of his welcome. Back in Pittsburgh, he renewed his acquaintances with the prominent and wealthy family of Mr. Nathaniel Richardson. Walter was invited to live in the Richardson's home to be the tutor of Robert Richardson, who was 14 years old at the time. Scott's fame as a teacher spread and Mr. Richardson provided space that he could use for a large class room. Scott opened a classical and English high school that was widely patronized. The number of his pupils grew to more than one hundred. The young classical scholar from Scotland was by far the best educator and teacher in the city. In addition to his duties in the class room, he insisted that his students read the New Testament every day. He felt that no education was complete without a knowledge of the Bible.

As a teacher, he was a strict disciplinarian. His rules were summed up in three words: obedience, order, and accuracy. In after years, some of his students ranked among the most useful men in the country. Young Robert Richardson, for an example, became an eminent physician, author and educator. After the death of Alexander Campbell in 1866, Robert Richardson wrote the famous history of the Restoration Movement called *Memoirs of Alexander Campbell.* In this work he wrote the following about his friend and teacher, Walter Scott:

> I would sometimes invite Mr. Scott to walk out of an evening in the Richardson garden in the vicinity of the city. Walter's mind could not be divorced from the high theme which occupied it. Nature, in all its forms, seemed to speak to him only of its Creator. Thus, for instance, if his pupil would present him with a rose, while he admired its tints and inhaled its fragrance, he would ask in a tone of deep feeling, 'Do you know, my dear, why in the Scriptures Christ is called the Rose of Sharon?' If the answer was not ready, he would reply himself: 'It is because the Rose of Sharon has no thorns,' and would then go on to make a few touching remarks on the beautiful traits of character of the Savior. The great central theme of the Christian religion is the Messiahship of Jesus. That Jesus is the Christ, the Son of God, is the theme of the Bible around which all other truths revolve as the planets revolve around the sun."

Robert Richardson tells how Mr. Scott took special pains to familiarize the students with the ancient tongues, with the Greek of the New Testament, for which purpose he caused them to commit to memory so that some of them could repeat the whole of Matthew, Mark, Luke and John in the Greek language. Students were also required to memorize portions of the ancient classic authors, as well as written translations of them. These tasks, to some, were irksome, but to others they tended to improve the pupils in taste and accuracy and to store their minds with charming passages for use in future life."[11]

It was during the winter of 1821-1822 that Walter Scott and Alexander Campbell met for the first time. Walter was 26 and Alexander was 34. A friendship was formed that lasted through life. Walter and Alexander were made for each other. Each complimented the life of the other. Without Scott, Campbell would never have become the great man that history knows. Without Campbell, Scott would never have accomplished the great things that are so well known to students of the Restoration Movement.

In many respects these two men were alike. For one thing, they were of Scotch ancestry. For another thing, they were intellectual giants and for another, they were men of spiritual stature. They were alike in that they believed that first century Christianity could be reproduced by using the New Testament as a blueprint.

Scott and Campbell were unalike in some respects. When Campbell made a speech it was always great. He never disappointed an audience. He knew what he wanted to say and he said it in the best possible way. On the other hand, Scott's efforts were not always equal. He often became depressed and despondent, and attempting to preach in this state of mind, he would make a complete failure and the people would go away disappointed. At times he was like Charles Kingsley (1819-1875), the English clergyman and novelist. On one occasion, Kingsley was invited to preach in Westminister Abbey. He accepted the invitation with fear and trepidation. On the day of his appointment, as he walked into the pulpit, he said to himself, "I wish I were dead." Kingsley preached his sermon and as he left the pulpit he said to himself, "I wish I were more dead." Scott felt that way at times, but on occasion when he was in good spirits and preaching on his favorite subject, "The Messiahship," he could reach heights of eloquence such as Campbell never reached in his best efforts. For example, in 1830 Scott was on his favorite theme before a large audience in a grove mid-way between Wellsburg and Wheeling, West Virginia, and Alexander Campbell was in the audience. Campbell was usually self-composed. But on this particular occasion, Walter Scott was so eloquent that he literally raised the people out of their seats including Mr. Campbell, whose emotions were so stirred and so intense that he arose and shouted, "Glory to God in the highest." Mr. Scott was at his best as an evangelist. He had a warm heart and a musical voice. His language was always chaste and exact - and at all times he exhibited a love and concern for the people that was easily recognized.

Robert Richardson, biographer of Alexander Campbell and student of Walter Scott, contrasts the two men:

> While Mr. Campbell was fearless, self-reliant and firm, Mr. Scott was naturally timid, diffident and yielding; and, while the former was calm, steady and prudent, the latter was excitable, variable and precipitate. The one like the North Star was ever in position, unaffected by terrestrial influences; the other, like the magnetic needle, was often disturbed and trembling on its center, yet ever returning, or seeking to return, to its true direction. Both were nobly endowed with the powers of higher reason—a delicate self-consciousness, a decided will and a clear perception of truth. But, as it regards the other departments of the inner nature, in Mr. Campbell the understanding predominated, in Mr. Scott the feelings; and, if the former exceeded in imagination, the latter was superior in brilliancy of fancy. If the tendency of one was to generalize, to take wide and extended views and to group a multitude of particulars under a single head or principle, that of the other was to analyze, to divide subjects into their particulars and consider their details. If one was disposed to trace analogies

and evolve the remotest correspondences of relations, the other delighted in comparison and sought for the resemblances of things. If one possessed the inductive power of the philosopher, the other had, in a more delicate musical faculty and more active ideality, a larger share of the attributes of the poet. In a word, in almost all the qualities of mind and character, which might be regarded differential or distinctive, they were singularly fitted to supply each other's wants and to form, a rare and delightful companionship."[12]

William Baxter wrote that "Mr Scott's meeting with Alexander Campbell naturally opened the way to an acquaintance with his father, Thomas Campbell, between whom and his gifted son there existed the most perfect sympathy of feeling in their religious views and efforts."

At that time there were few, if any, better educated ministers in America than the elder Campbell; he was not less remarkable for his perfect courtesy of manner and well developed Christian character than for his natural ability and literary culture; and looking at the trio, Thomas Campbell, Alexander Campbell, and Walter Scott, as we now can in the light of their finished lives and work, it may be said truthfully that they were not surpassed in genius, eloquence, talent, learning, energy, devotion to the truth and purity of life by any three men of the age in which they lived.[13]

It is my purpose at this time to note some contributions that Walter Scott made to the Restoration Movement—contributions that are commonplace to most students of this movement.

1) Walter Scott was the first to popularize the expression "Gospel Plan of Salvation." Since his time, it has been widely used by gospel preachers. In 1874, Dr. T. W. Brents (1823-1905) published his now famous book titled "The Gospel Plan of Salvation." In the judgment of this writer, Dr. Brents' book is the most important book written by anyone connected with the Restoration Movement during the nineteenth century. In addition to Dr. Brents' book being published in 1874, there were other events important to students of Restoration history. Tolbert Fanning (1810-1874), president of Franklin College, died that year. H. Leo Boles (1874-1946) and N. B. Hardeman (1874-1965) were both born in 1874. E. G. Sewell was well established as co-editor of the *Gospel Advocate* with David Lipscomb.

2) In his evangelistic meetings on the Western Reserve, Walter Scott introduced the custom of extending the gospel invitation at the conclusion of each sermon—inviting and admonishing people to come to Christ upon the terms set forth in the New Testament.

3) It was Walter Scott who emphasized the fact that the creed of the first century church was "Christ." We are reminded that our English word "creed"

is derived from the Latin verb "credo" which means "I believe." The creed of the early church was Christ Himself. Belief in Him as the Son of the living God and as a personal Savior was the one and only item of faith essential to valid baptism. Peter was the first to give utterance to this creed, Matthew 16:16. Note also John 20:30,31; 1 Corinthians 2:2. As we read the book of Acts we observe that people who became Christians gave expression to this creed: "I believe that Jesus is the Christ, God's Son," after which they were baptized (Acts 8:36-39). The unchangeableness of this divine creed is stated positively in Hebrews 13:8. This deathless creed is simple, profound, comprehensive, universal, living and heaven-born. Some one has put it this way: "The living creed of the living church is the living, ever-living Son of the living God."[13]

4) In the exercise of his analytical mind, Walter Scott soon discovered that the testimonies of Matthew, Mark, Luke and John were written for one great specific purpose, and that was to prove the proposition that "Jesus is the Christ, the Son of God" (John 20:30,31), and that this constituted the central truth and the great essential element of Christianity.[14] It was his idea that Christianity could be summarized in four words: "Jesus Christ, God's Son." This he referred to as the "Golden Oracle," and this became the subject of countless sermons, a sample of which will be given later in this chapter.

5) He emphasized in his preaching that "baptism is for the remission of sins." The idea came to him with great force (1821) after he read Henry Errett's pamphlet on Baptism, already referred to. In the same year, Alexander Campbell had access to this information.[15] It was some time later, however, before either Scott or Campbell publicly proclaimed this Biblical doctrine. Mr. Campbell gave brief mention of it in his debate with William McCalla in 1823. It soon became well established in the mind of Alexander Campbell, as seen in his first "Extra" titled "Remission of Sins," published in the *Millennial Harbinger*, July 5, 1830. (q.v.)

It should be noted that in 1826 Walter Scott, with his family, moved to Steubenville, Ohio, where he opened a school. Here he found a number of Baptists with views similar to his. They professed to be seeking the restoration of original Christianity. In the summer of 1826, the Mahoning Baptist Association held its annual meeting nearby and Scott attended. Although not a member, he was invited to participate as "a teaching brother." He delivered the sermon on Sunday morning. Alexander Campbell, who was present, was much impressed with Scott's eloquence and the finished nature of his sermon, which was based on Matthew 11. When the association met the following year in New Lisbon, Alexander Campbell travelled through Steubenville and prevailed upon Scott to accompany him. During the proceedings of the association, it was decided to employ an evangelist to labor among the Mahoning Baptists on the Western Reserve. The committee which had been appointed recommended Walter to this work. The invitation, when extended, was gladly accepted. It can truthfully be said that with this appointment, the

Restoration Movement got underway.

In 1827, the Mahoning Baptist Association consisted of seventeen churches, all in Ohio, except the one in Wellsburg, Virginia. From the beginning of Scott's labors on the Western Reserve as evangelist for the Mahoning Association, the Reformation gained momentum. New Lisbon, Ohio, where Scott had been chosen evangelist, became the center of his initial presentation of the "Ancient Gospel."

On November 18, 1827, Scott arrived at New Lisbon. He found that the Baptist meeting house, where he was to preach, was filled to capacity. He mounted the pulpit and took as his theme the confession of Peter as recorded in Matthew 16:16. This had been familiar ground to him for a number of years. In Pittsburg, he had discovered, to his joy, that the four gospels were written to prove the divinity of Christ. In his sermon he proceeded to show that the foundation truth of Christianity was the divine nature of Christ Jesus, and that the belief of it was designed to produce love in the heart of him who believed it as it would lead him to true obedience to Christ. In this connection Scott quoted the great commission, and called attention to the fact that Jesus had taught his apostles "that repentance and remission of sins should be preached in his name among all nations, beginning at Jerusalem." He then led his hearers to Jerusalem, on the day of Pentecost, and called upon them to listen to an authoritative announcement of the law of Christ, now to be made known for the first time, by the apostle Peter.

After a rapid, but graphic, review of Peter's sermon, Scott pointed out its effects on those who heard him, showing that they, being cut to their hearts, cried out in agony "men and brethren, what shall we do?" The inspired answer came in these words, "Repent, and be baptized, every one of you, in the name of Jesus Christ, for the remission of your sins, and ye shall receive the gift of the Holy Spirit." Then in his inimitable way, Scott made the application. He insisted that the conditions were unchanged and that the Word of God meant what it said, and that to receive and obey it was to obey God and to imitate the example of those who, under the preaching of the apostles, gladly accepted the gospel message.

When Scott was drawing to the conclusion of his sermon, he noticed a stranger enter the door. This man, as it turned out, was a highly respected citizen and a devout elder in the Presbyterian church. He was a diligent student of the Scriptures, and had long been convinced that the Savior's command to convert the world was not now obeyed as it was preached by the apostles. He often spoke to his wife about the matter saying, "When I find any person preaching, as did the apostle Peter in the second chapter of Acts, I shall offer myself for obedience and go with him." The name of this Presbyterian elder was William Amend, and just as he entered the building, Mr. Scott was pleading with the people to "Repent and be baptized every one of you in the name of Jesus Christ for the remissions of your sins, and you shall receive the gift of the Holy Spirit." Mr. Amend kept on walking until he got to where Scott was standing. He made the good confession and, along with others, was baptized for the remission of his sins. Scott used to say, referring to the incident, "Here is a case in proof that the Word of God can be understood alike by all who study it with unbiased mind."[16]

Several years after this incident, Mr. Scott wrote a letter to Mr. Amend in regard to his conversion. In a few days Scott received this reply:

> Now, my brother, I will answer your questions. I was baptized on the 18th of November, 1827, and I will relate to you the circumstances which occurred a few days before that date. I had read the second chapter of Acts when I expressed myself to my wife as follows: Oh, this is the gospel; this is the thing we wish, the remission of our sins! Oh, that I could hear the gospel in those same words as Peter preached it! I hope I shall someday hear, and the first man I meet who will preach the gospel thus, with him I will go. So, my brother, on the day you saw me come into the meeting house, my heart was open to receive the Word of God, and when you cried, 'The Scripture shall no longer be a sealed book, God means what he says. Is there any man present who will take God at His word and be baptized for the remission of sins—at that moment my feelings were such that I could have cried out 'Glory to God! I have found the man whom I have long sought for.' So I entered the Kingdom, when I readily laid hold of the hope set before me. William Amend.[17]

After receiving this reply from Mr. Amend, Walter Scott wrote: "The above letter is a very simple document, but on the occasion to which it relates, there certainly was resolved, not by words merely, but deeds also, questions the most interesting and important. The Rubicon was passed, and the church of God on that day, had restored to it, publicly and practically, the ancient gospel, and a manner of handling it, which ought never to have been lost by the servants of Jesus Christ." Scott continued by saying: "Permit me through this medium to acknowledge, publicly, my obligations to our beloved and justly esteemed brother Alexander Campbell, who, being the first to move for my appointment, which resulted in the restoration of the Ancient Gospel. May almighty God bless him through Jesus Christ."[18]

The movement to restore the church of the New Testament did not take hold with any marked degree of success until the thirty year old Walter Scott began his simplistic method of preaching on the Western Reserve.

The five-finger method of preaching the "gospel plan of salvation" took at once and the results were staggering. It was the common practice of Scott to illustrate the five items—viz: Faith, Repentance, Baptism, Remissions of sins, and Gift of the Holy Spirit—by holding up his left hand and using his thumb for Faith, and so on; then contrast it with the five points of Calvinism; thus, he made the Scripture order of the gospel so plain that little boys could carry it home. There was great excitement wherever he went.[19]

Such a change as took place on the Western Reserve (Northeast section of Ohio) under the labors of Scott have seldom (if ever) been equaled. The Bible was read with new interest, for the people had learned that it was not a "dead letter," but the living word of the living God. The Mahoning River became a second Jordan, and Scott another John the Baptist, calling on the people to repent and be baptized for the remission of their sins. "The good cause" had such a phenomenal growth that an excited onlooker remarked, "Campbellism, bourbon whiskey and dog fennel have taken over the blue grass of Kentucky and the first named of the Trinity will soon have captured the whole state."

Riding into a village near the close of the day, he would speak to the children returning home from school. As the children gathered around him, he would say: "Children, hold up your left hands." They all did so. "Now," said he, "beginning with your thumb repeat after me: Faith, repentance, baptism, remission of sins, gift of the Holy Spirit—that takes up all your fingers. Now, again: Faith, repentance, baptism, remission of sins, gift of the Holy Spirit. Now, again, faster altogether." He would go over these things repeatedly until the amused children could repeat the five items rapidly and in unison. He then would say: "Children, now run home—don't forget what is on your fingers, and tell your parents that a man will present the gospel tonight at the school house, as you have it on your hand." Away went the children, in great glee, repeating as they went: Faith, Repentance, Baptism, Remission of sins, Gift of the Holy Spirit. Soon the story would be repeated in every house of the village, and long before the hour of meeting, the house would be filled, the children sitting on the front seats. When Scott arose to preach he would hold up his left hand and the children would follow him eagerly as he presented his sermon. People were invited and urged to become Christians upon the terms of the gospel. Ordinarily, there were many responses with baptisms every day.

Scott made a special study of the New Testament with reference to the term "gospel". In his preaching and writing he would use such terms as "the true gospel," "the original gospel," "the pure gospel," "the Jerusalem gospel," "the Pentecostian gospel," and "the ancient gospel."

The "plan of salvation" as set forth by Walter Scott had wide acceptance among the disciples. According to this plan, God and man cooperate in the process of salvation; however, because before God can do anything for man, man must first recognize six existing evils and their cures. The six evils are: love of sin, practice of sin, state of sin, the guilt of sin, the power of sin, and the eternal consequences of sin. The six corresponding cures are: faith, which cures the love of sin; repentance, which cures the practice of sin; baptism, which cures the state of sin; forgiveness, which cures the guilt of sin; gift of the Holy Spirit, destroys the power of sin; and everlasting life, which is the escape from the eternal consequences of sin.[20]

Scott, in his study of the gospel, referred to it as having facts to be believed, commands to be obeyed, and promises to be enjoyed. He referred to the primary facts of the gospel as being the death, burial and resurrection of Christ; Primary commands of the gospel as faith, repentance and baptism; Primary promises of the gospel as remission of sins, gift of the Holy Spirit, and eternal life.

It was not long before the "Plan of salvation" was being preached with phenomenal success, not only on the Western Reserve, but throughout Ohio, Pennsylvania, Indiana, and Kentucky. In one year, Walter Scott baptized more than one thousand people. Talented men such as John Secrest, John Henry, A. S. Hayden, Adamson Bentley, William Hayden and many others were baptizing hundreds of people. In Kentucky, "Racoon" John Smith baptized 1400 during the years 1827-1829. In six months Jeremiah Vardeman baptized 550. This is just a sample of what was going on in the New Evangelism Movement.

In 1828, when the Mahoning Association met in Warren, Ohio, excitement was in the air. The new converts were numerous. Prospects were indeed bright. "This time the Association came together purely and simply as an assembly of Christians. Though under the form and name of a Baptist association, the creed system was abandoned, and neither that denominational name, nor any other, was on its standards."[21] The people had in mind the "possibility of the union of Christians on original Bible grounds."[22]

Alexander Campbell spoke upon this occasion to people in the "Movement" who had come from varied religious backgrounds. "With a correct discernment of the situation, and a profound and far-seeing appreciation of the necessity for a clearer and scriptural settlement of the grounds of true Christian union, Mr Campbell met the case fairly, fully, and manfully." His sermon text was Romans 14:1, which he classified under three heads, all subjects relating to the Christian religion: 1) Matters of knowledge—personal knowledge; 2) The things of faith, the facts reported to us, which we accept on testimony; 3) Matters of opinion.

Knowledge he defined as ones own personal experience. This term is confined to things which he sees, or hears, or discerns, either by his senses, or his own consciousness. A person can testify only to the things which he himself personally knows. It was asserted that the apostles knew the Lord Jesus, saw him, 'handled' him, heard him, and knew his miraculous works, and heard his gracious discourses, so that within this personal knowledge and consciousness they held the absolute certainty of knowledge of him—his character and his claims; that they were thus qualified to declare the gospel and to be his ambassadors, his apostles and witnesses to the world; that the apostles knew the gospel to be true, and none but they stood on this high ground of knowledge.

The subject of faith was treated in an equally clear and forcible style. Faith stands on testimony. No testimony, no faith. Testimony is delivered by witnesses. Christ's apostles are his witnesses, (John 15:27; Acts 1:8). Our faith in Christ is founded on the testimony of his witnesses. The apostles, the men of knowledge, testified, or declared, the things which they saw and heard; we receive their testimony and, thus, we believe, (Romans 10:17). It was next shown that the facts of the gospel are always one and invariable, and as the apostolic testimony or declaration of the facts never varies, the faith of all persons is a unit. The important conclusion was thus reached, that Christians are not divided on matters of faith.

> Touching the third division in this classification of knowledge, faith and opinion, he showed that opinion was the fruitful source of all the schism, which checkers, disgraces, and weakens the Christian profession; that creeds are but statements, with few exceptions, of doctrinal opinions or speculative views of philosophical or dogmatic subjects, and tended to confusion, disunion, and weakness; that as Christ receives us in the faith, without regard to questions of doubtful disputations, so we should receive one another, laying the basis of a rational and permanent union in faith, in the express matters of apostolic teaching, on which no differences obtain among the followers of Christ.[23]

The matter of re-appointing Walter Scott as evangelist of the association was unanimously resolved. Scott needed a companion to work with him, especially a good singer. Scott knew that William Hayden (1799-1863), a young man of dedication and promise would make an outstanding fellow-worker. Walter Scott stood before the association and said, "Brethren, give me my Bible, my head, and Brother William Hayden, and we will go out and convert the world."[24] The matter was settled in favor of Scott's proposal.

In choosing Hayden as his fellow-laborer, Scott was influenced not only by his preaching ability but also by his fine musical powers. He said, "There is not a man in the association that can sing like William Hayden." He had a voice of great depth and compass, at one time sweet and melodious, at another, swelling out in tempest tones. He instructed the people by his sermons, but he melted and moved them by his songs. He was truly "a sweet singer of Israel." A strong bond of friendship grew up between the two men. As they rode along on their horses, they enjoyed the opportunity of conversation.

As a father instructing his son who delighted to learn, so Walter instructed his young companion, whom he affectionately called "Willy." Hayden would sometimes spend so much time on his introduction as to shorten his sermon, throwing it out of proportion. The next day, riding along, Scott would break the silence by saying, "Willy, did you ever know a fish to be all head?" followed by instructions that were never forgotten. Occasionally, Hayden would be impelled by his feelings to exhort his hearers at the opening of his discourse, and the result would be that the sermon would all run to exhortation. Later, as they travelled, Walter would say, "Willy, did you ever see a fish all tail?" Hayden was an apt student, seldom was the same instruction needed twice. Hayden developed into one of the finest preachers in the Restoration Movement.[25]

During Hayden's ministry of thirty five years, he travelled ninety thousand miles, a full sixty thousand of which he made on horseback, a distance of more than twice around the world. The baptisms by his own hands were twelve hundred and seven. He preached over nine thousand sermons, that is over two hundred and sixty one discourses per year during his public life. He preached over fifty sermons in one month alone. Few men have equaled the record of William Hayden.[26]

The year 1829 was fruitful. Wherever Scott and Hayden went large audiences assembled and hundreds yielded to the gospel and were baptized into Christ. At Shalersville, on The Reserve, it was Scott's pleasure to baptize the distinguished Dr. Robert Richardson, who had been a student of his back in Pittsburgh, years before. For a good while a sentiment had been growing in the Association that they should repudiate human creeds and authorities and simply follow the Scriptures.

The years passed by and the Association met, as it proved to be, for the last time as an ecclesiastical body, at Austintown, Ohio. John Henry, who had been among the first to enter the ranks of reformers, moved "that Mahoning Association, as an advisory council, or an ecclesiastical tribunal, should cease to exist." This was in accordance with the general feeling, but Mr. Campbell was at the point of rising to oppose the motion. Scott, sitting nearby, placed his hand on the shoulder of Campbell and asked him not to oppose the motion. He yielded, the motion passed unanimously. This action at Austintown may be regarded as the formal separation from the Baptists.

In December of 1831, Walter Scott moved, with his family, to Cincinnati, Ohio. Eager to get his views before the public, he began editing and publishing a periodical "The Evangelist," which continued for a number of years. In a short time he removed to Carthage, a village some eight miles from Cincinnati. Here he lived and labored for thirteen years.

Alexander Campbell took note of Walter's work in Carthage (Millennial Harbinger, (1835), p. 329). "Brother Walter Scott has planted, and the Lord has made to grow up a congregation of one hundred and four members in Carthage, Hamilton county, Ohio—that being now the immediate theater of his domestic labors. The conversions in that place have not only been numerous for the time, but many of them extraordinary; so much so, that a village not long since distinguished for debate, fighting, and petty legal prosecutions, is now filled with the melody of praise and abounds in good order, joy and thanksgiving to the Lord.

His many essays in *The Evangelist* on a variety of subjects were widely and eagerly read. As we have already seen, a union between the "Christians" and the "Reformers" was affected on January 1, 1832 in Lexington, Kentucky.

In 1836, Scott published his book on *The Gospel Restored*. Baxter refers to this book as "a clear and systematic view of the Christian religion, of which it may be safely said, that no book of the present century has done more to explode common and popular errors and set forth the teachings of the Word of God in this pristine order, simplicity, and beauty." The effect of this book may be learned, in a measure, from an incident which took place about twenty five years later. While on a visit to Missouri, Walter Scott met with the well-known preacher, Moses E. Lard, who threw his arms around him and, with great warmth of feeling, said: "Brother Scott, you are the man who first taught me the gospel." "How so?" was the reply. "It was by your Gospel Restored," said Lard; and this was only one instance among hundreds.[27]

The first college to be founded by the Disciples was Bacon College, in Georgetown, Kentucky, 1836. Walter Scott was elected president. The college received its name in honor of Francis Bacon, the noted philosopher. J. T. Johnson was appointed vice president. Among the faculty, Tolbert Fanning was selected as professor of natural philosophy, chemistry, geology and mineralogy. It is said that Scott was president in name only. He "delivered a learned and lengthy inaugural address on the "Novum Organum" of Lord Bacon after which he went back home and, for some reason, never returned to assume the duties of his office."[28]

D. S. Burnett was soon chosen as president. In 1840, James Shannon, educator and preacher, was named president. He was an Irishman, who received a classical education from the famed Belfast Academical Institute. He came from Ireland to Georgia, where he taught four years in Sanbury Academy. In 1830, he was appointed professor of Ancient Languages in the University of Georgia, where he remained until 1836.[29] From 1836 to 1840, he served as president of Louisiana College at Jackson, where he came in contact with Alexander Campbell and The Reformation.

In 1840, Shannon was elected president of Bacon College, and during the first commencement exercises President Shannon conferred the LL.D degree on Alexander Carson of Tubbermore, Ireland. Shannon wrote that it was "not merely on account of Carson's work on Baptism, but his acknowledged merits as a scholar. . . .and having become the author of many works that have rendered his name deservedly celebrated throughout Christendom."[30]

Alexander Campbell said of the degree: "I willingly, indeed, accorded to Alexander Carson the literary honor intended and indicated by the degree. His work on Baptism alone merited such a distinction."[31] This, incidentally, was the first honorary degree to be bestowed on a person by a college connected with The Restoration. Many such degrees have been given since then.

At a state meeting held in Georgetown, Kentucky, in 1846, Walter Scott preached a sermon on a Sunday night. William Baxter, the biographer of Scott, was present and later gave an account of the sermon. Baxter said the audience was large and intelligent. People were there from all the principal towns of the Blue Grass region. Scott was at his best. His theme was "The Golden Oracle," as set forth in the statement of the apostle Peter, "Thou art the Christ, the Son of the Living God."

> His exordium was solemn, impressive, grave; his language reminded me of the finest passage of Milton and, almost with his first sentence, I saw that he had established a warm sympathy between himself and his hearers. He spoke of the nature of Christ as gold mingled with clay—the fine gold of divinity, with the clay of humanity; and then from the Old and the New Testament gathered all the glorious names which prophets and apostles applied to the Son of God—names of power, excellency, and glory, and showed how they set forth the nature of him around whom they clustered, who, not only were, but was worthy of them all.
>
> All felt that he was giving expression to their own highest conception of the Savior which they never had been able to embody in words, and so fixed and intense became the attention that the entire audience would sway to and fro, as waves at the will of the wind. . . .
>
> The interest was sustained throughout, and some of the passages were the finest I ever heard from the lips of man. In one portion of the discourse he spoke of Christ as Prophet, Priest, and King. He sought the prophet among all those who had delivered the messages of God to men; but found him not at Sinai, nor at Carmel, where God owned Elijah by fire, nor among the long lines of those who wept over Israel's sorrow and captivity like Jeremiah; or who, like Isaiah, heralded the dawning of a brighter day; but bowing in agony in the Gethsemane, the prophet he sought was found. He bade kings and conquerors, in pomp and majesty, march by— we saw Nimrod, and Nebuchadnezzar, and David, and Solomon in all his glory; Cyrus and Alexander, and the great Julius swelled the procession; but the king he sought was in Pilate's Judgment Hall, a soldier's purple cloak, thrown over him in mockery, for a royal robe; his scepter, a reed; for a diadem, a crown of cruel thorns; for subjects, rude soldiers with knees bent in scorn, and crying, in derision, Hail King of the Jews.
>
> Next, a procession of priests passed by—Abel, who reared his altar not far from the gates of Eden; Melchizedek, wearing crown and mitre; Aaron, in priestly robes, bearing the names of the chosen tribes on the breastplate near his heart, with all who ministered to God in Tabernacle or Temple. . . .but the priest he sought, he found on Calvary, offering himself to God on a bloody cross, at once both victim and priest, praying for those who nailed him there, and from whose bleeding heart the viler soldier soon plucked his vile spear away, but he left us not weeping, at least not in

sorrow, for he showed us the risen, glorified One, at the right hand of the Majesty on high, where he ever liveth to make intercession for us.[32]

The baptisms on the Western Reserve were so numerous and the excitement among the people was so great, that Alexander Campbell was concerned. He had some concern that the impulsive zeal of his ardent and able friend, Walter Scott, might, "in the quarter, wreck the vessel of reformation." At his suggestion, his father, the venerable Thomas Campbell, saddled his favorite sorrel and made an extensive tour of the "Reserve." Thomas visited first New Lisbon, then Fairfield, Warren, Mentor and various other places where there had been so many baptisms.

Thomas Campbell spoke to several groups and, because of his fame and scholarship, he drew large audiences. What he saw was simply an advance step in the great pleas of restoration that he, himself, initiated and advocated. After a thorough examination of Scott's work, he gave it his full endorsement. On April 9, 1828, from New Lisbon, Thomas wrote to his son as follows:

> I perceive that theory and practice in religion, as well as in other things, are matters of distinct consideration. . .We have spoken and published many things correctly concerning the ancient gospel—its simplicity and perfect adaptation to the present state of mankind, for the benign and gracious purposes of its immediate relief and complete salvation—but I must confess, that, in respect of the direct exhibition and application of it for that blessed purpose, I am at present, for the first time, upon the ground where the thing has appeared to be practically exhibited to the proper purpose. 'Compel them to come,' saith the Lord, 'that my house may be filled.'
>
> Mr. Scott has made a bold push to accomplish this object, by simply and boldly stating the ancient gospel and insisting upon it; and then by putting the question generally and particularly to males and females, old and young: will you come to Christ and be baptized for the remission of your sins and the gift of the Holy Spirit? Then come away, etc. This elicits a personal conversation; some confess faith in the testimony—beg time to think; others consent their hands to be baptized as soon as convenient; others debate the matter friendly; some go straight to the water, be it day or night and, upon the whole, none appear offended."[33]

Alexander Campbell was fully aware of what had happened on the early American frontier, where the spirit of evangelism was very emotional. Even though emotionalism was commonplace, at the time, Walter Scott did not become a part of it. "His sermons were clear, logical, well reasoned, carefully wrought out and finished."[34]

In 1839, Alexander Campbell wrote an article in *The Millennial Harbinger*, which reflects the thinking of churches of Christ around the world today. In this article, titled "The Religion of Excitement, and The Excitement of Religion" Mr Campbell says:

> In the present day we seem to have more of the religion of excitement than we have of the excitement of religion. The ancient and apostolic plan of first enlightening the understanding by declaring and illustrating the testimony of God seems to be both too rational and slow for the ardent demands of the proselyting spirit of the age. Our Savior and His apostles spoke plain good sense to the understanding of men, knowing it to be God's chartered way to the heart. Paul teaching that "faith comes by hearing"—that "hearing came by the Word of God"—and that as he "preached so the people believed," was only anxious to declare the whole testimony of God, with its innate and cognate evidences of the divine authenticity. His preaching being first understood, and then believed, he knew could not possibly fail to seize the heart with omnipotent power and turn it to God, Christ and Heaven. Therefore, he never made any effort to excite the feelings of any audience until he had "declared to them the whole counsel of God." He threw no artificial, exciting circumstances around them: he never thought of 'an anxious seat,' nor 'a mourner's bench,' and never called up convicted and trembling sinners to pray with them. These are all of the greenhouse or hotbed appliances of the present day. . .They have no root in themselves. They are born in the midst of excitement, and soon as it wanes they generally sicken and die. . .They are deluded by the idea that religion is the effect, and not the cause of feeling. Religion, with them, is the fruit of excitement, rather than the root and reason of it. . .
>
> The Christian religion is, indeed, a religion of the purest, noblest, and most refined feelings, and excitements of which our fallen nature is susceptible. It exerts a constant power upon all the affections and moral sensibilities of our hearts; but it is itself the offspring not of fancy, but of faith; not of excitement, but of reason; not of visions, dreams, or extraordinary impulses, but of the testimony of God, developed and confirmed by the Holy Spirit. It is, in one word, the effect of the Christian truth believed, and not the cause of faith: for it is faith, and not feeling, that works by love, that purifies the heart and overcomes the world.[35]

From the very beginning of the *Christian Baptist* in 1823, Walter Scott was a frequent writer under the signature of "Philip." He began a series of articles on the subject of "Teaching Christianity." Here he began to develop his favorite theme, the "Messiahship of Jesus," in which he showed that this majestic truth constituted the rock on which the church was founded and the great theme to be preached to the world. In 1859, Scott published what Robert Richardson called his "principal work."[36] Mr. Campbell referred to the book being a "very readable, interesting, edifying, cheering and fascinating volume from this most estimable, companionable and amiable fellow-laborer in the great cause of Reformation."[37]

Murch wrote that "Scott considered his book The Messiahship the crowning achievement of his literary career. It presented with logical force and deep spiritual power the centrality of Christ in the whole economy of God."[38]

Walter Scott had a full life. He was associated with a number of periodicals. He was a gifted writer. He conducted a number of schools with great success. As an evangelist, his labors were abundant and successful. He was married three times: 1823 to Sarah Whitsette who bore four sons and two daughters. Sarah died in 1849. The next year Walter married Nannie Allen. To this union one daughter was born. Nannie died in 1854. The following year he was married to Eliza Sandridge, a wealthy widow in Mayslick, Kentucky, where he spent the remainder of his life. Unfortunately, this third marriage was not a very happy one.

Though Walter was growing older, his faculties had suffered no decay; his form was erect, his hair but slightly changed, and the luster of his keen eyes undimmed. His invitations to preach were still numerous. He still preached with power and conviction.

During the last week of December, 1855, Walter paid a visit to Bethany, "and his spirit was greatly refreshed." He says that he was received with the greatest cordiality and hospitality in the home of Alexander Campbell. Together, Scott and Campbell had borne the heat and burden of the day; and both felt that their work was nearly done. It was refreshing to both faculty and students for Walter Scott to lecture every day at the college.

The clouds of Civil War were hovering over the nation. Scott was deeply concerned at the prospects of disunion. He grieved deeply at the strife that existed in the land. He loved his adopted country and feared for its future. In a letter to his eldest son, John, he wrote, "I can think of nothing but the sorrows and dangers of my most beloved adopted county. God is my witness to my tears and grief. I am cast down, I am afflicted, I am all broken to pieces. My confidence in man is gone. May the father of mercies show us mercy! Mine eye runneth down with grief."[39]

"Such were the feelings which overflowed from his pious and patriotic heart at the close of the year 1860, when only one state had seceded, when, as yet, no blow had been struck, when no blood had been shed."[40]

In reply to a letter from his son in Pittsburgh, dated April 10, he wrote that his worst fears were realized: "The fate of Fort Sumpter, which you had not heard of when you wrote - which, indeed, occurred subsequently to the date of your letter - will now have reached you. Alas, for my country! Civil war is now most certainly inaugurated, and its termination who can forsee? Who can predict? Twice has the state of things filled my eyes with tears this day. Oh, my country! My country! How I love thee! How I deplore thy present misfortunes!'[41]

Walter Scott took suddenly ill on Tuesday April 16, with a severe attack of typhoid pneumonia. His condition grew worse by the day. On April 23, at 10:30 p.m., he passed away at his home in Mayslick, Kentucky. He was buried in the village cemetery. Funeral services were conducted by John Rogers and L. P. Streater. The day following the funeral, Elder Streater wrote a letter to Alexander Campbell telling him of the death of his good friend.

In the next issue of *The Millennial Harbinger*, Campbell wrote an editorial under the caption, "Elder Walter Scott's Demise."

> No death in my horizon, out of my own family, came more unexpectedly or more ungratefully to my ears than this of our much beloved and highly appreciated brother, Walter Scott...Next to my father, he was my most cordial and indefatigable fellow-laborer in the origin and progress of the present reformation. We often took counsel together in our efforts to plead and advocate the paramount claims of original and apostolic Christianity...He was in his palmiest days, a powerful and successful advocate of the claims of the Lord Messiah...He had a strong faith in the person and mission, and the work of the Lord Jesus Christ...I knew him well. I knew him long. I loved him much...By the eye of faith and the eye of hope, methinks I see him in Abraham's bosom.[42]

Endnotes

Chapter IX. WALTER SCOTT, WARM-HEARTED EVANGELIST

1. J. J. Haley, *Makers and Moulders of The Reformation*, p. 59.
2. William Baxter, *Life of Elder Walter Scott*, p. 29.
3. A. S. Hayden, *A History of The Disciples on The Western Reserve*, p. 62.
4. Ibid, p. 63.
5. William Baxter, *Life of Scott*, p. 39.
6. Ibid, p. 40.
7. Walter Scott, *The Evangelist*, Dec. 1838, p. 283f. Original spelling and punctuation have been retained.
8. Ibid, p. 286.
9. Ibid, p. 288.
10. Ibid.

11. Robert Richardson, *Memoirs of Campbell*, Vol. 1, pp. 508, 509.
12. Ibid, pp. 510, 511.
13. William Baxter, *Life of Elder Walter Scott*, p. 66.
14. George Hamilton Combs, *The Call of The Mountains and Other Sermons*, p. 85; also C. C. Crawford, *The Restoration Plea*, p. 14.
15. Walter Scott, *The Evangelist*, (1838, Dec.). pp. 286-288.
16. A. S. Hayden, *History of The Disciples*, pp. 72-76; William Baxter, *Life of Walter Scott*, pp. 103-108.
17. Walter Scott, *Evangelist*, (1833), pp. 160-162.
18. Ibid, p. 162.
19. A. S. Hayden, *History of The Disciples on The Western Reserve*, p. 143.
20. Walter Scott, *The Gospel Restored*, pp. 39-44; William Baxter, *Life of Walter Scott*, p. 313.
21. Hayden, *History of Disciples*, p. 162.
22. Ibid.
23. Ibid, pp. 163-165.
24. Ibid, p. 174.
25. William Baxter, *Life of Scott*, p. 201.
26. Ibid, p. 209; Hayden, *History of The Disciples*, pp. 176-183.
27. Baxter, *Life of Scott*, pp. 313, 314.
28. A. W. Fortune, *The Disciples In Kentucky*, p. 185. Scott's scholarly inaugural address on the *Novum Organon* of Sir Francis Bacon is given in 'The Christian' (1837), pp. 3-72, edited by Walter Scott and J. T. Johnson.
29. Fortune, *Disciples in Kentucky*, pp. 188-9.
30. James Shannon, *Millennial Harbinger*, 1854, pp. 651, 652; 187-189.
31. Alexander Campbell, *Millennial Harbinger*, (1848), p. 516.
32. William Baxter, *Life of Scott*, pp. 347-349.
33. Hayden, *Western Reserve*, pp. 147-148.
34. Dwight Stevenson, *Walter Scott: Voice of The Golden Oracle*, p. 82.
35. Alexander Campbell, *Millennial Harbinger*, 1839, pp. 34, 35.
36. Robert Richardson, *Memoirs of Alexander Campbell*, Vol. 2, p. 641.
37. Ibid.
38. James DeForrest Murch, *Christians Only*, p. 106.
39. William Baxter, *Life of Scott*, p. 441.
40. Ibid, pp. 441, 442.
41. Ibid, pp. 444, 445.
42. Alexander Campbell, *Millennial Harbinger*, 1861, pp. 296-297.

Chapter 10

Some Restoration Views and Reviews

I.

Instrumental Music In Christian Worship

For some thirty years—from 1830 to 1860—there was almost universal unity among the Reformers. It was during this period that numerical growth was greatest. Excitement was in the air. There was active hostility from the "sects," but there was no retrenchment from presenting to the masses the "ancient gospel." The preaching of the pure gospel was having phenomenal results. Thousands were being baptized for the remission of sins. Churches were springing up throughout the land. Many men of prominence, including James A. Garfield (1831-1881), who became President of the United States, were active in this movement to restore First Century Christianity.

The Bible, and the Bible alone, was growing in favor. It was pointed out that the only message that will change the heart and save the soul is the New Testament in its purity and simplicity. The New Testament is quite sufficient to furnish the Christian unto every good work (II Timothy 3:16,17). A young preacher at David Lipscomb College approached the distinguished A. G. Freed (1863-1931) and asked if he could recommend a good book of sermon outlines. With a smile, Freed replied that he could and would. He reached in his coat pocket and pulled out a New Testament saying "This is the best book of sermons." The great teacher then admonished the student to "Preach the word!"

Even though things ran smoothly and successfully in the grand movement that was sweeping the country like a prairie fire, it was not long before some became dissatisfied with simply preaching and practicing the New Testament. A wave of innovations began to disturb the peace of Zion. Of the many, mention will be made of the introduction of instrumental music in Christian worship. There was strong opposition to this innovation as seen in the excerpts that follow:

Benjamin Franklin (1812-1878) was "a man of the people." He was baptized by Samuel Rogers (1789-1877) Though Franklin was lacking in formal education, he possessed a natural brilliance that served him well. His logic was based on common sense. He knew the Scriptures as few men of his day knew it. He was perfectly familiar with both the Old and New Testaments. In his preaching he declared, with boldness, what the Bible teaches. His illustrations were all drawn from the Bible. He was, indeed, a man of the book. People from all walks of life were moved by the grand and sublime truths which he preached. He always had capacity crowds. "His eloquence was original, simple, easy and natural.

One year before he died, two volumes of his sermons were published. These books, while rare, should be sought after with diligence; they contain the type of sermons that made us a great and viable people. In 1856, Franklin began to publish the *American Christian Review*, which he edited until his death. The "Review" was one of the most influential journals of the time. Franklin was second only to Alexander Campbell as a journalist, debater and preacher.

When instrumental music began to trouble the churches, he stood with Moses E. Lard (1818-1880), Tolbert Fanning (1810-1874), David Lipscomb (1831-1917), and J. W. McGarvey (1829-191) in opposing this innovation. In a published sermon (1878) he said,

> If any one had told us forty years ago that we would live to see the day when those professing to be Christians; who claim the Holy Scriptures as their only rule of faith and practice; those under the command to 'observe all things whatsoever I have commanded you' would bring an instrument of music into a worshipping assembly and use it there in worship we should have repelled the idea as an idle dream. . . .singing is the regularly ordained worship of the Most High; singing in obedience to the commandments of God. . . .This is prescribed in Scripture.

Franklin continues by giving invincible arguments against instrumental music in worship. His clincher was this:

> History shows that the use of instruments in worship finds no place among Christians in the time of our Lord and his apostles, nor for many centuries after their time. This ought to be enough for those who talk of the 'ancient gospel,' 'primitive Christianity,' 'the ancient order,' and the like.¹

Alexander Campbell "loved to see the utmost simplicity in the order and worship of the house of God. He delighted in the public reading of the Scriptures, the plain and earnest exhortations of the brotherhood, and in solemn psalms and hymns of praise. He had no relish for anything formal or artificial, such as repetitions in fugue tunes or the establishment of singing choirs. As to the use of mechanical instruments in worship, he was utterly opposed to it, and took occasion at a later period in regard to it that it was well adapted to churches "founded on the Jewish pattern of things" and practicing infant sprinkling."

Campbell said "that all persons who have no spiritual discernment, taste or relish for spiritual meditations, consolations, and sympathies of renewed hearts, should call for such aid is but natural. . . .so to those who have no real devotion or spirituality in them, and whose animal nature flags under the oppression of church service, I think that instrumental music would be only a desideratum, but an essential prerequisite to fire up their souls to even animal devotion. But I presume to all spiritually-minded Christians such aids would be as a cow-bell in a concert."[2]

Mrs. Alexander Campbell wrote after the death of her husband these words: "As there has been so much controversy amongst the brethren about the organ, I feel it to be a duty to refer to it. That it has, by its introduction into some of the churches, been the cause of sorrow and discord no one can deny. . . .I believe it to be a grievous innovation in the Christian church that our Heavenly Father does not approve of—I think will be discovered by the more reflecting brethren themselves—and that only a return to apostolic worship in our churches can be acceptable to the Great Head of the church, who has not left on record his sanction to add or to take from His institutions, ordinances and forms of worship."[3]

Writing in a tract called "What Shall We Do About The Organ?" J. W. McGarvey asserted: "We cannot adopt the practice without abandoning the only ground upon which a restoration of New Testament Christianity can be accomplished." McGarvey wrote in 1868, "I could once boast that there was not an organ or melodian in a single Christian church in Kentucky." (M. H., April 1868).

During the time that he conducted his column "Biblical Criticism" in the Christian Standard a brother wrote to McGarvey saying that a certain preacher "holds that instrumental music in the church is taught in Colossians 3:16, in the word 'psalm.' You will help a multitude of the brethren by giving your opinion on the above item."

McGarvey answered: "I doubt this last statement. . . .if any man who is a preacher believes that the apostle teaches the use of instrumental music in the church by enjoining the singing of psalms, he is one of those smatterers in Greek who can believe anything that he wishes to believe." (J. W. McGarvey, "Biblical Criticism," p. 116).

In 1851, John Rogers, of Carlyle, Kentucky wrote a letter to Alexander

Campbell lamenting the fact that "a popular preacher (would you believe it)" had written an article in the "E. Reformer" in favor of instrumental music in churches, and social dancing in our families! Rogers continued by saying, "Watchman, what of the night? I call upon you, my dear brother Campbell, in the name of God—in the name of the crucified one—in the name of poor, bleeding Zion; upon brothers Richardson, Pendleton, and every editor and every scribe who can lift a pen, and every orator of the Reformation to speak out in a voice of thunder and say, oh say! is this the goal to which you have been driving the car of this Reformation?" Rogers continued his lamentations by asking, "Has the subject of this warfare been to introduce instrumental music into our meeting houses?" The distraught Rogers concludes by repeating, "Are we to have instrumental music in our churches?"[4]

Moses E. Lard (1818-1880), one of the notable preachers and orators of his day, was strong in Christian worship. Concerning the gradual introduction of instrumental music in the worship he wrote, "Soberly and candidly we are pained at the symptoms of degeneracy in a few of our churches. The day on which a church sets up an organ in the house is the day on which it reaches the first station on the road to apostasy. From this it will soon proceed to other innovations, no stop can be put to it till ruin ensues. And then the spirit which proceeds and fosters these innovations is a most dangerous spirit—dangerous because it is cruel, intractable, and unreasonable. . . .unreasonable because it will heed neither the voice of God nor of man. Indeed, when a church has once introduced an organ we believe it is to be true, as a general rule, of those members who take the lead in the work, that they will suffer for its Bible to be torn into shreds before they will part from their pet. . . .These organ-grinding churches will, in the lapse of time, be broken down, or wholly apostitize, and the sooner they are in fragments the better for the Cause of Christ."[5]

David Lipscomb (1831-1917) wrote that "Alexander Campbell was so opposed to organs in worship that he would not preach where one was used." As quoted by John T. Lewis, Mr. Lipscomb continued, "I saw a statement made by his son-in-law, I reckon about the time of his death, or soon afterwards, when the organ question was up, he wrote an article that was published in 'The American Christian Review' that on one occasion, in New Orleans, a Presbyterian house was offered to Mr. Campbell to preach in (which had an organ in it). An organist that usually operated it during the services, taking for granted that they wanted the usual services, began the overture (or whatever part it was) and Mr. Campbell arose and requested it to be stopped, that he could not preach where the organ was used. He preached in McKendree church when he was here, which was offered him, and no organ was used. I suppose there was an organ in the house, but it was not used. I do not know how that happened, but I know it was not used. I was there."[6]

II

Indwelling of The Holy Spirit

My intention in this segment is simply to report the general thinking of Restoration personalities. It is admitted that there has been, and continues to be, diverse sentiments with reference to this question. The quotes which follow indicate that the major sentiments were in favor of the view advocating the personal indwelling of the Holy Spirit.

Shortly after Walter Scott's removal to Cincinnati, in 1831, he wrote his "Discourse on the Holy Spirit." Mr. Scott, in this work, attempted to show that "Christianity as developed in the Sacred Oracles is sustained by three divine missions." He said that the mission of Christ was to the Jews, and that of the apostles was to the world, and that the mission of the Holy Spirit was to the church. He pointed out that the Spirit came on the day of Pentecost, remaining in the church, dwelling in all its members, and acting through them to comfort the saints and convince the world of sin, righteousness and judgment. Only the apostles received the baptism of the Holy Spirit; the three thousand received the common measure of the Holy Spirit after baptism (Acts 2:38). He exposed the common notion that the Holy Spirit was sent to the world, as being opposed to the declaration of Christ that the world could not receive him. Scott insisted on the need of the indwelling of the Holy Spirit in every Christian. Finally, he argued that while the personal mission of Christ was to the Jews and that of the apostles to the world were limited in duration. The mission of the Holy Spirit to the church was permanent in its nature, since the Comforter was to abide with it forever. Scott went on to say, "There is no member of the body of Christ in whom the Holy Spirit dwelleth not...."[7]

This discourse was published by Alexander Campbell and widely circulated. It had a powerful effect in imparting clearness and definiteness to the views of the Reformers on this important subject.

In *The Millennial Harbinger* of September, 1831, Alexander Campbell had this to say:

> Brother Walter Scott who, in the fall of 1827, arranged the several items of Faith, Repentance, Baptism, Remission of Sins, Gift of the Holy Spirit, and Eternal Life, restored in this order to the church under the title of the "Ancient Gospel" which he successfully preached for the conversion of the world. He wrote a discourse on the fifth point, (viz The Holy Spirit) "which presented the subject in such an attitude as cannot fail to make all who read it understand the views entertained by us and, we think, taught by the apostles in their writings. We can recommend to all the disciples this discourse as most worthy of a place in their families, because it perspicaciously, forcibly, and with a brevity favorable to an easy

apprehension of its meaning, presents the subject to the mind of the readers....[8]

In commenting on Romans 8:9-11, Dr. T. W. Brents (1823—1905) observes:

> That this passage is applicable to Christians now is admitted by all; how strikingly similar the phraseology to that used by the Savior. He says, 'He dwelleth with you and shall be in you.' Paul says, 'If so be that the Spirit of God dwell in you.' 'If the Spirit of him that raised up Jesus from the dead dwell in you.' 'Shall also quicken your mortal bodies by his spirit that dwelleth in you.' What can this language mean? We cannot say that God will quicken our mortal bodies by His Spirit that dwelleth "figuratively" in us; and to say that He will quicken our mortal bodies by His Spirit that dwelleth "metonymically" in us would be no better. Nor will it do to say that God will quicken our mortal bodies by his "disposition" that dwelleth in us. To our mind, the passage admits of one interpretation, and only one; namely, that the Spirit of God—the Holy Spirit—dwells "literally and really" in every Christian, and by it God will re-animate his body in the great day."

In this connection read I Corinthians 6:19; 3:16.[9]

E. A. Elam (1855-1929) commenting on Acts 2:38 says, "The gift of the Holy Spirit" means to receive the Holy Spirit as a gift....All who obey God (Acts 5:32) will receive the Holy Spirit, but not in miraculous power or measure."[10]

In his commentary on Acts 2:38, the celebrated and learned J. W. McGarvey writes: "After commanding the enquirers to repent and be immersed for the remission of sins Peter adds the promise, 'and ye shall receive the gift of the Holy Spirit.' The gift of the Holy spirit should not be confounded with the Holy Spirit's gifts nor with the fruits of the Spirit. The fruits of the Holy Spirit are religious traits of character, and they result from the gift of the Holy Spirit. The latter expression means the Holy Spirit as a gift."

The People's New Testament with explanatory notes by B. W. Johnson (1833-1894) in his comments on Acts 2:38 says of the gift of the Holy Spirit: "Promised as a comforter to all who obey Christ, but whom the world cannot receive."

In "Questions and Answers," by Lipscomb and Sewell, edited by M. C. Kurfees, some one asked Sewell this question: "Does the Holy Spirit enter the heart to prepare us for baptism or because we have been baptised?" He answered by saying, "Paul says: 'And because ye are sons, God hath sent forth the Spirit of his Son into your hearts, crying Abba Father' (Galatians 4:6). This settles the question clearly and beyond all dispute....Let all read or hear and obey the Word of God, the gospel of Christ, and then have the promise of the Spirit to dwell in them, and by it their mortal bodies may be quickened."

172

On page 639 in the same book, another question about the gift of the Holy Spirit was asked. Sewell answered by saying, "We think it means that the Spirit of God itself was to dwell in Christians in an important sense."

The talented Gus Nichols (1892-1975) said, "The gift of the Holy Spirit comes immediately after we obey the imperatives in Acts 2:38, as promised in that verse, and in verse 39. Peter said, 'And we are his witnesses of these things; and so is also the Holy Spirit, whom God hath given to them that obey him' (Acts 5:32). NOTE: (1) The sinners must obey the Lord, as in Acts 2:38; Acts 5:32. (2) After they 'obey him' they are given the Holy Spirit himself to dwell in them, and (3) All who obey the gospel thus have this gift of the Spirit himself. He is given to all them that obey him (Acts 5:32). They have the Spirit, whether or not they realize it."[11]

In Great Britain there was a Restoration Movement that was concurrent with the one in America. There was a *British Millennial Harbinger* as well as an American *Millennial Harbinger*. One of the noted men identified with the Restoration Plea in Great Britain was Lancelot Oliver. Concerning the Gift of the Holy Spirit he wrote: "With the Bible to guide us we conclude that the promise of Acts 2:38, where the instructions to repent and to be baptized in the name of Jesus Christ unto the remission of sins is followed by the words, 'and ye shall receive the gift of the Holy Spirit' was intended for all who 'received his word.' As showing that the Spirit as a gift was limited to those qualified by their acceptance of Christ as Lord we have also Peter's word in Acts 5:32 where, after narrating the Gospel facts to the Sanhedrin, Peter said, "And we are witnesses of these things; and so is the Holy Spirit, whom God hath given to them that obey Him."[12]

One of the most popular books ever published by the "Disciples" was written by T. W. Phillips (1835-1912). It first appeared in 1905 under the pseudonym of "A. Layman." Since then, many editions have appeared. This book has been widely used by "our" people. Concerning the gifts of the Holy Spirit the author, no doubt reflecting the views of the majority, wrote:

> ....Miracles were confined to the first age of the church and connected with its establishment and were for the confirmation of the testimony, to prove the facts of the gospel and confirm its establishment for all times and then were to cease. They could not reasonably continue confirming facts which had transpired ages past and become history. We may, therefore, conclude correctly, too, that the baptism of the Holy Spirit and Gift of the Spirit conferred by the laying on of the Apostles' hands, both being miraculous, ceased also. These gifts fulfilled their end and passed away." The writer went on to say that the Gift of the Holy Spirit promised by Peter on the day of Pentecost abides. Phillips continues by asserting, "These were commanded to repent and be baptized, in order to receive remission of sins and the gift of the Holy Spirit.

This gift was exclusively promised to the obedient as the Scriptures abundantly testify. In closing this investigation we will direct attention to some of the testimony." He then quotes such passages as Acts 5:32; I Corinthians 6:19; I John 3:24. "How shall we know then that Christians have the Spirit? By their fruits ye shall know them . . . .The fruits of the Spirit are fully described by Paul in Galatians. But the fruit of the Spirit is love, joy, peace, long-suffering, gentleness, goodness, faith, meekness, temperance. Against such there is no law.[13]

Dr. Robert Milligan (1814-1875) was one of the great classical scholars and preachers of the Restoration Movement. He was the first president of The College of the Bible in Lexington, Kentucky, and he had this to say about the gift of the Holy Spirit in Acts 2:38: "By the gift of the Holy Spirit in this passage we do not understand the miraculous power of the Spirit bestowed on the apostles and many other primitive Christians, but the Holy Spirit itself." He went on to assert "that this gift was limited to the baptized." He continued by saying, "that this gift was promised to all who, like the three thousand Pentecostal converts, would comply with the prescribed terms and conditions of discipleship. 'For,' said Peter, 'the promise is to you and to your children and to all who are afar off, even as many as the Lord our God shall call' (Acts 2:39). Milligan pointed out that "the miraculous gifts or powers of the Spirit were bestowed on but a small portion of the primitive Christians."

To confirm his belief in the indwelling of the Spirit, Dr. Milligan quoted 2 Corinthians 1:22, "Who also hath sealed us, and given the earnest of the Spirit in our hearts." The word "earnest" as used here means simply the Spirit itself, which God has put into our hearts as a pledge that the eternal inheritance is ours. In the same sense it is used in 2 Corinthians 5:5, and Ephesians 1:14." God gives us his Spirit because we are his children (Galatians 4:6).

'From these, then, and many other similar passages, it is evident not only that the Holy Spirit dwells in us, but also of comforting us (John 14:16); helping our infirmities (Roman 8:26); and strengthens us with might in the inner man (Ephesians 3:16) that we may thus be made partakers of the divine nature. . . ." As to how the Holy Spirit accomplishes these things in our hearts Milligan says, "We must . . .confess our ignorance and humbly acknowledge our inability to answer the question."[14]

III

The Baptismal Question

Almost from the beginning of the Restoration Movement in America there has been a diversity of thought as to what a penitent believer must know about the design of baptism for it to be valid. There have been good and scholarly men who have discussed this matter pro and con. The sentiments which follow seem to reflect the majority of the scholars of the Restoration Movement. Read these quotations and compare them, not with what you might personally think, but what the Bible says. Follow the example of the Bereans as seen in Acts 17:11, "Now these were more noble than those at Thessalonica, in that they received the word with all readiness of mind, examining the Scriptures daily, whether these things were so."

One of the great principles of New Testament Christianity is "the right of private judgment." We are often too willing and too eager to withdraw fellowship from the brother who might have a different opinion or point of view from ours. We must respect the opinions of others as we would have them respect ours.

In 1832, when the union was affected between "The Reformers" and "Christians," Barton W. Stone and J. T. Johnson wrote about this union in *The Christian Messenger*:

> It may be asked, is there no difference of opinion among you? We answer, we do not know, nor are we concerned to know. We have never asked them what were their opinions nor have they asked us. If they have opinions different from ours they are welcome to have them, provided they do not endeavor to impose them on us as articles of faith. They say the same to us. We hear each other preach; and are mutually pleased and edified.[15]

The year 1845 was an important one for David Lipscomb. He is now fourteen years old. Tolbert Fanning, who only recently opened Franklin College near Nashville, made a journey through Franklin County, preaching on the way. Young David was just recovering from typhoid fever. He spoke to no one about it, but made up his own mind to send for Fanning. When Fanning tested David by asking him why he wanted to be baptized, David replied, 'To obey God.' With that statement, Fanning baptized him in a box."[16] Until the day of his death, David Lipscomb believed that the greatest motive for Christian baptism was simply "to obey God."

A question directed to editor David Lipscomb: "Is baptism for the remission of sins to one who has been baptized because of the remissions of sins?" Lipscomb answered, "I do not think anyone was ever baptized because his sins were remitted. They may have believed their sins were remitted before they were baptized, but remission of sins was not the moving cause. There is nothing in remission of sins as a motive to prompt one to be baptized. They may have thought inasmuch as God had forgiven their sins they ought to obey his command to be baptized; but in that case the desire to obey God is the moving cause. When a man is baptized to obey God, he is led by a proper motive; and I believe when he does this to obey him, God will forgive his sins, whether he knows the act in which God forgives him or not. Man cannot be led by a holier or more acceptable motive than the desire to obey God and so fulfill all righteousness. It is a dangerous thing to require more than God requires."[17]

In 1927 there appeared in the *Gospel Advocate* an exchange between J. D. Tant and F. B. Srygley on the subject of baptism. Among other things Srygley wrote: "One who would refuse to fellowship a man who had been baptized to honor and obey God, though he may have been mistaken as to when God pardoned him, needs baptism worse than the one who was thus refused. Brother Tant is a good man and knows a lot about the Bible; and if he will stick to that and preach all that it says and not try to cover too much ground, he can do a great deal of good. He has my hand and heart in the work of preaching all that God has said on this subject and all others, but he should cease to ride a hobby."[18]

In a later article Srygley writes: "Brother Tant then gives a statement which he believes, most of which I believe. He says, 'Sinners must hear and understand this gospel.' I think a sinner must understand all of it he has to obey. He is not required to understand God's side of it, but his side. 'For the remission of sins is God's side of the gospel, and no one is required to obey 'for the remission of sins.' It is a design of baptism and it is God's design, not the sinners." Later, in the same article, Srygley wrote: "There are many in the churches who are sectarian enough to believe that the body of Christ is made up of only those who are baptized 'for the remission of sins' whatever else they may have understood about it; but I have not reached that conclusion. Brother Tant knew my position, and he knew the position the *Gospel Advocate* has occupied for a half century. . . ."[19]

In a debate between J. A. Harding and A. McGary on "The Baptismal Question" Harding said in his first speech: "Let us notice carefully that famous verse, Acts 2:38, 'Repent, and be baptized every one of you in the name of Jesus Christ for the remission of sins, and ye shall receive the gift of the Holy Ghost.' To these believers who are crying out what to do, two commands are given to be obeyed and two promises to be enjoyed; they are commanded to repent and be baptized and they are promised the remission of sins and the gift of the Holy Spirit. . . If it is necessary to understand that baptism is in order to remission, is it not equally necessary to understand that it is for the purpose of securing of the gift of the Holy Spirit?"

Throughout the debate, Harding pointed out that one cannot obey a promise. One's concern should be to obey the Lord with assurance He will take care of the promises.

On January 16, 1941, Gospel Advocate editor, B. C. Goodpasture, published a thought-provoking article from the pen of J. W. McGarvey, a reprint from "The American Quarterly Review, 1862." The caption of the article was in the form of a question, "What is a Valid Immersion?" Among other things, McGarvey wrote, "As for the design of immersion, which expression means merely the blessing promised to those who are immersed, it involves no duty either of the immersion or of the immersed. It belongs to God and not to man. Having promised it on certain conditions, when the conditions are complied with, He will be as good as His word, and it would be most unreasonable to suppose that He would withhold the blessing simply because I do not know that I'm entitled to it. A man, therefore, cannot forfeit the blessing by mere ignorance of the promise unless a knowledge of the promise is found to be a condition of its fulfillment, which certainly will not be assumed by any reader of the New Testament."

John F. Rowe (1827-1897) "squarely opposed the 'rebaptism theory,' which its advocates upheld on the ground that as baptism is 'for the remission of sins' those who did not understand it so when they were baptized, ought to be baptized over again." He correctly held that "if it were necessary for a person to know all the reasons for obeying a command of the Savior in order to salvation, few would be saved."[20]

In *The Millennial Harbinger* of 1831, Mr. Campbell wrote an article on "Rebaptism" in which he asserted:

> I know some will say that the candidates which they immersed a second time did not rightly understand baptism the first time. Well, I am persuaded they did not understand baptism the second time; and shall they be baptized a third time! But did all the believers whom the apostles baptized understand their baptism in all its designs, meanings, and bearings? We presume not, else the apostles need not have written to them to explain it: 'Know you not,' said Paul to the Romans, 'that so many of us as were immersed into Jesus Christ were immersed into his death.' But did Paul command anyone to be baptized a second time because he did not fully understand the whole import of his baptism? Did Peter command Simon to repent and be baptized again for the remission of his sins?
>
> But were not many of John's disciples baptized again? Not one of them was baptized twice into John's baptism; but some of them were once baptized into Christ. John baptized not into the name of the Lord Jesus, but into reformation, saying that 'his disciples should believe in him that was to come after him.' There is neither precedent nor analogy to support this practice.
>
> Remission of sins is, indeed, connected with baptism; but so is adoption, sanctification, and all the blessings of the new institution. . . .No person, intelligent in the Christian religion, can be baptized for the remission of sins apart from all blessings.

Alexander Campbell points out with clarity that "baptism is no where proposed as an expiatory rite. He that regards it as such—he who goes to the water as a Jew to the altar, and is baptized merely to obtain remission of his sins, mistakes the whole matter.[21]

There are many purposes of water baptism mentioned in the New Testament, among which we mention the following: 1. Salvation, (Mark 16:16); 2. Sins remitted, (Acts 2:38); 3. Sins washed away, (Acts 22:16); 4. Puts on Christ, (Galatians 3:27); 5. Puts off past sins, (Colossians 2:11,12); 6. Gets one into Christ, (Galatians 3:27); 7. Gets into the body of Christ, (1 Corinthians 12:13); 8. Call on the name of the Lord, (Acts 22:16); 9. The right to wear the name of Christian, (1 Corinthians 1:10-15); 10. Raised with Christ, (Colossians 2:12); 11. Becomes a child of God, (Galatians 3:26,27); 12. Sins are forgiven, (Colossians 2:11,12); 13. Becomes a new creature, (2 Corinthians 5:17); 14. Contacts the blood of Christ, (Romans 6:3,4); 15. Receives a good conscience, (1 Peter 3:21); 16. Cleansed, (Ephesians 5:26); 17. Set apart for Christian worship and service, (Ephesians 5:26); 18. Baptized into the death of Christ, (Romans 6:3,4); 19. Born again, (John 3:3-5);[22] 20. Receives all spiritual blessings in Christ, (Ephesians 1:3); 21. Added to the Lord's church, (Acts 2:41,47); 22. We are baptized into the name of Christ, (Matthew 28:19); 23.

There are other purposes of baptism mentioned in the New Testament. The important point that needs to be emphasized is that immediately upon the baptism of a penitent believer he receives all of these benefits, whether he has a knowledge of this or not.

Robert Richardson wrote that "Mr Campbell greatly disapproved the practice of...using such expressions as the 'power of remitting sins' and 'washing away sins in baptism.' 'These,' said he, 'have been most prejudicial to the cause of truth, and have given a pretext to the opposition for their hard speeches against the pleadings of Reformers.' The habitual use of such expressions he also calculated to lead men to overlook or disparage that faith in the sacrifice of Christ from which alone baptism derived its efficacy. On this account, in baptizing persons, he used only the simple formula, 'Into the name of the Father and of the Son and of the Holy Spirit,' and forbore adding to it, like Mr. Scott and others, the expression 'for the remission of sins.' 'When any doctrine,' said he, 'is professed and taught by many, when any matter gets into many hands, some will misuse, abuse and pervert it. This is unavoidable. We have always feared abuses and extremes.'" (Richardson, Memoirs, Vol. 2, p. 288).

On June 12, 1812, Alexander Campbell was baptized, along with six others, in Buffalo Creek. As we have already seen, both Thomas and Alexander Campbell made speeches which lasted for seven hours prior to the baptism. Alexander spoke last. Robert Richardson asserts that Alexander made "an extended defense of their proceedings, urging the necessity of submitting implicitly to all God's commands, and showing that the baptism of believers only was authorized by the Word of God.

Richardson continues by saying that in Alexander's remarks he quoted, among other Scriptures, the command of Peter to the believers on the day of Pentecost: 'Repent and be baptized, every one of you, in the name of Jesus

Christ, for the remission of sins, and you shall receive the gift of the Holy spirit,' and he dwelt at length upon the gracious promises of God to all who shall obey him." After Mr. Campbell had concluded his remarks, James Hanen took his wife aside asking her what she thought of the declaration of Peter, 'You shall receive the gift of the Holy Spirit,' and how she understood it. Mrs. Hanen "gave a satisfactory reply," and both were baptized, along with the others.

In quoting Acts 2:38, Alexander, at that time, was not thinking of baptism for the remission of sins. Three things, according to Richardson's account of the event, were uppermost in Mr. Campbell's mind. (1) Baptism is for penitent believers. (2) He dwelt (at length) upon the "gracious promises of God to all who should obey him." (3) It seems evident that he had in mind "the gift of the Holy Spirit." This was a point that Mr. and Mrs. Hanen came to grips with prior to their baptism. It was not until 1820 that Mr. Campbell became seriously concerned with baptism for the remission of sins. Surely, when Campbell and the others were baptized they received the forgiveness of sins, along with all blessings promised to them who "Obey" God. Who doubts that the people who were immersed on this occasion were saved?[23]

At this point in The Reformation, immersion of the believers had been unanimously adopted as the only true scriptural baptism; infant baptism had been finally and absolutely rejected as an invention of man, and the simple confession of Christ, made by the early converts to Christ, was acknowledged as the only requirement which could scripturally be demanded of those who desired to become Christians—members of the Lord's church.

IV.

The Story of Aylette Raines (1788-1881)

In the year 1828, Thomas Campbell made an extensive tour of the Western Reserve, where Walter Scott was having such phenomenal success in preaching. It was during this trip that Campbell met Aylette Raines. Raines, though a Universalist preacher, had the highest regards for Thomas Campbell.

Raines said that he had seen Mr. Campbell, when he had no reason to believe that any eye saw him, in his closet, prostrate on his face, pouring out his soul in prayer to God. Raines had been preaching Restorationism, or Universalism, for five years when he came under the influence of Walter Scott and others who were preaching the Ancient Gospel on the Western Reserve. The first sermon that Raines heard Scott preach was "styled the six points of the gospel." The next day he heard him again; this subject being the "Resurrection of Christ." The text was the fifteenth chapter of 1 Corinthians. Raines was "exceedingly amazed. Germs of truth, and beauties and glories sprang from the bosom of that chapter" under the skillful handling by Scott.

The next day, Raines heard Scott preach on "The Two Covenants;" and "here again I was amazed." In a few days Raines heard Scott again, the subject being Hebrews, chapter eleven. Raines said "Scott convinced me that I ought to lay my philosophy aside and preach the gospel as the apostles preached." Raines parted from Scott for a while and journeyed to Warren, Ohio, to the house of Ebenezer Williams, a Restorationist preacher. Raines submitted his views of the gospel that he had learned from Scott. Williams accepted the views without question, and each immersed the other for the remission of sins.

The news of the conversion of these Universalist preachers spread all over the Western Reserve and caused much joy among the disciples. However, it was feared by some that Raines and Williams had not been thoroughly instructed in the fundamentals of the gospels. The brethren wanted proof of their abandonment of Universalism. It should be pointed out that Raines did not deny future punishment of the wicked, he simply believed it would be limited in duration and that, in time, the wicked would be made happy and holy.

The next meeting of the Association was to be held at Warren, Ohio. The worthiness of Raines would certainly be a matter of discussion. It was thought that Raines still held Universalist sentiments. If he advocated them, dissension would follow. Yet, there were many who were willing to receive him as a Christian brother. Raines greatly desired to be counted among the brethren, if he could be received as a brother without surrendering his liberty in Christ.

When the Association convened on Friday at one o'clock in the afternoon, Thomas Campbell preached. His text was Romans, chapter fourteen, verse one, "Receive him who is weak in the faith without regard to differences of opinions," (The Living Oracles). In his sermon, Mr. Campbell showed the difference between faith and opinion. He pointed out that "faith" is public property, and "opinion" is private property. Later, Campbell said, "Brother Raines and I have been together for the past several months, and we have mutually unbosomed ourselves to each other. I am a Calvinist, and he is a Restorationist, and although I am a Calvinist, I would put my right arm into the fire and have it burnt off before I would raise a hand against him."

Alexander Campbell arose and repeated what his father had said about faith and opinion. Then, Walter Scott arose and said that he concurred in what had been said. At the suggestion of Thomas Campbell, Raines addressed the assembly. Perhaps, for the first time, Raines realized that he was among friends and had the solid support of each of the Campbells and Walter Scott. He stated briefly that his "Restorationism was a philosophy." He further asserted that he would neither preach it nor contend for it, but would preach the whole gospel to the best of his ability. When the vote was taken it was in favor of Raines "by an overwhelming majority."

Aylette Raines became one of the truly great preachers in the Nineteenth Century. In 1868, Raines wrote that he had been treated by the Campbells with "kindness and wisdom. Had they attempted to brow-beat me, I might have been ruined forever. But treating me kindly convinced me that my opinion, whether true or false, dwindled into nothingness in comparison with the faith of the gospels. . .the opinions faded, and in ten months was numbered with all my former errors."

'The surest cure," H. Leo Boles wrote, "for any and all tendencies toward speculative views and opinions is an earnest, prayerful study of the plain and simple truths of the New Testament. If all will let opinions remain in the realm of opinions and all others treat with kindness and Christian fellowship those who may hold to speculative opinions, peace and harmony will prevail and the truth of God will be glorified."[24] Aylette Raines died on September 7, 1881, in his ninety fourth year. For several years before he died he wrote a number of articles in the "American Christian Review" warning the churches about various innovations that were appearing.

V.

Restoration Principles

A few days after the death of Alexander Campbell, a memorial service for him was conducted in Allegheny City, Pennsylvania, by Joseph King. In his discourse, Mr. King mentioned five "particular tenets" taught by Mr. Campbell:

1. The immersion of a penitent believer in water in the name of the Father, Son and the Holy Spirit as the only apostolic and scriptural Baptism. Infant sprinkling he regarded as a papal corruption of the New Testament ordinance of immersion.

2. The rejection of all creeds and confessions of human device as necessarily schismatical—as promotive of divisions and sectarianisms—and as tending to lead the mind away from the simplicity of the Gospel and the oneness of the Christian faith. For three centuries there was no creed in the church except the God-given creed, the Bible. The church, during these centuries, was more united, and enjoyed a degree of peace, harmony and prosperity, which she has never since enjoyed. The introduction of creeds was the beginning of sects, divisions and parties. . . .The church can be restored to her apostolic unity only by the destruction of evey human creed, and accepting the Bible as in all things sufficient, perfect and infallible.

3. The Spirit of God operates only through the inspired word in the conversion of sinners—that the word is the 'incorruptible seed' by which men are begotten—that the 'gospel is the power of God for salvation to every one that believes'—that the gospel is to be preached in its facts, commands and promises—that its facts are to be believed, its commands obeyed, and then its promises will be enjoyed, viz: the forgiveness of sins, the gift of

promises will be enjoyed, viz: the forgiveness of sins, the gift of the Holy Spirit, and the hope of eternal life; and that the Holy Spirit is given to dwell with, and to be in those who obey the Gospel. He rejoiced in the indwelling and communion of the Holy Spirit. . . .

4. The weekly observance of the Lord's Supper. This he regarded as a part of the regular Lord's Day worship of the primitive Christians. . . .

5. The rejection of all unscriptural terms, and the necessity of speaking of Bible things in Bible language to avoid misconception and misunderstanding. In the full inspiration of the Holy Scriptures, the Divinity of our Savior, the atonement made by His death in sin, the influence of the Holy Spirit through the truth in conversion and sanctification, the indwelling of the Holy Spirit, the resurrection of the dead, and the opposite destinies of the righteous and wicked, Mr. Campbell had full faith.[25]

Alexander Campbell "insisted that Bible things should be inculcated in Bible words, that all theological terminologies should be abandoned, and that the nomenclature of scholastic schools should be rejected, as only serving to confuse and discourage 'common people who gladly hear the Word,' and who cannot comprehend metaphysics, theological abstractions, and inferential deductions."[26]

In December of 1837, Mr. Campbell had an article in *The Millennial Harbinger* titled "Synopsis of Reformation Principles and Objects." He pointed out in the first sentence that "the healing of divisions among Christians and the understanding of the Christian institutions" depended on "the restoration of a pure speech, or the calling of Bible things by Bible names." This is one of the cardinal principles of the Restoration Movement and of New Testament Christianity.

Thomas Campbell put it this way: "Nothing ought to be inculcated upon Christians as articles of faith, nor required of them as terms of communion, but what is expressly taught and enjoined upon them in the Word of God. Nor ought anything be admitted as of Divine obligation in their church constitution and managements but what is expressly enjoined by the authority of our Lord Jesus Christ and his apostles upon the New Testament church; either in express terms or by approved precedent."[27] Thus, emphasis is placed on having a "thus saith the Lord" for what we teach and practice.

F. D. Kershner sets forth four things as "chief features of the Restoration Movement as follows:

1. The acknowledgement of the New Testament Scriptures as the only authorative rule of faith and practice for Christians.
2. The renouncing of all human creeds and the acceptance of Jesus

the Christ, the Son of God, as the only creed binding upon members of the church of Christ.

3. The restoration of the apostolic, or New Testament, church, with its ordinances and life as originally practiced in apostolic times.

4. The union of all Christians upon the basis of the platform laid down in the preceding propositions. The plea has some times been regarded as primarily a plea for Christian union, but it was upon the basis mentioned that union has been advocated."[28]

The very foundational principle of the Campbell-Stone Reformation was to be guided wholly and completely by the Bible and the Bible alone. Robert Richardson pointed out that "the best and highest reason that can be given for any action is that God commands it. Whatever it may have in itself of manifest suitableness or of probable utility will, if it becomes a motive to its performance, but detract to that extent from the obedience of faith. This seeks to be assured that it is God's will, and shines forth in a purer and holier light when the command seems strange, incomprehensible and even most unreasonable, as when Abraham laid Isaac, his son, upon the altar of sacrifice; the blood of the pascal lamb upon the Hebrew lintels; the mercy-seat covering in the law of human duty; the ashes of a red heifer sprinkling the unclean, nay, the whole rigid ceremonial of the Mosaic Law, may be given as ex-implications of ordinances and commandments, as unexplained as they were imperative, and as adequate to secure prosperity and life and pardon, as the obedience they demanded was simple and unquestioning.

As the child who refuses to obey his father until the latter first explains to him the particular reasons for his commands, shows that he acts not from love and trust, but that he disbelieves and doubts, and prefers the conclusions of his own feeble understanding to reliance upon the superior wisdom, so the individual who must know the philosophy of God's commandments, and satisfy himself as to their propriety before he will obey them, believes not in God, but in himself.

Dr. Richarson continued his penetrating comments by calling attention to the fact "that it would have been beneath the dignity of the Divine Lawgiver to make obedience to his laws contingent upon man's approbation of their fitness, so has he ever, in perfect harmony with his own character and truest interests of mankind, simply delivered his commands and prohibitions with their rewards and penalties. In all cases, it was sufficient for the true believer in abstaining from any act to know that God had forbidden it and, in keeping a divine command, to feel that "obedience" was "better than sacrifice," and "to harken than the fat of rams."[29]

In the foregoing, we have expressed views which dominated the thinking of the Reformers of the Nineteenth Century. We also see the emergence of these views in the *Gospel Advocate* under the editorship of David Lipscomb (1831-1917), E. G. Sewell (1830-1924), and most of their contemporaries. We not made laws.

Additional Principles of Restoration Movement

1. The all-sufficiency and alone sufficiency of the Scriptures in matters of faith and life (2 Timothy 3:16,17). Barton W. Stone: "We will that the people henceforth take the Bible as the only sure guide to Heaven." (Last Will and Testament of Springfield Presbytery).

2. The right of private judgement. Every person has the right to read the Bible in his or her native language (Acts 17:11).

3. A "thus saith the Lord" for what we preach and how we worship (2 Timothy 4:1,2).

4. Christian unity on the basis of the New Testament (John 17:20,21). Four things about unity in the Bible: (a) Prayer for unity (John 17:20,21); (b) Plea for unity (1 Corinthians 1:10); (c) Plan for unity (Ephesians 4:4-6); (d) Pattern for unity (Acts 2:44).

5. Calling Bible things by Bible names (1 Peter 4:11).

6. The living, interceding Christ our only creed (Matthew 16:16; John 20:30,31).

7. The name Christian to be worn to the exclusion of all human designations (Acts 11:26; 26:28; 1 Peter 4:16).

8. Liberty in matters of private opinion (Romans 14:13-23). In this connection we note: "in faith unity; in opinion liberty; in all things charity." Our plea is not for liberty to reject divine authority, but it is a plea for liberty to reject human authority, whenever and wherever found and to accept all truth revealed in God's Word.

9. The disavowal of all human creeds. Human creeds are nothing more than human opinions. Human creeds are divisive. The genius of the Christian creed is to unite on Bible teaching (cf. Matthew 17:5,6).

10. The autonomy of the local congregation. That is, each local congregation is free and independent under God to study, understand, worship and practice the Scriptures for itself.

11. Recognition and respect for the authority of Christ (Matthew 28:18-20).

12. Proper division of the Word of God (2 Timothy 2:15; Habakak 1:1,2). The pioneer preachers often used charts because they recognized that their auditors received more mental perceptions through their eyes than through their ears. They were acquainted with the old adage that "one picture is worth a thousand words." The sturdy frontiersmen were quick to respond to such preaching. The appeal was to the intellect and not the emotion. A favorite way of "rightly dividing the word of God" was as follows:

a. The Old Testament leads us to Christ.
b. The four gospels (Matthew, Mark, Luke and John) introduce us to Christ.

to Christ.

c. The book of Acts tells us how to get into Christ.

d. The twenty one epistles tell us how to live in Christ.

e. The book of Revelation tells us how to be victorious in Christ.

13. Conditions of pardon as set forth in the New Testament. Study carefully Acts, the book of conversions.

14. Restoration of the New Testament church in creed, name, doctrine, polity, worship and life.

15. Restoration of the ordinances of Christ to their proper place and meaning.

16. The emphasis on human responsibility in the Christian religion (Acts 2:27,40).

17. The exaltation of Christ as the creed, foundation and savior of the church (Ephesians 1:22,23; 5:22-24).

18. Loyalty to Christ, the first criteria of Christian character.

F. D. srygley tells this delightful story about David Lipscomb: "During the Civil War, Lipscomb took strong ground against Christians going to war, and preached his conviction with boldness that attracted much attention and excited bitter prejudice against him. Zeal for the Southern Confederacy ran high, and impetuous spirits denounced him as an abolitionist, a Yankee spy, an enemy to the South, etc., but none of these things moved him. When Forrest occupied Columbia, complaint was made to him that David Lipscomb was preaching doctrine that was disloyal, and he ought to be arrested and stopped. Forrest sent a member of his staff to one of Lipscomb's appointments where, by special announcement, he was to preach the disloyal doctrine that Christians cannot scripturally go to war. The staff officer took a seat immediately in front of the speaker, and gave close and respectful attention to the sermon. During the sermon, the military officer was moved to tears several times and, after the audience was dismissed, he remarked to a gentleman in the congregation: "I have not yet reached a conclusion as to whether or not the doctrine of the sermon is loyal to the Southern Confederacy, but I am favorably convinced that it is loyal to the Christian religion."[30]

Endnotes

1. Benjamin Franklin, *Gospel Sermons*, (Vol. II), pp. 411-432.
2. Robert Richardson, *Memoirs*, (Vol. 2), p. 366.
3. Selina Campbell, *Home Life and Reminiscences of Alexander Campbell*, p. 420.
4. John Rogers, *Millennial Harbinger*, (1851), pp. 467, 468.
5. Moses E. Lard, *Lard's Quarterly*, (Vol. 1), p. 332.
6. John T. Lewis, *The Voice of The Pioneers on Instrumental Music and Societies*, p. 117.

7. Robert Richardson, *Memoirs*, (Vol. 2), pp. 356, 358; Walter Scott, *Gospel Restored, Discourse on Holy Spirit.*

8. Walter Scott, *Gospel Restored, Discourse on The Holy Spirit; Richardson, Memoirs*, (Vol. 2), p. 350f.

9. Dr. T. W. Brents, *The Gospel Plan of Salvation*, pp. 639, 640.

10. E. A. Elam, *Elam's Notes*, (April 5, 1935), p. 108.

11. Gus Nichols, *Lectures On The Holy Spirit*, p. 172.

12. Lancelot Oliver, *New Testament Christianity*, p. 157.

13. T. W. Philips, *The Church of Christ*, pp. 219, 220. T. W. Philips (1835-1912) was founder of Philips Petroleum Company.

14. Robert Milligan, *Scheme of Redemption*, pp. 277-281.

15. Barton W. Stone, *Christian Messenger*, p. 7.

16. Earl West, *Search for The Ancient Order*, (Vol. 2), p. 9.

17. M. C. Kurfees, *Questions Answered by Lipscomb and Sewell*, p. 42.

18. F. B. Srygley, *Gospel Advocate*, (Dec. 1, 1927).

19. Ibid, (Dec. 29, 1927).

20. F. M. Green, *Life and Times of John F. Rowe*, p. 84.

21. Alexander Campbell, *Millennial Harbinger* (1831), p. 481.

(The following was pointed out in a letter by James Baird.) In the *Millennial Harbinger*, Extra, Number VII, August, 1834, in a section entitled, "Induction into the Kingdom of Heaven," bro. Campbell said, "In naturalizing aliens the commandment of the King is first to admit to them the Constitution, or preach to them the gospel of the Kingdom. Soon as they understand and believe this, and are desirous of being translated into the kingdom of Christ and of God, that 'they may receive the remission of sins and inheritance among all that are sanctified,' they are to be buried in water, into the name of the Father, Son, and Holy Spirit, and raised out of it confessing their death to sin, their faith in Christ's sacrifice and resurrection; and thus they are born of water and the Spirit, and constituted citizens of the kingdom of heaven." p. 413. In his book *Christian Baptism With Its Antecedents and Consequents*, 1913 edition (originally published in 1851), bro. Campbell said, "Baptism, a new institution, is an ordination of great signification, and of the most solemn and sublime importance. It is a sort of embodiment of the gospel; and a solemn expression of it all in a single act. Hence the space and the place assigned it in the commission. It is a monumental and commemorative institution, bodying forth to all ages the great facts of man's redemption as developed and consummated in the death, burial, and resurrection of the Lord Jesus Christ. Hence, immediately upon the first constitutional promulgation of it on the part of the Christian

Lawgiver and Saviour, he adds, 'He that believeth and is baptized shall be saved.'" p. 206.

". . . Peter, after the new light imparted in the commission, feared not to say to the inquiring Jews, 'Repent and be baptized, every one of you, in the name of the Lord Jesus, for the remission of sins,' Nor did any one, so far as the history of the apostolic labors is reported, ever express a doubt or an inquiry upon the connection thus solemnly established between faith, repentance, baptism, and remission or salvation. So far from this, that the Apostles frequently allude to the subject in their epistles as though, by universal consent, it was understood to be a symbol of moral purification—a washing away of sin in a figure, declarative of a true and real remission of sin—*a formal and definite release of the conscience from the feeling of guilt and all its condemnatory power.*" (emphasis Campbell's), pp. 206, 207.

"True, when immersed into Christ, we have 'put on Christ;' and, of course, are in him and under him, interested in all the provisions of that covenant of life and salvation of which he is the Alpha and the Omega, the Author and the Mediator. Still, through faith and repentance, we are commanded to be baptized for one specific purpose, just as much as we celebrate the Lord's Day and the Lord's supper for a specific purpose. Every Christian institution has, indeed its own peculiar and specific object, which can be neither secured nor enjoyed so well any other way." pp. 202, 203.

22. With reference to the relationship between the New Birth and Baptism we have this: James A. Harding (1848-1922) in his debate with J. B. Moody (Baptist) May, 1889, in Nashville, Tennessee, maintained that J. R. Groves, Brother Moody's senior editor, says that 'born of water refers to baptism. It means nothing else, and no Baptist that we ever heard or read of ever believed otherwise until Alexander Campbell frightened them away from an interpretation that is sustained by the consensus of all scholars of all denominations in all ages.' *Harding-Moody Debate*, p. 142.

23. Richardson, *Memoirs*, (Vol. 1), p. 397.

24. A. S. Hayden, *A History of The Disciples*, pp. 149-170; William Baxter, *Life of Elder Walter Scott*, pp. 170-180; H. Leo Boles, *Biographical Sketches of Gospel Preachers*, pp. 50, 51.

25. Joseph King, *Millennial Harbinger*, (1866), pp. 203, 204.

26. John F. Rowe, *A History of Reformatory Movements*, p. 184.

27. Thomas Campbell, *Declaration and Address*, (Proposition 3 in Address).

29. Richardson, *Memoirs*, (Vol. 1), pp. 406, 407.30.
30. F. D. Srygley, *Biographies and Sermons*, p. 161.

Chapter 11

Epilogue

It would be unfortunate to close a work of this kind without making mention of some notable preachers of more recent date. First of all, we mention B.C. Goodpasture (1895-1977), Bible scholar, peerless pulpiteer, and long-time editor of the Gospel Advocate; serving from 1939 to his death. Only David Lipscomb served longer. The Gospel Advocate was founded in 1855 by Tolbert Fanning (1810-1874) and William Lipscomb (1829-1908), "that prince of scholars" who was a member of the first faculty of Franklin College.

In the 1945 issue of the *Millennial Harbinger*, Alexander Campbell mentions Bacon College, Franklin College and Bethany College as "our colleges." "Bacon is the oldest and Franklin the youngest. It has some eighty students; and, under the presiding genius of the active, enterprising, and persevering brother Fanning, is rising in usefulness." Some of the great men of the church were trained at Franklin College including David Lipscomb, T. B. Larimore, J. E. Scobey, E. A. Elam, E. G. Sewell, etc.

Publication of the *Gospel Advocate* was suspended at the outbreak of the war in 1861. On January 1, 1866, publication was resumed with David Lipscomb as editor. Lipscomb, at the time, was 35 years old; he continued his editorial work for the next 50 years. Tolbert Fanning served on the paper with Lipscomb until 1868. At the beginning of 1870, E. G. Sewell (1830-1924) joined Lipscomb as associate editor and served until his death in 1924. Sewell and Lipscomb "were in sacred league and hallowed covenant with each other for more than half a century." H. Leo Boles points out that Lipscomb and Sewell "did more to encourage the churches in the South to remain faithful to the New Testament than any other men." (Boles, *Biographical Sketches*, p. 241.)

The *Gospel Advocate* is unique in that it has the longest history without change of name, location, and uninterrupted service of any religious journal of the restoration movement. Moreover, it has never changed its objective.

In the first issue of the *Gospel Advocate*, July, 1855, Tolbert Fanning and William Lipscomb wrote the following editorial concerning the name and aim of the paper:

THE NAME OF OUR PAPER

Men speak idly and irreverently, when they affirm 'There is nothing in a name.' There are words and names, which, from their association, are the source of infinite mischief in the world. Hence, the anxiety of men to stigmatize each other with opprobrious names; as "Shaker," "Quaker," "Campbellite," etc. Politicians and religionists are equally adroit in turning to account every advantage offered from offensive names; but it is singularly strange that few study or appreciate the value of sacred, or even appropriate names. God's power to save the Jews was in his name as recorded at Jerusalem; and there is no name under these heavens in which can be found life, save that of Jesus, the despised Nazarene. Whilst we are free to admit that names, apart from their associations, are meaningless and empty sounds, we are free to say that no corrupt people cleave alone to the sacred styles of the Bible. True, the vilest wish to appropriate some of the sacred designations of the New Testament to consecrate their own "outlandish" names, but all that is imported by the divine vocabulary they despise.

In constructing a name for our paper, our first study was to find a style that would smack of nothing immodest or immoral; and secondly, we endeavored to select a name which would express, as nearly as possible, the work we have in view. Hence, 'The Gospel Advocate.' By which we mean to say, that if God has been revealed in the universe, if there is a moral truth in heaven or on the earth, and if men have a right to speak with even the certainty of belief upon spiritual matters, there is something in the world, but not of the world, called *The Gospel,* through which the obedient are saved, and the wicked are condemned. If these are correct conclusions, we think we see peculiar fitness in employing a name for our journal which offends no good man, and expresses a labor worthy of the purest beings in existence. We claim not the right to advocate any measures of our own, neither the claims of any party; but we regard our position as entirely catholic. Our work is to defend the sayings and doings of Jesus Christ against the assaults of the enemy, whether covert or avowed; and we can meet all who do in fact acknowledge the authority of the New Testament, on common ground. With us, the Gospel is everything or nothing. If true, all good men will, sooner or later, unite under its ample folds; and if false, we can have the consolation of pleading for the cause which has done more for the amelioration of the condition of the world than any other.

Hence, the appropriateness of the name, Gospel Advocate.

We doubt not our friends will properly consider the dignity and value of their labor in advocating the high claims of the Gospel, even in the circulation of our humble sheet. Every effort to turn the attention of the world from men, and all their works, to the sacred institutions of God, must result favorably."

Editors

B.C. Goodpasture carried on the original objectives of The Gospel Advocate throughout his tenure as editor. He was a clear and forceful writer. He was like David Lipscomb in that "his pen was facile and vigorous in 'contending for the faith which was once for all delivered to the saints."

We next mention that "prince of preachers," N. B. Hardeman (1874-1965). For more than fifty years Hardeman was perhaps the best known preacher in "our brotherhood." He possessed a commanding appearance, always immaculately dressed. As a preacher, he was thoroughly prepared. His language was chaste and convincing. He was as familiar with the Greek New Testament as he was with the English New Testament. He was a polished and eloquent speaker.

With A. G. Freed, he founded Freed-Hardeman College, Henderson, Tennessee, where he served as president and taught for more than a quarter of a century. Hardeman was great in the class room and he was equally great in the pulpit.

The nineteen-twenties ushered in a new era for the churches of Christ in Middle Tennessee. In 1920, there were more than fifty congregations in Nashville alone. In 1921, a decisive step was made by the Nashville churches to cooperate in conducting a great central meeting. Plans were finalized: Ryman Auditorium was rented and N. B. Hardeman was selected as the preacher. The a capella singing was unlike anything that had ever been heard in Nashville on so large a scale.

The Nashville Tennessean reported on the opening service, March 28, 1922, as follows:

Crowds, representing every walk and avocation of Nashville's life and citizenship, packed the Ryman Auditorium Sunday afternoon and Sunday night to hear N. B. Hardeman, the evangelist."

Hardeman preached every day at noon and every night through April 22, with more than two hundred baptized and a large number reclaimed. Both of the Nashville papers, *The Tenessean" and The Banner* published in full every sermon that was preached by Hardeman. It is doubtful whether any preacher of the Restoration Movement previously was ever so extensively quoted or had his sermons printed in full for so long a series by the secular press. The Hardeman Tabernacle meeting covered a span of twenty years, from 1922 to 1942. All the sermons were printed in book form.

A short article called *Hardeman's Sermons*, by Guy N. Woods, appeared in the *Gospel Advocate* of March 26, 1959, as follows: "The Hardeman Tabernacle Sermons, all things considered, is the finest series ever published in the English language. As long as the world stands, they will never be surpassed for their amazing simplicity of style, striking clarity of diction, and widest possible inclusion of basic and fundamental truth."

In all of his meetings at Ryman Auditorium it was filled to overflowing. Every night between two and three thousand people were turned away for lack of room.

It was the privilege of this writer to hear N. B. Hardeman preach in a meeting at Kimball Street Church of Christ in Memphis in 1958. My appraisal of the meeting appeared in the *Gospel Advocate*, December 18, 1958. "Recently, N. B. Hardeman, who is in his eighty-fifth year, conducted a meeting at the Kimball church in Memphis. It was my privilege and pleasure to attend this meeting. Brother Hardeman is still vigorous in mind and body. He has the learning of a Bacon and the eloquence of a Demosthenes. He stands erect and deports himself with his usual dignity. His preaching of the gospel is unexcelled. His diction is flawless. His voice is well-modulated; it is firm and clear.

The first time I ever heard Brother Hardeman was in his third Tabernacle meeting in Nashville in 1928. At the time, I was a student at David Lipscomb College. He was magnificent then, as he is now.

It was heartening to hear Brother Hardeman preach on the Old Bible themes—the themes which made our people a distinctive people. But it seems that we are getting away from real Bible preaching. Is it possible that we are more concerned with method than message? It is hoped that we will indoctrinate the people with the word of God, so that we may retain our distinctiveness."

B.C. Goodpasture and N. B. Hardeman were luminous advocates of the Biblical principles enunciated by the Campbell-Stone Movement.

'And what shall I more say?" for time will fail me if I tell you of F. W. Smith, Foy E. Wallace, Jr., C. R. Nichols, Gus Nichols, G. C. Brewer, F. B. Srygley, S. H. Hall, A. B. Lipscomb, M. C. Kurfees, T. W. Brents, A. R. Holton, J. M. McCaleb, T. Q. Martin, Hall L. Calhoun, J. M. Barnes, Price Billingsley, E. A. Elam, James A. Harding, J. C. McQuiddy, Marshall Keeble, and a host of other worthies who, through faith, preached with telling effect, converted thousands, established churches patterned after the New Testament, not only in this country, but in lands abroad.

BIBLIOGRAPHY

Periodicals

Bible Advocate, (Paris, Tennessee) 1842-1847
Christian Baptist, (Bethany) 1823-1830
Christian Standard, (Cincinnati, Ohio) 1866-
Christian Messenger, (Georgetown, Kentucky) 1825-1844
Evangelist, The, (Cincinnati) 1832-1842
Gospel Advocate, (Nashville, Tennessee) 1855-
Herald of Gospel Liberty, (Portsmouth) 1808-1817
Lard's Quarterly, (Georgetown and Frankfort) 1863-1868
Millenial Harbinger, (Bethany) 1830-1870

Historical Background

Abbott, B. A. *The Disciples, An Interpretation*. St. Louis: Christian Board of Publications, 1924.

Ahlstrom, Sidney. *A Religious History of the American People*. New Haven: Yale University Press, 1972.

Bainton, Rolland. *The Reformation of the Sixteenth Century*. Boston: The Beacon Press, 1952.

Banowsky, William S. *The Mirror of a Movement*. Dallas: Christian Publishing Company, 1964.

Boles, H. Leo. *Biographical Sketches of Gospel Preachers*. Nashville: Gospel Advocate Company, 1932.

Brents, T. W. *The Gospel Plan of Salvation*. Nashville: J.T.S. Fall, 1868.

Brown, John. *Churches of Christ*. Louisville: Morton, 1904.

Campbell, Alexander. *Memoirs of Thomas Campbell*. Cincinnati, 1861.

Campbell, George. Doddridge, Philip, and MacKnight, James. *The New Testament, Translated from the Original Greek*. Aberdeen: George King, 1827.

Campbell, Selina H. *Home Life and Reminiscences of Alexander Campbell by His Wife*. St. Louis: John Burns, 1882.

Choate, J. E. *I'll Stand on The Rock: A Biography of H. Leo Boles.* Nashville: Gospel Advocate, 1965.

Cramlet, Wilbur H. *The Christian Church (Disciples of Christ) In West Virginia.* St. Louis, Missouri: The Bethany Press, 1971.

Davis, M. M. *The Restoration Movement of the Nineteenth Century.* Cincinnati: Standard Publishing Company, 1913.

Fitch, Alger Morton, Jr. *Alexander Campbell—Preacher of Reform and Reformer of Preaching.* Austin: Sweet Publishing Company.

Fortune, Alonzo W. *The Disciples In Kentucky.* The Convention of Christian Churches in Kentucky, 1932.

Gardner, James. *The Christians of New England.* Unpublished Manuscript.

Hailey, Homer. *Attitudes and Consequences In the Restoration Movement.* Rosemeed: Old Paths Book Club, 2nd Edition, 1952.

Haldane, Alexander. *Memoirs of the Lives of Robert Haldane of Airthrey, and of His Brother, James Alexander Haldane.* New York: Carter and Brothers, 1857.

Haley, Jesse J. *Debates That Made History.* St. Louis: Christian Board of Publication, 1920.

Hayden, A. D. *Early History of the Disciples on the Western Reserve.* Cincinnati: Chase & Hall, 1875.

Hopson, Ella Lord. *Memoirs of Dr. Winthrop Hartley Hopson.* Cincinnati: Standard Publishing Company 1887.

Jennings, Walter Wilson. *Origin and Early History of the Disciples of Christ.* Cincinnati: The Standard Publishing Company, 1919.

Jones, Abner. *Memoirs of the Life and Experience, Travels and Preaching of Abner Jones.* Boston: Crosley, 1842.

Lewis, John T. *The Voice of the Pioneers on Instrumental Music and Societies.* Nashville: Gospel Advocate Company, 1932.

Marro, W. C. *Brother McGarvey.* St. Louis: The Bethany Press, 1940.

Minutes of the Redstone Baptist Association, Convened at George's Creek, George Township, Fayette Co., Virginia, September 3rd, 4th, and 5th, 1824. Reprint Ed. M. T. Cottrell, 1964.

MacClenny, W. E. *The Life of Rev. James O'Kelley.* Indianapolis: Religious Book Service, 1950.

McGarvey, John W. *The Autobiography of J. W. McGarvey.* Lexington: The College of the Bible, 1960.

McMillon, Lynn A. *Restoration Roots.* Dallas: Gospel Teachers Publications, Inc., 1983.

McNemar, Richard. *The Kentucky Revival.* Cincinnati: John W. Brown, 1807.

Murch, James DeForest. *Christians Only, A History of the Restoration Movement.* Cincinnati: Standard Publishing Company, 1962.

Neth, John Watson. *Walter Scott Speaks.* Milligan College Tennessee: Emanuel School of Religion, 1967.

Newman, A. H. *American Church History. A History of Baptist Churches in the United States.* Philadelphia: American Baptist Publication Society, 1894.

Norton, Herman. *Tennessee Christians.* Nashville: Reed and Company, 1971.

Oliver, Lancelot. *New Testament Christianity.* Birmingham, England: Publishing Committee of Churches of Christ, 1911.

Owen, Robert, and Campbell, Alexander. *The Evidences of Christianity, A Debate.* Cincinnati: Jethro Jackson, 1852.

Page, Emma, Ed. *The Life and Works of Mrs. Charlotte Fanning.* Nashville: McQuiddy Printing Company, 1907.

Phillips, Thomas W. *The Church of Christ.* New York: Funk and Wagnalls, 1905.

Powell, J. M., and Powers, Mary Nell. *N. B. H. A Biography of Nicolas Broady Hardeman.* Nashville: Gospel Advocate Company, 1964.

Power, Frederick D. *Life of William Kimbrough Pendleton.* St. Louis: Christian Publishing Company, 1902.

Qualben, Lars P. *A History of the Christian Church.* New York: Thomas Nelson & Sons, 1904.

Randall, Max Ward. *The Great Awakening and the Restoration Movement.* Joplin, Missouri: College Press, 1983.

Richardson, Robert. *The Principles and Objects of the Religious Reformation Urged by Alexander Campbell and Others.* Bethany: 1853.

Richardson, Robert. *Memoirs of Alexander Campbell.* Philadelphia: Lippincott, 1871.

Rogers, James R. *The Cane Ridge Meeting House.* Cincinnati: Standard Publishing Company, 1910.

Rogers, John. *The Biography of Elder Barton Warren Stone, written by himself with Additions and Reflections by John Rogers.* Cincinnati: J. A. and U. P. James, 1847.

Rogers, Samuel. Autobiography of Elder Samuel Rogers. Cincinnati: Standard Publishing Company, 1880.

Scobey, James E. *Franklin College and Its Influences.* Nashville: Gospel Advocate Company, 1954.

Smith, Elias. *The Life, Conversion, Preaching, Travels and Sufferings of Elias Smith.* Portsmouth: Beck and Foster, 1816.

Srygley, F. D. *Larimore and His Boys.* Nashville: Gospel Advocate Company, 1891.

Stevenson, William. *The Story of the Reformation.* Richmond: John Knox Press, 1959.

Thomas, Leslie G. *Restoration Handbook.* Nashville: Gospel Advocate Company, 1954.

Tucker, William E. and Lester G. McCallister. *Journey in Faith.* St. Louis: The Bethany Press, 1975.

Walker, Williston. *A History of the Christian Church.* New York: Charles Scribner and Sons, 1947.

Ware, C. C. *Barton W. Stone*. St. Louis: Bethany Press, 1932.

Waters, A. C. *A History of the British Churches of Christ*. Indianapolis: Butler School of Religion, 1948.

Welshimer, P. H. *Concerning the Disciples*. Cincinnati: Standard Publishing Company, 1935.

West, Earl. *The Search for the Ancient Order, Vol. 1*. Nashville: Gospel Advocate Company, 1949.

Wilburn, James R. *The Hazard of the Die: Tolbert Fanning and the Restoration Movement*. Austin: Sweet Publishing Company, 1969.

Williams, John Augustus. *Life of Elder John Smith*. Nashville: McQuiddy Printing Company, 1908.

Young, Charles Alexander. *Historical Documents Advocating Christian Union*. Chicago: The Christian Century Company, 1904.

Young, M. Norvel. *A History of the Colleges Established and Controlled by Members of the Churches of Christ*. Kansas City: The Old Paths Book Club, 1949.

INDEX